Teaching Preaching as a Christian Practice

A New Approach to Homiletical Pedagogy

Edited by
Thomas G. Long
and
Leonora Tubbs Tisdale

Westminster John Knox Press
LOUISVILLE • LONDON

Scripture quotations, unless otherwise indicated, are from the New Revised Standard Version of the Bible, copyright © 1989 by the Division of Christian Education of the National Council of the Churches of Christ in the U.S.A., and used by permission.

Some material in chapter 15 is reproduced herein with the permission of Gregory Heille, O.P. Some other material in chapter 15 is reproduced herein with the permission of Mary Margaret Pazdan, O.P. Material in chapter 15 from "Preaching from the Scriptures: New Directions for Preparing Preachers" (Chicago: Catholic Theological Union, 1998), Barbara E. Reid, O.P., and Leslie J. Hoppe, O.F.M., is reproduced herein with the permission of Barbara E. Reid, O.P. Material from *We Speak the Word of the Lord: A Practical Plan for More Effective Preaching,* © 2001 by Daniel E. Harris, CM. Used with permission of ACTA Publications, Skokie, Illinois, www.actapublications.com. All rights reserved. Material herein from Anna Carter Florence's *Preaching as Testimony* is reprinted with permission of Westminster John Knox Press. Excerpt (170 words) from pp. 42–3 from *The Master Butchers Singing Club* by Louise Erdrich is copyright © 2003 by Louise Erdrich. Reprinted by permission of HarperCollins Publishers. Excerpt (202 words) from "Jonah's Gourd Vine" by Zora Neale Hurston is copyright © 1934 by Zora Neale Hurston; renewed © 1962 by John C. Hurston. Reprinted by permission of HarperCollins Publishers. Excerpts from *Social Analysis: Linking Faith and Justice* by Joe Holland and Peter Henriot, 1980 edition, pages 42–43, is reprinted with permission from the Center of Concern, www.coc.org. Excerpt from *A River Runs through It, and Other Stories* by Norman Maclean, © 1976 by The University of Chicago, is used with permission of The University of Chicago Press. All rights reserved. Every effort has been made to determine whether texts are under copyright. If through an oversight any copyrighted material has been used without permission, and the publishers are notified of this, acknowledgment will be made in future printings.

Book design by Drew Stevens
Cover design by Pam Poll Graphic Design

First edition
Published by Westminster John Knox Press
Louisville, Kentucky

This book is printed on acid-free paper that meets the American National Standards Institute Z39.48 standard. ♾

PRINTED IN THE UNITED STATES OF AMERICA

08 09 10 11 12 13 14 15 16 17 — 10 9 8 7 6 5 4 3 2 1

Library of Congress Cataloging-in-Publication Data

Teaching preaching as a Christian practice : a new approach to homiletical pedagogy / edited by Thomas G. Long and Leonora Tubbs Tisdale. — 1st ed.
   p. cm.
  ISBN 978-0-664-23254-2 (alk. paper)
  1. Preaching—Study and teaching. I. Long, Thomas G. II. Tisdale, Leonora Tubbs.
  BV4211.3.T43 2008
  251.0071—dc22

                         2007050333

To our colleagues in the discipline of homiletics who, with wisdom, dedication, and faithfulness, teach the practice of preaching

Contents

Preface

This book was developed by a team of scholars, colleagues, and friends, all of whom are teachers of preaching in theological schools. The book reflects both our convictions about teaching homiletics and our experiences over the years in the classroom.

In recent history, homiletical pedagogy has wavered between a teacher-centered approach and a learner-centered approach, that is, between the notion that the teacher held all the wisdom and the notion that the learner held all the potential. The basic thesis of this book is that, while teacher-centered and learner-centered approaches in homiletics have their virtues, neither is finally satisfactory. The purpose of this book is to encourage the field of homiletics to move away from teacher-centered and learner-centered pedagogy and toward a *learning-centered* methodology. Specifically, we are calling homiletics to recognize that preaching is a Christian practice, with a centuries-long tradition. Over the many years, Christian preachers have discovered what is wise, good, and true about preaching, and new preachers are the heirs of this wisdom. This homiletical tradition is not static, of course, but evolving and changing. Still, there is a fine and rich tradition, to which new preachers both need and deserve to be introduced.

Section 1 of this book develops this idea of preaching as a practice and explores further the impact of this idea on the teaching of preaching. In Section 2, we name and discuss some of the key components of the practice of preaching. It is important to note that these components are listed in random order and not according to any chronological or hierarchical scheme. None of the components named is by definition more important than any other, and preaching courses will present these components in a variety of sequences, not necessarily in the order in which they appear here. Section 3 raises the issue of standards of excellence and evaluation in preaching, and approaches the classic question of the formation of the preacher, this time from a practice-oriented perspective. Section 4 examines possible designs for a basic course in preaching and addresses the question of how preaching courses fit into the larger patterns of seminary curricula.

Not every component of preaching is discussed in this volume. Preaching is an enormously complex practice, involving the integration of numerous skills and drawing upon a wide array of knowledge bases. To the list of components treated here could be added others, such as theological analysis, the use of electronic media, and the spiritual disciplines needed for the formation of a preacher. The discussions included here stand, then, not as a complete survey but as an invitation to others to add their voices and analyses to ours.

The authors of this book were the participants in a two-year consultation on the teaching of preaching sponsored by the Wabash Center for Teaching and Learning in Theology and Religion. Every participant in this consultation has considerable experience teaching preaching in seminaries and theological schools. A list of the contributors is found on page 239. We are grateful to the staff of the Wabash Center, especially to Lucinda Huffaker, who was then director of the Center, to Associate Director Paul Myhre, and to Director Emeritus Raymond Williams, for their support, hospitality, and encouragement in this project. All royalties from this project will go to support the work of two of the homiletical professional societies to which the authors belong: the Academy of Homiletics and the Catholic Association of Teachers of Homiletics.

Thomas G. Long
Bandy Professor of Preaching
Candler School of Theology
Emory University

Leonora Tubbs Tisdale
Clement-Muehl Professor of
    Homiletics
Yale Divinity School
Yale University

SECTION ONE

Preaching as a Christian Practice

1

A New Focus for Teaching Preaching

THOMAS G. LONG

The main purpose of this book is to call for a change in how Christian preaching is taught today. Or, more accurately, this book describes a pedagogical change that is already underway, sometimes intuitively, in many places where preaching is taught—in theological schools, in lay preaching academies, in preaching seminars in continuing education centers, and in other settings. In the pages that follow, the authors want to try to name this change clearly, to make it more visible and understandable, and to urge that it be embraced more fully and intentionally.

We are not talking merely about the kind of change that routinely occurs in homiletics, that is, the constant search for new teaching techniques, innovative ways to employ the latest electronic media, or fresh pedagogical exercises designed to nurture styles of preaching currently in vogue. At this level, the teaching of preaching is forever under construction, subject to the shifting fashions of rhetoric, culture, technology, and church life, and there is always some "new homiletic" emerging to challenge the reigning wisdom, accompanied by innovations in pedagogical methods. Changes of this sort are nothing new in the homiletics classroom.

Rather, we are talking about a change that is deeper than surface alterations to the syllabus or to classroom teaching techniques. We have in mind a radically different way of framing the ministry of preaching altogether, and thus a radically different way of viewing the task of those who seek to learn and to teach preaching. Specifically, we propose that *the ministry of preaching should be understood as a Christian practice and that the whole task of teaching preaching be reenvisioned from this perspective.*

We need to say clearly, of course, what we mean by understanding preaching as "a Christian practice" and why doing so should call for a new approach to the teaching of preaching. One way to begin to highlight the change we have in mind is to see it in contrast to what has gone before. In 1989, a team of eight superb teachers of preaching, all members of the Academy of Homiletics, the oldest and largest professional society of homileticians in North America, published *Learning Preaching: Understanding and Participating in the Process.*[1] This book was the result of nearly three years of collaborative effort, and it stands as a state-of-the-art description of 1980s homiletical pedagogy. *Learning Preaching* was a manifesto of how the most accomplished teachers of preaching in that day thought that preaching was best learned, and, therefore, best taught. The book opens with this important and revealing claim:

> Each of us has within us already the effective preacher God wants us to become. We teachers of preaching know that when we guide wisely in the process of learning preaching, we help students cultivate and harvest what God has planted in them, through genetic inheritance, personality, life experience, and church background. We aim to help each person in class start on the road to becoming with God's help the best preacher each has it in them to be.[2]

This was a fine statement in its day. Indeed some of the authors of the present volume who were already active in teaching when *Learning Preaching* was published eagerly applauded its approach. Today, however, we find that we can no longer endorse the central doctrine of that volume. Put simply, we no longer believe that "each of us has within us already the effective preacher God wants us to become."

Our doubt does not arise because we have lost faith in our students. To the contrary, we are as confident as ever in the gifts, commitments, talents, and faith that the great majority of our students bring to the classroom. Instead, our departure from the view of *Learning Preaching* comes because we have refocused our attention on the ministry of preaching itself—its history; its problems and virtues; its deep customs and ways of acting; its internal standards of excellence. Becoming a competent preacher is not simply a matter of drawing out and strengthening inner traits and gifts, important as that is, but it is instead a matter of critical learning about traditions and patterns of thinking and acting that have been honed over the centuries of Christian preaching. Our primary pedagogical emphasis now is not on what is allegedly "in there" in each student, a "little preacher" waiting to grow, but on what is "out there," namely the age-old practice of Christian preaching into which each student must be initiated.

What first commands our interest, then, is not the inner life of the persons who feel called to preach, but the ministry of preaching to which these people are called. Obviously, good teachers are always mindful of the needs and capacities of their students, and learning how to preach is not like learning the multiplication tables or the names of the kings of Israel. Becoming a preacher demands costly personal involvement, and students need to be taught and cared for in attentive and personal ways. Nevertheless, becoming a preacher is more than self-development, more than having the internal seeds of homiletical gifts watered and cultivated. Rather, it is to be instructed in and equipped for a practice of the church that has its own canons and norms, that is older, larger, and more vital than the capacities of any one person.

By analogy, it would make little sense to say that each of us has within us already the effective neurosurgeon or torts litigator God wants us to become. Medicine and law are widely recognized as practices, and aspiring physicians and attorneys must learn the skills, procedures, traditions, and ways of thinking appropriate to these practices. Personal gifts and aptitudes are important, but there are also habits of mind, patterns of action, and ways of being that must be acquired for the effective practice of law or medicine. Of course, there are important differences between practicing law or medicine and engaging in ministry, and these differences should not be forgotten in the homiletics classroom, but in this critical sense the analogy holds: like law, medicine, and accounting, and perhaps even like sailing, gardening, cooking, playing baseball, and making music, preaching is a living, developing practice that has an identifiable shape, a literature to support it, a broad set of norms, and desired outcomes. For twenty centuries, Christians have been engaging in this practice, and those who have gone before us have fashioned paths in the forest that can be discovered and traveled by new practitioners.

This does not mean that there is only one way to preach effectively and that students must be pounded into this single template regardless of their personalities or backgrounds. To the contrary, there are thousands of ways to preach well. It does mean, though, that all of these thousands of ways participate in and are variations of a common activity known as Christian preaching. The Mormon Tabernacle Choir and the band U2 have markedly different ways of making music. They have their own ways of vocalizing and harmonizing, their own styles and repertoires, but, different as they are, both of them engage in the same activity, singing. Both groups have learned and follow the conventions of musical time, tonality, pitch, and chord structure, and both have studied and to some degree been shaped by accomplished musicians before them, and, in turn, each group has its followers, fans, and imitators. Similarly, a new preacher will inevitably and joyfully develop a personal style, but this will be done as a part of joining the great company of Christian preachers and by seeking to enter the grooves and learn the rhythms and excellences of this historic practice.

THE SEARCH FOR AN ORGANIZING
FRAMEWORK IN HOMILETICS

For nearly as long as there have been Christian preachers, there have been others helping, coaching, encouraging, and teaching them. The earliest homiletical textbook we know about, Book 4 of Augustine's *De doctrina christiana*, dates from the early fifth century, but even before Augustine there were those who reflected on the methods and mission of preaching and helped Christian preachers negotiate the work of proclaiming the gospel amid the rhetorical traditions of the Hellenistic world.

When we watch across the centuries as such teachers have stood in the wings and encouraged the ministry of preaching, what can we say about the nature of their work? What is the main task of the teacher of preaching? On the one hand, preaching is a complex activity composed of many moving parts. Preaching involves the interplay of several kinds of knowledge and a number of specifiable skills, and the job of a homiletical teacher is to ensure that people know what they need to know and are able to do what they need to do to engage in faithful preaching. At the seminary level, even very basic courses in preaching touch on such disparate matters as biblical interpretation, theological reflection, cultural and social analysis, historical inquiry, ethical discernment, pastoral care, structure, language, illustration, and the use of voice and body. Many of these topics are covered, often at greater length, elsewhere in the seminary curriculum, but they come together in the act of preaching. Being a specialist in homiletics, then, necessarily entails also being a generalist in almost everything else, a theological jack-of-all-trades.

On the other hand, the very fact that all of this knowledge and all of these skills do come together in preaching means that preaching is an integrative activity, and preaching is more than the sum of its parts. Preaching makes use of many pieces of knowledge and many rhetorical skills, but there is something about preaching that is not simply borrowed from other disciplines. The teacher of preaching should have some larger vision of how the parts work together to form a whole. What is this larger vision? What is the sense of the integrated whole that can serve as an organizing framework, a pedagogical focal point, for teachers of preaching?

The answers to the question of what constitutes a fitting organizational framework for homiletics have changed and migrated over the centuries. We can catch the flavor of these shifts by surveying the transformations in homiletical teaching that have occurred just over the last 125 years. In the late nineteenth century, when the distinguished Boston cleric Phillips Brooks delivered the Beecher Lectures on preaching, he famously coined this definition of preaching:

> What, then, is preaching, of which we are to speak? It is not hard to find a definition. Preaching is the communication of truth by man to men. It has in it two essential elements, truth and personality.
> . . . Truth through personality is our description of real preaching.[3]

Brooks spoke for a whole generation when he defined preaching as "truth through personality," but even though Brooks named both truth and personality as the essential ingredients of preaching, it was actually personality that captured his imagination. Indeed, he was four lectures into the Beecher series before he managed to get off the topic of the preacher's personality. Even after he tried to change the subject, the preachers' needs, passions, character, and authority continued to resonate on almost every page of the lectures. The reason was that Brooks considered truth to be "a fixed and stable element" of preaching, while personality was "a varying and growing element."[4] According to Brooks, every preacher, whether in the pulpit next door or in a missionary congregation on the other side of the globe, preached the very same truth. The truth was a constant poured into the variable mold of human personality.

The implications of Brooks's influential lectures for a theological curriculum generally and for homiletics in particular were staggering. Brooks's description of preaching implied a sharp division of labor in the training of ministers. On one side there was truth, the timeless message of Christianity, and this was the responsibility of dogmaticians and biblical scholars. It involved a stable body of knowledge that could be taught and learned systematically. On the other side, there was the personality of the preacher, and the development of the preacher was the responsibility of the teacher of preaching and the focal point of homiletics. Ideally, students came to the preaching class with the fixed truth already mastered, and the teacher of preaching could turn to the variables—the shaping of the preacher's personality, the molding of character, and development of the student's ethos.

So Brooks's answer is clear: the organizing frame for homiletics is the personality of the preacher. In this regard, Brooks's lectures marked for homiletics the turn into the modern period, a shift away from the canons of classical "sacred rhetoric" and a move toward psychology and personalism. Also, it can be said that Brooks's powerful and articulate brief for the preacher's personality foreshadowed the concern of the authors of *Learning Preaching*, a century later, for the interior life of the developing preacher.

However, the path from Brooks to *Learning Preaching* was neither straight nor unbroken. By the middle of the twentieth century, Brooks's notion of a personally luminous preacher passionately communicating timeless truth began to give way to another organizing frame for homiletics, namely, the understanding of preaching as a peak function of biblical hermeneutics. Homiletics, under the influence of Barth and others, began to reject both propositional truth and personality as legitimate homiletical categories. A sermon was now seen not as some fixed doctrinal truth absorbed into the preacher's personality but as the immediate claim of God experienced as the biblical Word comes alive in the sermon. As Gerhard Ebeling, a student of Rudolf Bultmann, put it:

> [T]he sermon as a sermon is not exposition of the text as past proclamation, but is itself proclamation in the present—and that means, then, that the sermon is *execution* of the text.[5]

In other words, a sermon is not a vessel containing timeless truth with the value-added voice of the preacher's personality, but is instead the expression of God's own voice speaking through the biblical text. In this view of the sermon, the job of the preacher is to get out of the way, and the preacher's personality is at best irrelevant and at worst a vain intrusion.

Barth, in his lectures on preaching delivered at Bonn in the early 1930s, rehearsed a number of unsatisfying (to him) nineteenth-century definitions of preaching, including that of Christian Palmer, professor of homiletics at Tübingen and a contemporary of Phillips Brooks, who said, "To preach is by living witness, and in the name of God, to offer the salvation which appeared and is present for human beings in the person and work of Christ."[6] Barth was offended by the very idea that preachers would presume that they had anything to offer at all. Was it not God, and God alone, who did the offering? Barth scolded Palmer, wondering if "the preacher's offer is anything more than the offer of his own pious personality." Pious personality? Whether that dart found its target in Palmer or not, it struck Brooks right between the eyes. As an antidote, Barth offered his own definition of preaching:

> Preaching is the Word of God which he himself speaks, claiming for the purpose the exposition of a biblical text in free human words that are relevant to contemporaries by those who are called to do this in the church that is obedient to its commission.[7]

Thus, under the influence of Barth and his successors, the sermon is understood as a moment in the process of biblical interpretation. Therefore, homiletics pedagogically melds into biblical hermeneutics. The organizing frame for everything taught in preaching courses—content, structure, style, and all the rest—is shaped by the momentous and definitive act of biblical interpretation. While this approach to homiletics dominated the classroom for a season, such a concentrated focus on the event of biblical exegesis as the sum and substance of preaching was bound to collapse under its own weight. As Heinz Zahrnt, writing in the heyday of the biblical theology movement, complained,

> Nothing reveals the lack of contact with the contemporary historical situation in the theology of Barth so much as the fact that the problem of the *language of preaching* plays virtually no part in it.[8]

And again,

> There is no question that preaching in Germany today, and not only in Germany, would be very different without Karl Barth and his theology. But the effect of Barth has been twofold. On the one hand, without it present-day preaching would not be so pure, so biblical, and so concerned with central issues, but on the other hand, it would also not be so alarmingly correct, boringly precise, and remote from the world.[9]

Indeed, it was the neglected matters of sermonic form and language that became the next fascination of North American homiletics, and its next organizing principle. The burst of energy springing forth from a highly charged encounter with the biblical text was important, but one could not, after all, build an entire homiletics out of that alone. There was the matter of the sermon itself, its shape and vocabulary. Fred Craddock's enormously engaging and influential 1971 monograph *As One without Authority* was the right book at the right time, with its call to what Craddock termed "inductive movement." Craddock claimed,

> Anyone who would preach effectively will have as his primary methodological concern the matter of movement. Does the sermon move and in what direction? Movement is of fundamental importance not simply because the speaker wants to "get somewhere" in his presentation but because the movement itself is to be an experience of community in sharing the Word.[10]

Craddock's call to focus on sermonic movement eloquently represents yet another shift in the central emphasis of homiletics, this time to sermon form. By the late 1970s, this enchantment with dynamic sermon form had fallen in love with narrative theology, and the love child was a brand-new emphasis on "narrative preaching." In the popular 1980 textbook *Preaching the Story*, Charles L. Rice and Morris J. Niedenthal named their broad-ranging quest:

> Anyone who has experienced preaching, whether in pulpit or pew, knows that it is an event—a moment, a meeting, a sudden seeing—in which preacher, listener, the message, and the impinging social environment all come together. Can we find a word for that event, a paradigm which will recognize all the elements and in doing so tell us what preaching is, and how it is done when it is done well?[11]

Rice and Niedenthal answer their own question:

> If we were pressed to say what Christian faith and life are, we could hardly do better than *hearing, telling, and living a story*. And if asked for a short definition of preaching could we do better than *shared story*?[12]

Shared story—throughout the 1970s and early '80s, this was a powerful metaphor and a strong organizing concept for homiletical pedagogy, but it was not without its critics. Early on, Richard Lischer objected to the tendency of the story image to reduce the full span of homiletical issues to questions of form. He scoffingly called this season in homiletics the "Cinderella period":

The implicit hope is that if we could find the perfect glass slipper of form, not only would the sermon be transformed into a beautiful princess, but we (the preachers) would also be transformed.[13]

Despite the criticism, the metaphor of storytelling held sway in homiletics for many years. Eventually, though, the idea of storytelling began to shine the spotlight once again on the role and person of the preacher. It was, after all, the preacher who tells the story, and before long teachers of preaching began to ask about the traits of character, oratorical skills, and personality required to tell stories well. They wondered and worried about how much of the preacher's own story should be revealed in sermons. In other words, the homiletical world had, in its own meandering way, come full circle to Philips Brooks's focus on the preacher's personality and character. In 1989, when the authors of *Learning Preaching* stated their conviction that each person "has within us already the effective preacher God wants us to become," they were not merely repeating nineteenth-century ideas about personality and morals. They had moved beyond the definitions and terms of Phillips Brooks, but in their quest for a frame to organize the teaching of preaching, they had pointed to the very same location: the inner life of the developing preacher.

So, in the last 125 years all the bases have been occupied at one time or another, and almost every conceivable category—the personality of the preacher, the encounter with the Bible, the form of the sermon, the inner capacities of the preaching student, and the inner life of the listener—has been put forward as the organizing center of preaching and, consequently, of homiletical pedagogy. Where should homiletics go next?

PRACTICING PREACHING AND PREACHING AS A PRACTICE

What we want to claim is that the time has come not only for a new answer, but this time for a quite different kind of answer, to the question posed by Rice and Niedenthal: Is there a way of describing the field of preaching such that "preacher, listener, the message, and the impinging social environment all come together"? In other words, is there an organizational framework for homiletics that can better focus our teaching and strengthen the learning of our students? The authors of this volume are persuaded that the answer is not to be found in some controlling metaphor, such as "storytelling," nor is it to be found in some place or moment in the preaching process, such as biblical interpretation, the psychology of listener, or the personality of the preacher. Rather, we suggest that the focus of homiletical teaching should now fall on the concept of *preaching as a practice*.

But what, exactly, does it mean to call Christian preaching a practice? The term "practice" is not new in theological circles, of course, but it has lately reentered the theological stream with revived energy. Dorothy Bass and Craig Dykstra, theologians who have been influential in the recent practices conversation, have provided a broad working definition of Christian practices as *"things Christian people do together over time to address fundamental human needs in response to and in the light of God's active presence in the world."*[14] This description points toward understanding the Christian life not as mere adherence to doctrines nor as prescribed rules of pious action, but as a way of life, a way of being in the world. To be a Christian means joining with others to engage in an ensemble of practices such as showing hospitality, bearing witness to God, praying, and working for reconciliation. Each of these practices has developed patterns and traditions over time and is pregnant with theological meaning.

Under this definition, preaching certainly qualifies as a practice. Christians have been preaching sermons and listening to them since the very beginning, so preaching is "[done] together over time." Theologically, preaching is not ornamental or mere oratorical entertainment. People need to hear the gospel, need to attend to the speech of the living and present God. Thus, preaching also addresses "fundamental human needs in response to and in the light of God's active presence in the world."

So Bass and Dykstra's definition is helpful in identifying preaching as one of the essential practices of the Christian life,[15] but it is too broad to function as an organizational frame for a complex activity like the teaching of preaching. Not moving away from this definition, but turning up the magnification somewhat, we put forward the following marks of a practice, a statement first crafted by James Nieman and developed by him in chapter 2 in this volume:

> *A practice is a constellation of actions that people have performed over time that are common, meaningful, strategic, and purposeful.*

This definition of a practice highlights certain key elements of preaching:

—A practice is *a constellation of actions*. Christian preaching is not merely an intention, a mood, a thought, or an emotion. Preaching simply does not happen until somebody *does* something. It is an embodied, physical event. The actions belonging to preaching can be named (and potentially taught and learned). Drawing a bow across a string and melting butter in a sauté pan are actions, but they are actions belonging to music and cooking, not to preaching. Exegeting a passage from the Bible with a sermon in view, crafting a sermon structure, and opening one's mouth to speak the sermon in the presence of others are preaching actions. Also, unlike threading a needle or flipping on a light switch, preaching is not a single, simple action, but a *constellation* of actions, all of which should work in concert to form the practice. The proportions and inner harmonies of the various actions of preaching can be taught and learned.

—The actions of a practice have been *performed over time*. Like musical composers, preachers do not start de novo, but step into a deep stream of tradition. Christian preaching has been done for twenty centuries, and it draws on Jewish and rhetorical traditions even older. Over time, much wisdom has accumulated about the practice of preaching, and competent preaching involves an informed awareness of preaching's historical treasures and discoveries.

—The actions of a practice are *common*. Christian preaching is always performed in the context of Christian community. This does not mean that every aspect of preaching is a group activity and that preachers do nothing alone, but even the parts a preacher may do in private—prayer, reflection, and study—are not finally in isolation from other Christians. Preaching is a common practice also in the sense that a storefront preacher in inner-city Detroit and a preacher in a country parish in the south of France are, for all their obvious differences, engaged in the same practice. Each preacher will, naturally, tailor the sermon to speak to the immediate context, but the very idea that sermons ought to be shaped to fit their contexts is a mark of preaching that applies everywhere and a sign that this is a commonly shared practice.

—A practice is *meaningful*. Preachers do not just talk about theology; preaching embodies theological meaning. Preachers do not work out their theological ideas in the study and then merely refer to them in the sermon. The act of preaching is itself theologically pregnant, and preaching generates and participates in theological meaning. Decisions about manner, language, style, structure, and so on are not just technical matters, but matters of meaning.

—A practice is ***strategic and purposeful***. The measure of a fruit tree is not finally the beauty of its leaves or the sturdiness of its trunk, but its fruitfulness. Just so, Christian preaching is assessed not by its poetic charm or even its popular reception, but by its fruits, its ultimate purpose. A faithful Christian sermon participates through language in the action of God in the world, and invites hearers to enter into this event. Preachers hope that sermons will become places where hearers encounter the living God, are called to deeper faith, and are formed in discipleship. These aims form the telos of preaching; every aspect of the sermon is strategically designed to accomplish these purposes, and the sermon is evaluated in light of them. This overarching telos can be refracted into a set of desired goals or fruits for preaching and further refined into standards of excellence for sermons. Sermons can be said to be faithful or not, good or bad, better or worse, not merely on the basis of taste or popular appeal but in terms of how well the parts of it were fitted and fashioned to the goals of preaching.

When Christian preaching is seen as a practice and when this is employed as the organizational framework for the teaching of preaching, several important advantages result:

1. *A focus on the practice of preaching provides a balance between commonalities and distinctives in homiletics.* Physicians may disagree about diagnoses and plans of treatment while still considering themselves to be involved in the common practice of medicine. In like manner, preachers—because of denominational traditions, theological perspectives, gender, race, or other variables—may have widely varying understandings of what constitutes good exegesis, acceptable sermon structure, level of listener involvement, and the like, but still be aware that they participate in an overarching and common domain of action. When a liberal Episcopal priest in Connecticut, an independent fundamentalist minister in East Texas, a National Baptist pastor in Chicago, and a small-town Methodist preacher in Kansas preach, there will, of course, be remarkable differences in style and content, but they are all still preaching, all participating in the same practice.

What generates the distinctiveness in preaching is clear, but what is it that creates the commonalities, the unity of a practice? In part the unity is created by the fact that preaching, no matter where it is done or by whom, always involves an identifiable core of actions. Even when preachers differ in this or that aspect of preaching, there are enough areas of overlap and congruency for sermons to be seen as participating in a common domain of action. Just as lunch at McDonalds, a formal dinner party, a picnic on a blanket spread beside the lake, and a casual family dinner at home can be seen as different expressions of the same human activity, so a homily at a Catholic Mass and an evangelistic sermon at a tent revival possess sufficient symmetry and similarity to be understood as variant expressions of the same practice.

Also, the commonality of preaching may be seen, ironically, in the vigorous debates about method that constantly ripple through the field of preaching. When one preaching scholar advocates the use of autobiography in sermons and another scholar counters that pulpit self-disclosure is a theological and rhetorical disaster, the argument itself discloses the fact that the two sparring partners believe themselves to be trying to articulate norms for a common practice.

2. *A focus on the practice of preaching begins with a description and an understanding of actual performance.* In contrast to some homiletical approaches that begin by developing a theological or ethical theory of what preaching ought to be, a practice-oriented approach begins with actual on-the-ground preaching as currently performed. Moreover, a practice-oriented approach to homiletics does not consider an act of preaching to be simply the application of a theory or a theological position, but rather as itself theory-laden and theologically imbued. Critical evaluation, comparative studies, and strategies for reform of the practice are not abandoned, but are developed in response to actual performance. The question "What should preaching be?" is posed only after the question "How are things done here?" is answered.[16]

3. *A focus on the practice of preaching demands that the history and sociology of preaching be aspects of the student's learning.* Since Christian practices are social and corporate and have developed over time, the practice cannot be learned without attention to the communal and historical dimensions of preaching. Preaching is not simply a clerical activity but an action of the whole church, and a church set down in a particular place and time. Moreover, there is a continuity in the practice over time. Augustine, Sojourner Truth, and the pastor down the street are all participants in an evolving practice. Whatever expectations and standards have grown up

around the practice have developed over the history of Christian preaching and cannot be grasped apart from an understanding of that history.

4. *A focus on the practice of preaching allows for the naming of and training in standards of excellence.* While there will obviously be areas of disagreement among traditions, it is possible to think of preaching being done well and being done badly and to describe internal measures and criteria by which such standards of performance are assessed. A sermon may employ the Bible responsibly or irresponsibly. A sermon's structure may be clear and coherent or not. The sermon may be delivered effectively or not. It will be a constant challenge to develop standards of excellence by which a practitioner can measure performance, but it is not impossible—indeed, it is necessary—to do so.

5. *A focus on the practice of preaching that possesses namable standards of excellence allows for the creation of pedagogical strategies designed to engender competent preaching.* Every event of preaching involves multiple actions and skills for which preachers can be educated and trained. In other words, good preaching can be taught and learned. Obviously, good preaching, like good musicianship, requires a basic level of giftedness, but when this is in place the actions and habits of thought involved in competent practice can be communicated and nurtured. The fact that most basic preaching courses in American seminaries are quite similar in the topics they treat and the educational goals they set, despite the fact that these schools are literally and figuratively all over the map, points to a tacit consensus about the necessary skills and knowledge for effective practice.

As stated in the preface, some teachers of preaching have recently described their own pedagogical evolution in terms that also accurately describe the movement of the field of homiletics, namely, that they had moved from a teacher-centered approach to a learner-centered approach, and then to a learn*ing*-centered approach.[17] In other words, the field has gone from thinking of the teacher as the source of knowledge and the model for good preaching, through a period when the student's internal development was the focus of teaching, and now on to a time when there is something outside of both teacher and student to be learned, namely, the practice of preaching itself. The goal of this book is to place the idea that preaching is a practice that can be taught and learned firmly in view, to explore the learning-centered approach, and to examine pedagogical approaches that will introduce students to the practice of preaching and encourage a lifelong process of becoming effective practitioners.

NOTES

1. Don M. Wardlaw, ed., *Learning Preaching: Understanding and Participating in the Process* (Lincoln, IL: Lincoln College and Seminary Press and the Academy of Homiletics, 1989). In addition to Wardlaw, other contributors to this volume are Fred Baumer, Donald F. Chatfield, Joan Delaplane, O. C. Edwards Jr., James A. Forbes Jr., Edwina Hunter, and Thomas H. Troeger.

2. Ibid., 1.

3. Phillips Brooks, *Lectures on Preaching* (New York: E. P. Dutton, 1888), 5, 8.

4. Ibid., 28.

5. Gerhard Ebeling, "Word of God and Hermeneutics," in *The Company of Preachers: Wisdom on Preaching, Augustine to the Present,* ed. Richard Lischer (Grand Rapids: Wm. P. Eerdmans Publishing Co., 2002), 210, emphasis his.

6. Christian Palmer, as quoted in Karl Barth, *Homiletics* (Louisville, KY: Westminster John Knox, 1991), 26.

7. Ibid., 44.

8. Heinz Zahrnt, *The Question of God: Protestant Theology in the 20th Century* (New York: Harcourt, Brace, and World, 1966), 116.

9. Ibid., 118.

10. Fred B. Craddock, *As One without Authority* (Nashville: Abingdon Press, 1971), 54.

11. Charles L. Rice and Morris J. Niedenthal, "Preaching as Shared Story," in Edmund A. Steimle et al., *Preaching the Story* (Philadelphia: Fortress Press, 1980), 9.

12. Ibid., 12–13, emphasis theirs.

13. Richard Lischer, "Preaching and the Rhetoric of Promise," *Word and World* 8, no. 1 (Winter 1988): 69.

14. Craig Dykstra and Dorothy C. Bass, "A Theological Understanding of Christian Practices," in *Practicing Theology: Beliefs and Practices in Christian Life,* ed. Miroslav Volf and Dorothy C. Bass (Grand Rapids: Wm. P. Eerdmans Publishing Co., 2002), 18, emphasis theirs.

15. In *Practicing Our Faith,* ed. Dorothy Bass, 91–118, preaching is actually not itself named as a practice but as one form of a larger, more inclusive, practice called "testimony."

16. See Penny Edgell Becker, *Congregations in Conflict: Cultural Models of Local Religious Life* (Cambridge: Cambridge University Press, 1999), 1 and passim.

17. David Lose, in remarks made to the Wabash Center Consultation on the Teaching of Homiletics, May 2003.

2

Why the Idea of Practice Matters

JAMES NIEMAN

Just over fifty years ago, a West Coast correspondent for *Time* glimpsed a rising musical star at the Tiffany Club in Los Angeles, the then twenty-eight-year-old jazz pianist Oscar Peterson. As the reporter watched Peterson, who was a big man at well over six feet tall and 250 pounds, settle heavily on the bench and place his long fingers over the keys, he strained for the right language to tell of a rare moment whose full impact could not be held in words. "Each tune . . . ," he wrote, "began with a fast, straightforward version of the melody, then, after a few bars, swung into Peterson's impromptu variations—interlaced arabesques, rhythmical counterpoints, stream-of-consciousness insertions from other tunes—then back to the original melody." Peterson accompanied his playing with "scat-singing," and "his fingers frisked the keys," marveled the reporter, "with the precision of a hell-bent Horowitz."[1] That moment came early in the remarkable career of Peterson, who, with apparent ease and astonishing skill, attained an excellence at the keyboard no one could repeat but everyone could recognize.

Twenty years earlier, Zora Neale Hurston wrote of a life about to plummet. In her first novel, she described characters closely patterned on her own childhood home, including one particularly tortured life.

Sunday afternoon, the sunlight filtered thru the colored glass on the packed and hushed church. Women all in white. Three huge bouquets of red hibiscus below him and behind the covered Communion table. As he stood looking down into the open Bible and upon the snow-white table, his feelings ran riot over his body. "He that soppeth in the dish with me." He knew he could not preach that Last Supper. Not today. Not for many days to come. He turned the pages while he swallowed the lump in his throat and raised: "Beloved, Beloved, now are we the sons of God. . ." The audience sang with him. They always sang with him well because group singers follow the leader. Then he began in a clear, calm voice. "Brothers and Sisters: De song we jus' sung, and seein' so many uh y'all out here tuh day, it reaches me in uh most particular manner. It wakes up uh whole family uh thoughts, and Ahm gointer speak tuh yuh outa de fullness uh mah heart. Ah want yuh tuh pray wid me whilst Ah break de bread uh life fuh de nourishment uh yo' souls. Our theme this morning is the wounds of Jesus. . . ."[2]

Even with the remarkable sermon of John Pearson that followed, the preaching included much more than words. Hurston saw it as an event amidst a people, their passions, and a relationship that began with respect but ended in rejection.

These two incidents may seem an odd way to start a journey toward better teaching of preaching. Even so, they help demonstrate a key concept on which this entire collection rests. Oscar Peterson and John Pearson were both engaged in activities that do not involve natural phenomena (like earthquakes or storms), accidental events (like collisions or illnesses), or mental realities (like worldviews or ideas). Instead we see people doing recognizable tasks that call for much preparation and not a little skill. When powerfully done, these events may reach beyond themselves, delighting and inspiring others, perhaps even carrying them away. Each depiction therefore shows a kind of *practice*, a term very important for all that follows. Admittedly, there is little gained by simply introducing some new term, calling preaching a practice instead of something else. But our aim in this book is to show not only that the concept of practice helps us better understand how preaching actually works, but also how we can teach that practice more effectively.

Vague terms and fuzzy thinking could quickly lead us off course. Thus, we first need to develop a clear and durable understanding of the concept of practice. Although this might sound rather theoretical, it carries the benefit of connecting our discussion with a larger body of scholarship. If we can get a firm grasp on the larger idea of practice, we can see how Christian preaching manifests the typical features of practices generally while retaining its own uniqueness. This will in turn provide a broad orientation for many of the topics explored in the chapters that follow, particularly underscoring the connection between the practice of preaching and the methods used to teach it, and pointing to reliable measures for the assessment and improvement of preaching.

Our route will proceed through three stations. First, I will develop a compact but wide-ranging view of practices, reflecting the current scholarly discussion. Second, I will show that preaching is a particular instance of this larger concept of practices. We will see how understanding preaching as a practice gives new perspectives on what preaching is and allows us to consider how to employ broadly recognized standards of excellence to evaluate particular instances of students' preaching. Third, I will explore how the teaching of preaching is a practice in its own right. The value of this insight is that it allows us then to explore how the character of the teaching and the character of what is taught can be consonant with each other, and in ways that can guide our pedagogy.

PRACTICES

Any definition of practices must avoid the extremes of either false simplicity or mind-numbing detail. On the one hand, we want to use the term "practice" to refer to more than any sort of human activity or behavior. Calling any and everything a "practice" is obviously unhelpful. On the other hand, an overly elaborate and technical definition of practices—and there are several examples of such in the Western philosophical history[3]—would be cumbersome and equally unusable. We simply seek here a portable, supple, durable heuristic definition of practice that is attentive to the philosophical streams of development without becoming swept away in their detail.

Surveying the range of contemporary approaches to practice, it appears that five basic features often appear. A practice can be recognized as including *common, meaningful, strategic, purposive actions.* Unpacked just a bit, this phrase conveys the "who" (common), the "why" (meaningful), the "how" (strategic), the "where" (purposive), and the "what" (actions) of a practice. Let us take a closer look at each element of this compressed list of features, beginning with the noun at the end of the list, *actions.*

Actions

The most basic feature of practices is perhaps also the most challenging to specify. How do we explain something as simple as action? Of course, we can begin by saying that actions involve energy and effort in the material realm. They involve doing something with the stuff of our lives and world, and in a way that is more than the private manipulation of thoughts or ideas. Attitudes and dispositions alone, therefore, do not qualify as practices. The action of practice is manifested in a public and substantial way that others can see and acknowledge.

At the same time, practices are not identical with actions. A practice involves a group of component actions that have been shaped into a larger pattern. In a practice multiple actions are arranged into an overall structure, and thus not every random or haphazard action or set of actions counts as a legitimate practice.[4] Consider one concrete instance of how actions and practices relate, namely the pitching of the legendary Tom Seaver, as described by baseball writer Roger Angell:

> One of the images I have before me now is that of Tom Seaver pitching; the motionless assessing pause on the hill while the sign is delivered, the easy, rocking shift of weight onto his back leg, the upraised arms, and then the left shoulder coming forward as the whole body drives forward and drops suddenly downward—down so low that the right knee scrapes the sloping dirt of the mound—in an immense thrusting stride, and the right arm coming over blurrily and still flailing, even as the ball, the famous fastball, flashes across the plate, chest-high on the batter and already past his low, late swing.[5]

As a practice, pitching (or playing the piano à la Oscar Peterson) involves many actions working together as an integrated whole, and not just a single action or a series of discrete actions.

A single practice is often governed by a larger *domain* of endeavor. The practice of pitching, while certainly understandable by itself, makes better sense when we see it within the domain of baseball. In that context, pitching conforms to the assumptions and rules of baseball and is linked to other practices, such as batting, running, and coaching. Put pitching into another context—say, the game of cricket—and of course it has a different meaning and purpose.

Someone who wishes to teach a practice, whether pitching or preaching, needs to know the component actions, the shape of the pattern into which they are arranged, as well as the larger domains that give those practices meaning and purpose.

Understood in this multilayered way, practices clearly also require the development of proficiency. We need to "practice" the practice, and we commonly speak of "practicing" something, like practicing the oboe or practicing basketball, for just this reason. To engage in a practice with skill and competence requires repeating the patterned actions and their components. When the practitioner has reached a sufficient level of competency with the coordinated actions of a practice, the result is a seeming effortlessness, "a disposition of the mind and heart from which action flows naturally, in an unself-conscious way."[6] This naturally moves beyond mere skill development with constitutive actions toward the way social character formation occurs among those who engage a particular practice within its governing domain. This matter of character formation leads us on to explore the next feature of practices.

Common

The actions coordinated into practices can be further refined by noting their social or collective quality. This does not mean that a practice always and only exists as a group activity. While practices certainly can be collectively enacted (and often are, when we fully see how they operate), this is not the primary sense in which they bear a social quality. They are more importantly a product of groups, using group resources, and serving group interests, even when they are performed by individuals. This is why I have used the modifier "common" to convey this quality. It refers to the social dimension of practices as something that is held and known in common, whether or not performed in common or having a commonplace aesthetic.

In particular, practices are common by existing in and across time. They have common origins and goals. Regarding their origins, they emerge from groups and their long-standing patterns and ways of being. Practices are always traditioned, standing within and in turn shaping the stream of how a group operates. Regarding their goals, practices exist for groups in relation to their larger purposes. Practices are not privately held, but serve collective outcomes, creating mutual goods that benefit more than just those who enact them. Common origins and goals are evident in a chef's recollection of his first solo preparation of a meal for paying customers:

I went to work, hesitant and uncertain at first, but more confident as the ingredients began to react to my techniques and feel. Working from memories of what I had seen Chef and the *commis* do when they made *poulet à l'estragon*, I cut a chicken into four pieces, two legs and two breasts. I then cooked the pieces *à blanc*, so they did not take any color, slowly in butter. I added white wine, along with a little chicken stock. Next in were a small onion and a bouquet garni, consisting of a few sprigs of thyme, parsley stems, and a bay leaf, tied together. I seasoned my dish with salt and pepper, covered it, and cooked it over medium heat for about thirty-five minutes. I then removed the chicken from the broth, keeping it warm on a serving dish, and created a sauce by whisking a *beurre manié*, a mixture of butter and flour in equal proportions, into the broth with rich, thick farm cream and fresh tarragon. Finished forty minutes later, the dishes looked right, felt right, and smelled right.[7]

The actions of this practice were not arbitrary, but coordinated in light of a received tradition with its tested insights and procedures. Naturally, these actions and objects used by another tradition would result in a quite different meal. Moreover, this practice did not exist for its own sake. Its goal was to produce a meal on this new occasion that would benefit those who partook of it, who would in turn assess it in light of group standards.

The common quality of practices in light of their traditioned origins and goals does not render them stodgy or unchanging. Instead, practices seek to bring a shared tradition to bear on the present situation. They must always be contextually responsive. Practices will therefore attend to and interact with the specific traditions out of which they operate, reinforcing these at some points while rupturing them at others. Such responsiveness is not an optional extra added to proficient performance, but is integral to it. This holds important implications for how practices are best taught and the standards to which they are held, items to which we will return later.

This common quality also explains how an individual and group relate in their use of practices. Practices are "socially shared forms of behavior that mediate between what are often called subjective and objective dimensions. A practice is a pattern of meaning and action that is both culturally constructed and individually instantiated."[8] Group interests are embodied in the practices of specific individuals performing them, without whom those interests (and the group itself) would grind to a halt. This suggests once again that practices contribute to character formation. The regular and repeated performance of practices offers a way for individuals reliably to display who they truly are in relation to others. Development of a consistent character has impact not only on individuals, of course, but also on the subsequent practices performed within a group. In this sense, practices serve as the basis for inherent standards of excellence within a group, such as professions and guilds. Character formation and standards of excellence generate a deep awareness of values, which opens onto the next feature of practices.

Meaningful

A practice involves more than just the actions it is able to do. It also bears various meanings within those actions. It is typical and mistaken to assume that such meanings are somehow clarified in advance and then put into force through the mechanism of actions, so that a practice is simply the result of applied ideas. Instead, the actions within a practice convey meaning and intentionality already, to which the assignment of explicit thoughts or reasons is usually a later step. We therefore must inductively discern the meanings inherent in practices, reviewing a series of them for the significance they most centrally and consistently seek to convey. In this way, not only is a practice not reducible to its constituent actions, but in turn these actions are enhanced by contributing to a larger practice, receiving a greater horizon of meaning than they would ever have on their own.

Since a practice carries significance in this way, it operates as an iconic sign. Some signs convey what they mean indexically, referring to an outside reality that is conventionally associated with the sign. This is how an alphabet relates to a living language or a gravestone denotes a place of burial. Other signs, however, convey what they mean iconically, actually participating in the reality they signify.[9] This is how practices operate, whether in jazz, baseball, preaching, or the following example of communal song:

> That first night, with an air of exquisite discovery, the men drank beer and sang until dawn. They sang their favorites to one another, taught each other the words. Their voices rose singly and then by the second chorus swept in fervent unison through the night. On the more familiar melodies, they instinctively harmonized. Sheriff Hock possessed a heartrending falsetto. Zumbrugge's baritone had a cello-like depth and expression surprising in the author of so many heart-

less foreclosures. As long as he had a glass of schnapps in one hand, Roy Watzka could sing all parts with equal conviction, but he found that his voice was so similar to Chavers' that they sometimes dueled instead of harmonized. Eva fell asleep, as she would once a week from then on, to the sound of the men's voices. The singing club became the most popular meeting in town and began to include listeners, those of ragged or pitchless voice, who came to sit on the outskirts of the core group and listen.[10]

By entering into the singing, these men entered a deeper meaning that only made sense through the participatory performance itself. Meaning was also available beyond these singers, for those who simply listened also shared in the significance of the practice. Because practices involve a complex of actions, moreover, this implies that they hold the potential to bear multivalent meanings, such as (in this example) camaraderie, musical growth, and pleasure. In this way, a single practice can carry manifold intentions for its diverse participants.

Practices are "focal" about meaning, drawing us through a practice into a closer engagement with what is signified. At their best, practices focus us in a way that is integrative and sustaining. Contrast this with how we are involved with techniques. Because they separate reality to means and ends or problems and solutions, techniques may help us briefly satisfy a particular challenge but fail to offer the broader patterns of significance that practices can convey. In their tendency to fragment and isolate, techniques are quite literally meaningless.[11] This distinction is important because the meaning-laden quality of practices affects how they must be taught. Without this realization, practices can become distorted in a problem-solving pedagogy as a set of techniques to be mastered. The result may be technical proficiency at a task robbed of its ability to convey wisdom or value. Effective teaching of practices is judged, instead, by the way it retains a concern for focusing and thus conveying significant meaning.

Over time, it is possible to step back from a series of similar practices and begin to name the embedded meanings they bear. That is, practices can be theorized, again not in advance as abstract ideas applied in action, but as concrete performances that, as such, convey intentional themes. This means that the inherent wisdom of a group can be known through what its practices convey. We can specify the traditions that shape such a group and which are reshaped by every subsequent deployment of that practice. Beyond this, a larger account of practices can be offered to others not part of the group. We can indicate the rationale for practices that can be especially valuable in unsettled or crisis times when reorientation is needed. Uncovering these traditions and their rationale is extremely important when it comes to explaining and teaching these practices to others. Not only is the inductive discernment of meanings embedded in practices pedagogically important, but it also suggests further standards by which excellent performance can be gauged.

Strategic

The use of a practice, especially when done consistently over a long period of time, is not a speculative exercise or a parlor game. Instead, its intent is to accomplish specific, recognizable ends for the group in which it arises. We will turn more directly to those ends in a moment. For now, it is worthwhile to note that practices not only bear meanings important to a group, but also a plan of action by which ends may be achieved. They offer guidance and strategies toward attaining group aims and goods, suggestions for how to proceed, respond, and even rethink the practice in its continued use. For example, the practice of driving an automobile, while also governed by physical and legal forces, is replete with strategies for how individual practitioners interact with unforeseen situations in order to attain a broad social goal of safe and efficient personal transportation.

Like the meanings that practices bear, the strategies implicit in practices are better assessed by inductive review of actual cases than treated as mental schemes first deduced and then implemented. They are often not logically ordered or meticulously reasoned in advance of action. At first glance, the following example of fly-fishing may seem contrary to that claim.

> The four-count rhythm, of course, is functional. The one count takes the line, leader, and fly off the water; the two count tosses them seemingly straight into the sky; the three count was my father's way of saying that at the top the leader and fly have to be given a little beat of time to get behind the line as it is starting forward; the four count means put on the power and throw the line into the rod until you reach ten o'clock—then check-cast, let the fly and leader get ahead of the line, and coast to a soft and perfect landing. Power comes not from power everywhere, but from knowing where to put it on. "Remember," as my father kept saying, "it is an art that is performed on a four-count rhythm between ten and two o'clock." My father was

very sure about certain matters pertaining to the universe. To him, all good things—trout as well as eternal salvation—come by grace and grace comes by art and art does not come easy.[12]

Remember, though, that we meet these tightly scripted strategies as they were taught to a son and conveyed to readers. Lifelong practice preceded reflection on it and its economical summary. A recipe also abbreviates strategies for the practice of cooking, as does musical notation for the practice of performance. Effectively conveying or teaching a practice's strategies is therefore like learning to use durable, time-tested forms of narrative emplotment that have a proven ability to produce desired effects upon an audience. Put another way, it resembles de Certeau's notion of "tactics," a series of moves or principles that may ultimately contribute to a consistent and comprehensive plan, but along the way remain open to constant adaptation and adjustment.[13]

Plainly, the kind of competence needed to grasp such embedded strategies takes time and exposure to develop. This highlights again how learning a practice, including its strategies, has such an impact on character formation. Moreover, this accounts for why competent teachers of a practice must be similarly shaped in character by vast experience with its strategies in order effectively to mentor others in learning those same strategies. This relationship between strategies and character, which I am suggesting applies to both teachers and learners, is what Bourdieu meant by *habitus*, a kind of "practical sense for what is to be done in a given situation—what is called in sport a 'feel' for the game, that is, the art of *anticipating* the future of the game, which is inscribed in the present state of play."[14] Adept practitioners are so formed by a practice that they naturally have this feel for it, a repertoire of strategies that both guides their own actions and becomes a key component in teaching the practice to others. Since strategies are intimately connected with a practice's aims, however, this teaching and formation cannot be reduced to simply handing on tricks of the trade. It is to these larger purposes of a practice we must therefore finally turn.

Purposive

While this modifier is the last to be treated, in many respects it is the most important feature of a practice. The several actions at the heart of a practice have a forward energy to them, a teleological drive that is central to the existence of any practice in the first place. Therefore, aims can be seen as directing every other feature of a practice. Its common or social origins are extended into the future insofar as they continue to work toward these aims. Its implicit meanings operate as condensed expressions of the aims it seeks to attain. Its strategies have nowhere else to go unless these aims are already given, at least in some suggestive way. Beyond this, however, the aims of a practice establish its ethics, the ultimate values to which excellent performance will be held accountable. Once again, the intersection of practices and character is evident.

Any practice is related to its own aims in two important ways that have significant ethical implications. First, a specific practice is something of a synecdoche of its aims, with the ultimate values of that practice expressed in microcosm within its actual performance. For this reason, the moral dimension of a practice is not a value added to it, but integral within its very structure. In well-formed practices, the ends never (and simply cannot) justify the means, no matter how lofty those ends. Instead, the means (both the actions constituting a practice and the practices comprising a domain) already and unavoidably express the ends they seek to attain. (This, of course, is why Alasdair MacIntyre was so careful to attend to practices within his broader effort to recover a virtue ethics.) Second, a specific practice never exists to repeat or perpetuate itself, even if performed with great skill or excellence. Meaningful practices push past any admiration or emulation to implement ends beyond themselves. Indeed, the final assessment of the excellence of a practice is governed by this question of the aims it attains, including how the character of its practitioners has been formed along the way.

While any of our earlier anecdotes could be used to display this, another example shows the importance of aims in an unmistakable way.

Gill dusts his fingers with gymnasts' chalk and walks purposefully up to the boulder's base. By clinging to small nicks on the rock's surface and balancing on pea-sized nubbins, he somehow manages to pull his body off the ground, as if by levitation. To Gill, the boulder's steep face is a puzzle to be solved with finger strength, creative movement, and force of will. He puts the puzzle together piece by piece, delicately shifting his weight from tiny hold to tiny hold until he finds himself hanging from his fingertips three feet beneath the boulder's crest. Here he seems stymied; his feet dangle uselessly in space and his position is so tenuous that he can't let go with either hand to reach higher without falling. Wearing an expression of beatific calm that gives no clue to the terrible strain his muscles are under, Gill fixes his eyes on the top, dips his shoulders slightly, and then springs suddenly for the crest from his pathetic handholds. Completely airborne, his body travels upward mere inches before the apogee of its flight is reached, but in that moment, just as he begins to be pulled earthward, his left hand shoots for the crest of the boulder like a snake striking a rat and clamps onto it securely. A few seconds later Gill is standing on top.[15]

Note the tight connection here between the practice and its aims. Any component or action in this practice that fails to contribute to reaching the top is not just wasted energy but even contrary to the practice itself. Turned on its head, only the seekng of the aim gives meaning to its actions or components. No matter how well done, they are worthless apart from this aim.

Since the aims of a practice establish how its other features are understood, this can guide us in conceiving how that practice is taught. Just as a practice is governed by the aims it seeks, so the teaching of that practice is likewise subject to the same framework. This is not for the sake of mere consistency between what a practice does and how it is taught. Instead, teaching a practice requires discerning its several features, assessing their actual implementation in specific cases, and critiquing that performance based on standards inherent to the practice itself. Since the features of a practice are governed by a purposive framework, the teaching of that practice cannot be otherwise. This prevents teaching from becoming detached from its object in an endless quest for the latest educational gimmicks. Effective teaching of a practice requires entering into its very worldview and values, crafting a form of teaching from within that remains attentive to the larger aims that practice seeks to bring into being.

PREACHING AS A PRACTICE

This analysis of the features of practices might by now seem far removed from the task of preaching, let alone how it is taught. For this reason, let us revisit the idea that preaching does, in fact, embody the view of practices described in this elaborated definition.[16] All five features are easily discerned in this famous depiction of the task crafted by Herman Melville:

There was a low rumbling of heavy sea-boots among the benches, and a still slighter shuffling of women's shoes, and all was quiet again, and every eye on the preacher. He paused a little; then kneeling in the pulpit's bows, folded his large brown hands across his chest, uplifted his closed eyes, and offered a prayer so deeply devout that he seemed kneeling and praying at the bottom of the sea. This ended, in prolonged solemn tones, like the continual tolling of a bell in a ship that is foundering at sea in a fog—in such tones he commenced reading the following hymn; but changing his manner towards the concluding stanzas, burst forth with a pealing exultation and joy—"The ribs and terrors in the whale, arched over me a dismal gloom. . . ." Nearly all joined in singing this hymn, which swelled high above the howling of the storm. A brief pause ensued; the preacher slowly turned over the leaves of the Bible, and at last, folding his hands down upon the proper page, said: "Beloved shipmates, clinch the last verse of the first chapter of Jonah—'And God had prepared a great fish to swallow up Jonah.' Shipmates, this book, containing only four chapters—four yarns—is one of the smallest strands in the mighty cable of the Scriptures. Yet what depths of the soul does Jonah's deep sealine sound! What a pregnant lesson to us in this prophet! What a noble thing is that canticle in the fish's belly! How billow-like and boisterously grand! We feel the floods surging over us, we sound with him to the kelpy bottom of the waters; seaweed and all the slime of the sea is about us! But *what* is this lesson that the book of Jonah teaches? Shipmates, it is a two-stranded lesson; a lesson to us all as sinful men, and a lesson to me as a pilot of the living God."[17]

As a complex of actions, this preaching combined human effort, sound, and movement into a coordinated and skillful performance. As a common feat, it deployed a rich tradition of group expectations and patterns, implementing these within and through a social gathering to further its work. As a meaningful sign, it engaged a significant and warranted reality, using patterns of language accessible to all participants. As a strategic effort, it used the power of vivid language and images in the hope of giving shape to human living. As a purposive event, it pointed to a horizon of values and encounters that oriented all the other features.

Of course, simply to describe preaching as a practice would be more at home in an anthropologist's field notes than a work that claims to help our teaching of a vibrant part of Christian ministry. Indeed, what I have offered so far could justifiably be criticized for failing to differentiate the practice of preaching from a motivational speech or a poetry reading. We would certainly want to press for an understanding of preaching as not simply any practice, but a distinctively *Christian* one. The problem is that such assertions so easily import essentialist assumptions that actually obscure our ability to understand the practice of preaching in all its uniqueness and depth, let alone how we might best teach it. While there is still ample debate on the subject, I remain unconvinced that there are practices (preaching or otherwise) whose Christian character makes them sui generis in relation to all others.[18] I do not question that preaching is a Christian practice, but instead how that claim is advanced and understood.

Our broader discussion of all practices can again be helpful here. We accurately refer to Christian practices in the same way that we might speak of a Christian auto repair shop. By such a title, we typically do not mean that the business itself has an inherent trust in God or pattern of beliefs, but rather that its owner does, which affects how business is conducted and who might therefore wish to use those services. Likewise, preaching is a Christian practice not because the practice as such is innately Christian. There are enough analogues to Christian preaching in other religious traditions,[19] let alone other societies and cultures, to doubt such an assertion. Instead, we mean that the practice of preaching deploys actions that Christians have traditionalized in familiar patterns that bear faith meanings, using warrants recognized within a particular community of belief, in order to express God's ways for the world known chiefly in Christ Jesus. That is, preaching is a constellation of common, meaningful, strategic, purposeful actions governed by and contributing to the aims of Christians (such as witness to Christ, enactment of the gospel, and reconciliation with God), especially but not strictly as a community of believers in the church.[20] It is in this sense that preaching accords with the narrower definition of Christian practices mentioned earlier by Long, which is an important and helpful subset of the general theory of practices I have provided.

That being said, our broad approach to practices allows us to do more than simply state that preaching is a practice and in what sense it can be considered a Christian one. A further step comes in realizing that the features integral to all practices provide a powerful way for more closely examining what is actually occurring within any instance of preaching. Borrowing a term from organizational studies, the five features of all practices can be treated as "frames" on the distinctive practice of Christian preaching.[21] A frame is simply a way of adopting one perspective on group work in order to notice it more deeply. Each frame foregrounds a special aspect of such work that others might diminish or ignore. At the same time, no frame is utterly discrete from the rest, so that all are required in order to provide an ensemble account. For these reasons, the features I have presented serve well as frames for examining what distinguishes the practice of preaching.

To explore this further, let us consider the feature of "actions" as a frame for closely examining the practice of preaching, particularly an instance quite influential on Martin Luther King Jr., that of William Holmes Borders.

> What young King heard in Borders was an educated man who had learned to speak the language of his people. Borders did his exegetical homework and prepared an exposition of the text in manuscript form that he delivered in a reedy baritone not nearly as powerful as Daddy King's. Then he would literally step back and let it out, and the stories would begin. He told stories with the vividness and abandon of a child. In Borders's pulpit the great Old Testament stories came to life, their setting translated from ancient Palestine to black Atlanta, their heroes the familiar denizens of Auburn Avenue. David was a "country boy," said Borders in a late sermon, who whipped a big man with a "Cassius Clay tongue." When the boy slung his smooth stone at Goliath, everybody in the church could hear Borders's imitation of a stone whistling through the air and splatting into the giant's forehead. Soon the manuscript would be forgotten, and Borders would be crouching on the stage to fetch five smooth stones, lurking in wait behind the organ, or lying full length on the sanctuary floor like a dead giant. As Borders lost himself in the event of preaching, he transported his audience to another realm.[22]

It is easy to recognize the most familiar actions of this practice, Borders's oral presentation and expression accompanied by bodily gesture and physical movement. However, these obvious manifestations hardly encompass the entire range of actions that comprised his preaching. For instance, they immediately cause us to wonder about the decisions that led up to what was said and how it was presented. The actions frame therefore causes us to notice the preparatory efforts that were essential for and integrated with the public performance. A full discussion of this practice would have to include actions such as attention to theological warrants or reflection on how words might be understood. Nor does this exhaust the actions that contributed to such preaching, since we have named only those centered on the preacher. Even if we chose for now to set aside the actions of hearers, Borders was still obliged to engage with them. This suggests a further set of actions during and outside the sermon that were also part of the overall practice. The ability to gauge reactions while preaching or to listen to community discourse (including reactions to the sermon itself) were surely crucial to his practice. What we begin to see through this one frame, therefore, is that this practice was less an event than a process, and one that involved the actions not just of one practitioner but of many. This in turn has significant implications for all that must be included if this approach to preaching is to be taught well.

We could continue this analysis of preaching by looking through the remaining features of a practice. Each one would provide a distinct angle of vision on the practice as well as a richer rationale for why so many items must be addressed in order to grasp the complexity of preaching. There are two particular advantages to such a painstaking procedure. On the one hand, the sense of what matters within preaching is then inductively derived from within the practice itself, rather than from conventional topics, generic categories, or abstract ideals imposed from outside. Framing the practice in this way will make us far more likely to address the realities of actual preaching. On the other hand, disciplining ourselves to look through all of the frames will attend to those parts of the practice that may otherwise be overlooked. For example, the "purposive" frame of preaching, which would foreground its missional aims, could easily be downplayed if we were to look through the actions frame alone, which might produce a view of preaching dominated only by matters of technique.

Rather than looking through each of the frames at this point, however, I wish to remark on the significant interaction between them. A frame-based approach to practices will allow one frame to inform or correct another, with the benefit of helping us understand more deeply what makes preaching a distinctive practice. Let us return to the actions frame explored earlier. Bearing in mind the various coordinated actions of preaching within the following example, consider how they receive further specificity when laid alongside the "common" frame.

> Everywhere people marveled at Sister's ability to persuade people. To ordinary Protestants who needed someone and something to believe in, she seemed made-to-order. The child who had won a gold medal for elocution had become a woman with magnificent oratorical power. "Never did I hear such language from a human being as flowed from the lips of . . . Aimee Semple McPherson," one seasoned reporter wrote in 1920. "Without one moment's intermission, she would talk from an hour to an hour and a half, holding her audience

spellbound." She spoke with impressive simplicity, another wrote. Perhaps her experience with the Salvation Army made her comfortable talking to people in brothels, dance halls, pool rooms, theaters, and restaurants. In such settings, reports regularly noted with amazement that she never preached against vice; she declared a simple gospel message and made the people—however socially marginalized or outcast—feel welcome to her meetings. She sang, laughed, and cried with them as compellingly as she did with the more respectable crowds who flocked into the churches.[23]

In light of the common frame, we can now especially notice how McPherson's actions operated within particular Christian assumptions, shaped by distinctive faith group traditions, engaged various social resources and capacities, and mediated between individual faith formation and collective theological identity. That is, a common framing of her practice prevents the actions frame from overlooking, say, the strong faith warrants or sociocultural qualities peculiar to her background and setting. Put another way, the work of attending to Scripture or listening to situation (actions frame) receive greater precision in light of the specifics of the assembly in question (common frame). To go farther, we could bring these remarks into conversation with what the "meaning" frame exposes about McPherson's preaching. Through that frame, we note how her practice of preaching incorporated a view of human beings as boundlessly valued by God. This would surely carry implications about the concept of church her preaching presumed and reinforced (common frame) as well as how she selected forms of speech that honored rather than degraded her hearers (actions frame).

No doubt, this level of analysis at first appears daunting. Even so, we already attempt something like it when we try to justify what makes preaching good or bad. Reflect, for example, on your own intuitive responses to this all-too-familiar incident.

> Leeds Memorial was a stately brick building with a white interior and dark, varnished pews. The choir sounded professional, and they sang the opening hymn on their own while the congregation stayed seated. Maybe that was why Ian didn't have much feeling about it. It was only music, that was all—something unfamiliar, classical-sounding, flawlessly performed. Maybe the whole church had to be singing along. The theme of the day was harvest, because they were drawing close to Thanksgiving. The Bible reading referred to the reaping of grain, and the sermon had to do with resting after one's labors. The pastor—a slouching, easygoing, just-one-of-the-guys type with a

sweater vest showing beneath his suit coat—counseled his listeners to be kind to themselves, to take time for themselves in the midst of the hurly-burly. Ian felt enormous yawns hallowing the back of his throat. Finally the organist began thrumming out a series of chords, and the sermon came to an end and everyone rose. The hymn was "Bringing in the Sheaves." It was a simpleminded, seesawing sort of tune, Ian felt, and the collective voice of the congregation had a note of fluty gentility, as if dominated by the dressed-up old ladies lining the pews. Walking back to the bus, Eddie asked if he'd be coming every Sunday. Ian said he doubted it.[24]

Something is wrong here, we suspect, but what is it exactly, and how do we guard against it in the teaching of preaching? Our best efforts to answer these questions can be easily dismissed as the result of taste or cultural bias, however, were the method for assessment to remain hidden, which in turn prevents the development of mutual standards for preaching that still allow for diverse implementation. By contrast, a practice-based approach that uses frames to explore preaching can provide a truly disciplined, comprehensive, densely textured, and accountable way of asserting and using such standards. Not incidentally, it also suggests both the range of items that should be taught and why these are so important for the practice of preaching.

TEACHING PREACHING AS A PRACTICE

In a fashion parallel to what has been said above about preaching, we could also present teaching as a practice. Effective, compelling pedagogy surely utilizes common, meaningful, strategic, purposive actions, like any practice. Indeed, it might be quite helpful to seek a deeper understanding of the practice of teaching through a framing process like the one just demonstrated in reference to preaching. However, our narrower interest in this final section is to examine how two different practices are related when preaching is taught. That is, we will explore how the practice of preaching sets certain frameworks for how the practice of teaching preaching is conducted.

I claimed earlier that there ought to be consonance between the teaching of a practice and the practice being taught. This is because, at the level of the focal practice itself, its aims or purposes govern all its other features and how they interrelate as an ensemble. For this reason, and since effective teaching of any practice requires approaching it in an accurate and ample fashion, teaching a practice is also governed by the aims and purposes bearing upon the practice itself. Consider again the practice of cooking. One of several imaginable aims for such a practice would be the creation of cuisine that is delicious and nourishing. This aim would affect other features of the practice as well, such as selection of raw ingredients (actions) or aesthetics of meal presentation (meaning). To teach the practice of cooking in a way that is inattentive to these various relevant features of the practice of cooking would undermine that larger aim and therefore be considered an inept pedagogy. This is what students mean by the complaint "I'm getting nothing out of that class." Assuming they have first invested effort, the remark implies that the method and content of the teaching have not attended to the aims of a practice students know they will have to attain as practitioners. As a result, they cannot grasp or use the features of that practice that will reach its aims.

No less is true when it comes to teaching preaching. For example, consider how the practice of preaching involves purposive actions. By "purposive," I mean the ends or aims a Christian assembly hopes will be reached through preaching. One such aim might be that of divine encounter. Through the sermon, the assembly desires to meet God and hear God's ways directly bearing upon human life. I noted earlier that the aims ought to affect the complex of actions that comprise preaching. One such action would be the form and content of language used during the sermon. Given the aim of divine encounter, then, the action of language use would likely tend toward dynamic and engaging modes of performative utterance, seeking to do something with words and thereby evoke the divine encounter that is the aim of such preaching. When it comes to teaching preaching in light of such aims and how they affect the action of language use, it should be fairly clear that the *content* of the instruction would reflect the same aims and thus focus on performative utterance as an action to be introduced, learned, and reinforced. Are we also willing, however, to accept the far more controversial implication that the *method* of instruction would also be governed by this kind of aim, using evocative language or intending divine encounter within the teaching?

This connection between teaching a practice and the practice being taught thus makes the teacher's task vastly more complex. Teaching preaching cannot be reduced to content delivery or skill development that keeps teacher and student at a safe distance. A practice-based approach to preaching leads to teaching that practice as a mutual risk and investment on the part of everyone involved in the learning environment. This mutuality also extends far beyond the preaching classroom itself to include the curriculum in which preaching instruction is located. For instance, the practice of preaching often includes the meaning-laden task of attending to a community's traditions, including its strong theological warrants. One way that the teaching of preaching addresses this is by modeling a respectful, creative, and discerning engagement with Scripture. Yet this sort of connection between teaching and the practice of preaching is quickly undercut if biblical instruction elsewhere in the curriculum utilizes strategies of textual mastery or cognitive analysis. At best, students will naturally be confused about how to take Scripture seriously in the practice of preaching. At worst, they will conclude that it is easier to analyze and report on a text in preaching than to produce an open and liberating engagement. Teaching preaching in a practice-based way extends to how the entire curriculum is conceived and implemented.

A practice-based approach also means that teaching preaching is unavoidably concerned with the formation of preachers, not just learning a practice. I remarked earlier that the character of practitioners is implicated in any serious examination of the features of a practice. The repeated tasks needed to appropriate the coordinated actions or multiple strategies of effective preaching require long-term effort that shapes how students perceive themselves, not just how others perceive them. Serious respect for the deep meanings within a faith community while learning to preach also forms preachers in those same values and communal roles. This is what is meant by the "habitus" of the practice, a feel for the game by which preachers realize their transformation from novices to adepts. The core issue is not about becoming more confident, but about growing in faithfulness in order to be open for others when preaching. This is why students who struggle with the practice of preaching often face deeper issues of faith formation and readiness for ministry. In my estimation, this is the invisible part of preaching instruction, rarely reflected in the course syllabus but instantly recognized by those who teach the practice. Learning to preach includes, as a necessary and vital component, being shaped by the practice in one's own character and faith. This aspect of preaching instruction is seriously understated in existing resources on the subject, and calls for much closer attention.

One final way that a practice-based approach to preaching affects how it is taught relates to assessment. Once again, my earlier discussion of the features of practices noted the implicit standards each feature suggests. For example, because preaching emerges as something "common," having a social origin and goal, attention to the local situation is not a decoration added to an otherwise completed sermon, but an integral question from the outset. This in turn means that contextual engagement is a standard by which preaching can be assessed. Just such an ability to make connections is at the heart of the following example.

> True to the church's heritage in the Reformed tradition, the sermon is the focal point of worship at FCC. Attention is riveted on the preacher as she steps up to the podium and begins to paint vivid word pictures, making real and present a vision of what the Christian life can be. Twenty minutes later she sits down, but the time passed seems but a moment. It is a moment (*kairos*) in which these worshippers are gathered together into a community. They have shared this experience, glimpsed the vision, and by so doing have affirmed the connections among them. Not many are able to explain what makes Reverend Kilsby's preaching so remarkable, so important to them, but all agree that it is.[25]

In this case, the standard of contextual engagement (one reason why this preaching was seen as remarkable) was not some abstract ideal imposed from elsewhere, but can be derived inductively from the specifics of the situated practice itself. Unlike Kilsby's hearers, however, the task for those who teach this practice would be to explore exactly how she embodied that standard within her preaching, as well as how other practitioners might do likewise in unforeseen settings.

Of course, preaching is not just any practice or even a generic speech act, but a Christian practice embedded within communities attentive to an overarching theological tradition and mission. For this reason, assessment standards in the teaching of preaching cannot be, say, the functional categories one would find in a communication arts course, as technically helpful as those might be. Those categories might help us refine the *components* and *actions* within the practice, but not the governing *domain* of endeavor that provides its reason for being. Instead, assessment of preaching looks at how the practice contributes to larger theological and ecclesial commitments, both within a confessional tradition and in relation to the church catholic and the *missio Dei* it embodies. Therefore, the marks for preaching that David Lose presents in the ensuing chapter can be conceived as the start of a practice-based approach to assessment standards.[26] Such marks are broad enough to be claimed by a range of Christians, while allowing for particular manifestations appropriate to the communities in which the practice actually occurs. Indeed, all the subsequent chapters in this volume operate out of a similar practice-based view of preaching, creating a general vision for how it might be taught that still remains open to specific adaptation.

NOTES

1. "Swing, with Harmonics," *Time,* December 28, 1953, 36.

2. Zora Neale Hurston, "Jonah's Gourd Vine," in *Novels and Stories* (New York: Library Classics of the United States, 1995), 144–45.

3. Nikolaus Lobkowicz, *Theory and Practice: History of a Concept from Aristotle to Marx* (Notre Dame, IN: University of Notre Dame Press, 1967); Richard J. Bernstein, *Praxis and Action: Contemporary Philosophies of Human Activity* (Philadelphia: University of Pennsylvania Press, 1971).

4. Alasdair MacIntyre explored this distinction between simple actions and fuller practices in his famous definition, although he often and unhelpfully blurred the same line in the examples he chose. See *After Virtue: A Study in Moral Theory* (Notre Dame, IN: University of Notre Dame Press, 1981), 187–88.

5. Roger Angell, *Late Innings: A Baseball Companion* (New York: Simon and Schuster, 1982), 43.

6. Duncan B. Forrester, *Truthful Action: Explorations in Practical Theology* (Edinburgh: T.&T. Clark, 2000), 4–5.

7. Jacques Pépin, *The Apprentice: My Life in the Kitchen* (Boston: Houghton Mifflin Co., 2003), 61.

8. Rebecca S. Chopp, *Saving Work: Feminist Practices of Theological Education* (Louisville, KY: Westminster John Knox Press, 1995), 15.

9. Charles S. Peirce, in *Collected Papers*, ed. Charles Hartshorne and Paul Weiss, vol. 2, *Elements of Logic* (Cambridge, MA: Belknap Press, 1931–58), 247.

10. Louise Erdrich, *The Master Butchers Singing Club* (New York: HarperCollins, 2002), 42–43.

11. Albert Borgmann, *Technology and the Character of Contemporary Life: A Philosophical Inquiry* (Chicago: University of Chicago Press, 1984), 196–210.

12. Norman Maclean, *A River Runs Through It* (Chicago: University of Chicago Press, 1989), 5–6.

13. Michel de Certeau, *The Practice of Everyday Life*, trans. Steven Rendall (Berkeley, CA: University of California Press, 1984), 34–39.

14. Pierre Bourdieu, *Practical Reason: On the Theory of Action* (Stanford, CA: Stanford University Press, 1998), 25, cf. 80–81.

15. Jon Krakauer, *Eiger Dreams: Ventures among Men and Mountains* (New York: Lyons & Burford, 1990), 14–15.

16. For an examination of preaching using MacIntyre's definition of practices, see Charles L. Campbell, *The Word before the Powers: An Ethic of Preaching* (Louisville, KY: Westminster John Knox Press, 2002), 136–39.

17. Herman Melville, *Moby Dick* (New York: Barnes & Noble Books, 1993), 33–34.

18. Kathryn Tanner, "Theological Reflection and Christian Practices," in *Practicing Theology: Beliefs and Practices in Christian Life,* ed. Miroslav Volf and Dorothy C. Bass (Grand Rapids: Wm. B. Eerdmans Publishing Co., 2002), 228–29.

19. For example, compare Christian preaching with the practices described in Robert V. Friedenberg, *"Hear O Israel": The History of American Jewish Preaching, 1654–1970,* Studies in Rhetoric and Communication (Tuscaloosa: University of Alabama Press, 1989); and Richard T. Antoun, *Muslim Preacher in the Modern World: A Jordanian Case Study in Comparative Perspective* (Princeton, NJ: Princeton University Press, 1989).

20. This relates also to Campbell's larger proposal that the practice of preaching should empower authentic Christian practices. Campbell, *The Word before the Powers*, 128–56.

21. Lee Bolman and Terrence Deal, *Reframing Organizations: Artistry, Choice, and Leadership* (San Francisco: Jossey-Bass, 1991), 11, 15–16, where the term was first defined as "a perspective or a distinctive group practice, a way of noticing a special sphere of activity ordered by certain predominant meanings, values, and purposes."

22. Richard Lischer, *The Preacher King: Martin Luther King Jr. and the Word That Moved America* (New York: Oxford University Press, 1995), 49.

23. Edith L. Blumhofer, *Aimee Semple McPherson: Everybody's Sister* (Grand Rapids: Wm. B. Eerdmans Publishing Co., 1993), 153.

24. Anne Tyler, *Saint Maybe* (New York: Alfred A. Knopf, 1991), 107.

25. Nancy Tatom Ammerman, et al., *Congregation and Community* (New Brunswick, NJ: Rutgers University Press, 1997), 176.

26. For another example of this procedure, see James Nieman, "What Is Preaching?" in *What Is Changing in Eucharistic Practice?* Open Questions in Worship, ed. Gordon Lathrop, vol. 5 (Minneapolis: Augsburg, 1995), 6–13.

3

Teaching Preaching as a Christian Practice

DAVID J. LOSE

In the summer of 1931, an eager father brought his four-year-old son to one of the instructors at the Imperial Musical Conservatory of Japan with a simple request: "Teach my child to play the violin." As straightforward as his petition was, however, it was also highly unusual, as training in such a difficult instrument did not normally begin until children were much older. Yet the father persisted and the instructor was intrigued, if somewhat baffled about how to begin. In seeking the means by which to train his young charge, the teacher was eventually struck by an observation as revolutionary as it was ordinary: all Japanese children learn to speak fluent Japanese. Though few of his contemporaries were immediately impressed by this insight, for Shinichi Suzuki it became the key to his now world-famous method of violin instruction.[1]

In a nutshell, what Suzuki discovered was that successful training in the violin springs neither from the innate musical ability of the student to become proficient with the instrument nor from the genius of the instructor to impart knowledge; rather, successful training comes from adopting a method of instruction in consonance with the basic human capacity to learn. Japanese, after all, is one of the most difficult languages in the world, and yet no child reared in Japan fails to master it. If so, concluded Suzuki, why not also the violin. What eventually resulted from these reflections, and his subsequent experience with thousands of young students, was his commitment to a method of instruction based on his convictions regarding how humans learn, an activity he observed most concretely in a child's acquisition of language. By carefully observing how children learn to speak their "mother tongue," and by applying and testing what he learned in his conservatory, Suzuki developed a pedagogy for musical instruction that has been used throughout the world to train hundreds of thousands of children in a variety of musical instruments.

Suzuki's work three-quarters of a century ago—and the tremendous success it continues to enjoy as a method of instruction—is illustrative because he intentionally developed a method by which to train students to become proficient in a specific *practice:* playing the violin. In recent decades, educators working in a variety of other practices as diverse as medicine, community organizing, and foreign language instruction have developed pedagogical principles that bear a distinct resemblance to Suzuki's.[2] While particular aspects of the training involved in such different disciplines may vary widely, what binds them together is a commitment to a pedagogy rooted in observations and convictions about the basic processes by which people acquire proficiency in some discipline, occupation, or practice. So while it is important for us to note and expect that the pedagogy of any given practice will entail specific requirements of teacher and student, we can nevertheless detect similar convictions about the type of educational environment most conducive to learning.

These developments in teaching specific practices mirror much recent literature in education theory more generally that shifts primary responsibility for learning away from the teacher toward the student.[3] The central conviction animating this work is that students learn most effectively when they are actively engaged in the material at hand. As a result of this trend, there is growing disdain for models of teaching centered exclusively on the abilities and actions of the teacher or lecturer (described pejoratively as "the sage on the stage" model), because the methods arising from such convictions often render students passive recipients of knowledge rather than active participants in the learning process. Instead, educators are advocating a variety of means by which to increase student participation in the learning process, including negotiating elements of the syllabus with students in order to increase their investment in the course, employing discussion and other teaching methods that nurture active and democratic engagement with the material, inviting students to take an active role by offering presentations, affirming in the construction of the course and the tone and manner of the instructor that students have valuable contributions to make to the learning process, and structuring the means by which students can provide critical feedback to, and learn from, each other.[4]

Although this pedagogical shift is most regularly described as moving from a "teacher-centered" to a "learner-" or "student-centered" approach, I suggest that a more apt description is "learn*ing*-centered," as the goal of engaging student participation reflects beliefs about the actual *process* of learning. That is, we shift our attention and energy from either the teacher or the learner per se to the common pursuit and activity of *learning* that joins the two. Similar to Suzuki, educators embracing this model have dismissed the myth of innate genius, whether lodged in the student or the teacher, in order to focus instead on creating structured learning environments that can be sustained across a variety of disciplines and settings, including even recent moves to instruction via the Internet.[5] Further, these educators have moved beyond conceiving of learning primarily as an act of transmitting and receiving information toward viewing learning as an act of transformation by acquiring new habits, practices, and perspectives in addition to new insight and information.[6]

While teachers of a variety of subject matter have found it helpful to adopt and adapt a learning-centered method of teaching to their fields, for those who teach a particular discipline—be it violin performance, medicine, or preaching—it is simply crucial. Practices, as discussed in the previous chapter, are patterned, common actions that are strategically undertaken toward realizing distinct communal goals.[7] Therefore, for any practice to continue serving its communal end, at least two things need to happen. First, for a practice to persist, let alone to flourish, it must pass on to its students—that is, the practitioners of the future—the discrete knowledge, skills, and attitudes that describe and define the practice in the first place and thereby enable those students to participate in, and realize the goal of, the practice. Because becoming proficient in a practice has never been simply a matter of absorbing information, our chances of training students to become adept practitioners increase immeasurably as we engage them in active, participatory, learning-centered methods of instruction. (Dare we suggest that one of the reasons preaching has suffered so considerably in recent decades is because we have taught it as a body of static information rather than as a living practice?) Second, flourishing practices are not static institutions, but are always evolving to be responsive to the needs and demands of the current age. For this reason, educating students to be critically reflective practitioners is simply essential if we wish not simply to repeat a tradition, but to perpetuate a living practice.

On both of these counts, learning-centered pedagogy lends itself particularly well to teaching a practice. First, it proposes uniform structures by which students may gain proficiency in any given practice while also honoring the varying discipline-specific knowledge, skills, and attitudes each individual practice will demand. Second, it seeks to train students to be critically reflective practitioners by drawing them into active engagement with the material at hand, by immersing them in the actual execution of the practice, and by encouraging them to take responsibility for their own learning.

In addition to these benefits, a learning-centered approach to teaching practices also places the relationship of the teacher and student on the solid ground of a shared commitment to learning the practice at hand. The central issue is neither the teacher nor the student, it is learning; and the shared commitment of teacher and learner to this larger goal helpfully clarifies the tasks and roles at hand while distributing both the power in the relationship and the responsibility for learning more evenly. Finally, a learning-centered approach to teaching, because it identifies the discrete elements that constitute the practice, provides internal, objective, and discipline-specific standards of evaluation that assist both teacher and learner in assessing progress, correcting errors in theory or execution, and celebrating development. Because of these and other benefits, it is my intention in this chapter to adopt and adapt such an approach to the teaching of preaching. Toward this end, the remainder of this chapter divides into two parts. In the first I will outline five elements of learning-centered, practice-oriented pedagogy I have found most helpful and describe some of the implications of each for the teaching of preaching. In the second section I will offer a description of preaching as a practice based on its particular goal or, to borrow from the Greek, telos. From there we will be able in the rest of this volume to delve more successfully into a discussion of the various constituent parts of the practice of preaching and construct effective strategies to teach these to our students effectively.

ELEMENTS OF TEACHING PRACTICES

Not surprisingly, different incarnations of learning-centered, practice-oriented approaches to teaching and learning manifest different pedagogical elements or components. Despite there being, therefore, no "master list" of formally agreed-upon dimensions of "practice-oriented" teaching, I am drawing on literature I have read across specific disciplines and in educational theory generally, as well as my own experiences as a teacher and learner in several distinct settings, in order to distill five central components: (1) the frequent exposure to examples of excellent practice (and the importance of role models); (2) creating a supportive environment of high expectations; (3) identifying and teaching the distinct, interrelated parts that constitute the specific practice; (4) engaging in an action-reflection model of learning; and (5) instilling a commitment to lifelong learning and development in the practice. In addition to describing each of these briefly, I will also highlight some of the concrete pedagogical implications that emerge in relation to the teaching of preaching.

1. *Frequent exposure to examples of excellent practice.* An implicit conviction of learning-centered, practice-oriented education is that it is difficult to do what you cannot imagine and even more difficult to imagine what you have not experienced. For this reason, frequent exposure to exemplary practice is crucial to the teaching and learning of any discipline. Examples of this abound. What, for instance, is the single greatest predictor of a child's ability to read, write, and eventually succeed in academics? The amount of time the child was read to by an adult or older child. Being read to, as numerous studies have demonstrated, not only inculcates basic dimensions of grammar, but more importantly creates in the child positive experiences of, and expectations for, the experience of reading books.[8] Similarly, consider the vastly superior results that immersion courses in a foreign language have over translation-based classes. Students who are consistently immersed in a foreign language eventually not only internalize the basic grammar and vocabulary of what they are hearing, they also develop along the way evaluative standards regarding pronunciation, accent, and so forth by which they can "self-correct" their own learning and thereby accelerate their progress. Perhaps not surprisingly, we learn a second language most easily the way we learned our first: by constant exposure, listening for great lengths of time, making connections between various symbols, actions, and things, before attempting active production. For this reason Suzuki students spend hours listening to masterful performances of the music they will eventually play long before they set bow to string. By this constant exposure to, and even immersion in, excellent examples of the practice, students make all kinds of conscious and unconscious observations and connections and internalize norms about what constitutes effective practice.

This, in turn, highlights the importance role models can play, although we should be cautious not to elevate the teacher or any other role model to the status of "guru." Rather, what is called for is the availability of a more advanced practitioner who not only can provide examples of effective practice but is also willing to offer guidance to the student covering terrain the mentor has already traveled.[9] In fact, the teacher does not have to be the only or primary role model. Other professionals in the field, senior colleagues, and more advanced students can serve in this capacity. To acknowledge the importance of role models for students entering into a disciplined practice is simply to reclaim the critical role apprenticeships once played across disciplines, and can still be seen not only in various trades but also in professions like medicine, with its mandatory residency under a supervisor, and law, where those interested in pursuing a seat on the judicial bench will first clerk with an experienced justice.

For this reason, the students in our preaching classes would be well served if we offered them numerous examples of good preaching. Certainly these do not need to be similar types of preaching, all in one form or style or even from one theological point of view. What must be consistent is the excellence of the sermons. Instructors can provide these examples by using audio- or videotapes of sermons in class, encouraging students to draw on the video and audio resources most seminary libraries offer, highlighting the strong elements of student preaching when it occurs in class, and encouraging attendance at chapel and Sunday worship. As I tell my students, I learned more about preaching from regularly going to chapel in seminary than I did from any single class in preaching.

At the same time, we must also take into account the negative impact of bad examples. Some theorists believe that tone deafness, for instance, is not the result of a physical defect of the ear or brain but rather the result of repeated exposure to an out-of-tune musical gamut.[10] The solution, in such a case, is to overwhelm the history of negative examples with positive ones, eventually erasing and replacing the defective learning with the proper one. Might it be that part of the challenge of teaching students to preach is that they have heard so much bad preaching in the church? Our response as instructors can only be to provide them with numerous examples of excellent preaching and to serve as experienced guides as they attempt to learn how to preach well themselves.

2. *Creating a supportive environment of high expectations.* Learning is a discretionary activity. That is, it will not take place until other more basic needs have been met. These include basic requirements of shelter and food (hence the success of free-breakfast programs at many schools) and the need for a sense of safety, well-being, and affirmation. In short, there must

be a high level of trust between students and instructors.[11] Perhaps nowhere is this more evident in the seminary curriculum than in an introductory preaching course, where students bring all the normal trepidations about public speaking and combine them with a salutary awe of being charged to proclaim the Word of God. For this reason it is simply imperative that students experience the preaching classroom as a place of safety, trust, and mutual respect. This is not to advocate an "I'm OK; you're OK" approach to preaching. Rather, it is to insist that the teacher's role is to "tell the truth in love," commending what is strong and pointing out what needs to be corrected or improved, in a manner that never jeopardizes the students' sense of self-worth. Instructors not only model such behavior, but they also are in a position to actively create such an environment by intentionally structuring the class or workshop with basic ground rules for the giving and receiving of critical feedback.

When such a climate of trust and respect is created, then critical feedback itself becomes a tool not only of instruction but also of affirmation, as students believe that the instructor and peers offer critical input on their performance because they want the preacher to improve. Further, the high expectations set by the instructor—both for performance of the practice and the giving of feedback—convey the instructor's belief that students are capable of reaching such standards. Ensuring that the critique is balanced between the strong elements of a student's attempt and areas for the student's improvement is important not only because it safeguards the environment of trust but also because it lifts up positive examples for all the students to emulate as well as celebrate.

In order to maintain an environment of support and trust, instructors must also be clear about their expectations, both in terms of (a) student participation in the course and (b) what constitutes effective practice. That is, high expectations that are not clear will only be frustrating and confusing, and will very quickly undermine the climate of trust we desire to create. Discipline-specific standards of effective practice will emerge from immersion in the constituent elements of the practice. Elucidating these will nurture a supportive classroom environment, aid instructors and students in the task of evaluation, and help students internalize norms of excellent practice and thereby enable them to become more critically reflective practitioners capable of taking responsibility for their ongoing development.

3. *Identifying and teaching the distinct, interrelated parts that constitute the specific practice.* Every practice can be subdivided into distinct components or constituent parts that, when governed by the internal

logic of the discipline, constitute practice. These may include the distinct actions, unique history, and particular terminology that distinguish the practice and without which it is difficult to enact the practice. A primary element of practice-centered teaching is therefore to identify these components and train students in their execution.[12] The constituent parts are interrelated, of course, and from the outside may in fact be difficult to separate. That is, when an untrained listener hears either a sermon or a performance of Bach's "Double Concerto," he or she may not be aware of, let alone able to isolate, the various distinct actions, skills, and abilities that go into the performance; nevertheless, the student has studied and mastered each element, and the mark of such mastery is, in fact, their seamless employment.

Some components or elements may simply be intentional actions or skills employed to execute the practice—like pitching in baseball or bowing in violin performance, neither of which make much sense apart from the practice they serve. Other components may themselves be traditioned practices in other circumstances—like biblical exegesis— which are employed in this case to reach the distinct goal or telos of some other practice. In either case, instructors can greatly assist their students not only by identifying such constituent parts, but also by structuring their basic classes around them so as to lead students through the various elements, moving either from the easiest to the more difficult (as in working on a three-minute summary of a sermon, to a longer one with an illustration, to a full-fledged sermon), or in an order of logical succession (e.g., choosing a biblical text, interpreting the text, distilling a central focus from the text on which to preach).[13]

The distinctiveness of the particular practice in question emerges most clearly at this point, as students are learning the knowledge, skills, and attitudes that actually constitute the practice they seek to master. Like the grammar of a language, such constituent parts, when mastered, allow students to "converse" in their chosen discipline fluently. In my classes and writing I have described the constituent components of preaching as the "marks" of a good sermon, intentionally borrowing the paradigm of identifying the classic "marks of the church." Such marks, grammar, constituent parts, or elements are each necessary but not sufficient to constitute the practice. That is, without pitching baseball would not be baseball, but pitching apart from the other constituting elements of playing baseball seems rather pointless. Much of the rest of this volume, as with much of our preaching classes, will delve into these constituent elements.

4. *Engaging in an action/reflection model of learning.* To emphasize the importance of actual participation in a practice is not simply to underscore the basic fact that we "learn by doing"; it is also to join in challenging the Enlightenment and modernist penchant for privileging the theoretical over the practical. All too often, the actual practice of a discipline has been seen as merely the application of previously derived theory.[14] What is called for in response is a more organic sense of the relationship between theory and practice, emphasizing the necessary interdependence between the two, in that while theory informs practice, practice in turn not only assesses, validates, and extends theory but is also often the source of theory in the first place. That is, often it is only by participating in a practice and reflecting on that participation that we can deduce its internal logic.

Further, accentuating the importance of actually engaging in the subject at hand turns over significant responsibility for learning to the students. In a practice-oriented learning environment students cannot afford to sit back as passive recipients, but rather are encouraged to participate, to learn about both the practice and themselves by actually engaging in it, and in this way to actualize the dynamics of the practice in their own being through constant and repeated critical engagement with the knowledge, skills, and attitudes the practice demands. By constant immersion in the discipline of "reflection-in-action," students become far more critically aware—of themselves and of the practice at hand—and in this way experience the transformative power of education.[15]

To go a step farther, we might better capture the importance of repeatedly engaging in a practice in order to master it by describing this as an "action/reflection, action/reflection, action/action/action/reflection" model, as only repeated participation leads to mastery. Or, as Suzuki once said, "Knowledge is not skill; skill is knowledge practiced one thousand times."[16] Further, as with other action-reflection pedagogies, a practice-centered vision of teaching has as its goal not simply sharing information, but transformation, as through repeated practice students come to realize and participate in the teleological goal of the practice.

In terms of preaching, this means we need to maximize the number of preaching opportunities available to students. Preaching once and then trying it again a second time, as has been the norm in many basic preaching courses, simply will not do. Rather, students should preach in an environment of supportive critique five, six, seven, or more times during their seminary experience. Through repeated participation in the practice students will be more likely to develop a measure of proficiency and thereby both gain a degree of self-confidence that comes only from competency, as well as realize the intrinsic ends and good of the practice. In this way, students experience the penultimate transformation that proficiency in a practice offers, as they can now do something well they could not do before, and, because they can do it, they are different people than they were before.

Privileging the actual experience of preaching over other aspects of course work will necessitate some difficult choices, but can often be accomplished by strategically drawing on other elements of the curriculum. Certainly if we trust the exegetical training students are receiving from our counterparts, we can spend less time covering such material in class, instead offering instruction on how that training can be adapted to feed and fuel the preaching process. At the same time, we might cultivate conversations with colleagues in other disciplines about how the central task of proclamation might surface more immediately in other classes. I have been impressed, for example, by the number of my colleagues who include writing or preaching a sermon based on their exegetical or theological work as part of their course requirements. We might also explore with colleagues possibilities for cross-discipline team teaching in order to invite students into deeper immersion in the practice of preaching as it intersects with other Christian disciplines.

5. *Instilling a commitment to lifelong learning and development in the practice.* Any practice worth giving your professional life to will not be mastered during one's years at seminary, let alone in a single course. For this reason, it is important that we nurture in students the awareness that their course work at seminary is merely the good beginning of a lifelong journey. This is particularly true of preaching, where once a minister is engaged in regular preaching it becomes increasingly difficult for him or her to continue to be exposed to excellent examples of practice; therefore, a commitment to ongoing hard work, professional development, and continuing education are paramount. Further, most practices require consistent attention and, well, *practice!* It is not only athletes and performers who describe themselves as "rusty" when they have been away from the rigors of their practice; preachers, too, suffer in their efforts when they do not keep up-to-date on recent homiletical theory or have not kept their skills sharp by availing themselves of structured feedback.[17] Discipline is one of the most predominant attitudes that proficiency in any practice demands, and students should be

encouraged to develop a disciplined approach to sermon preparation while still at seminary. At the beginning of my latest preaching courses, I have told my students about recently taking up the violin after an almost entirely nonmusical childhood, and then describe my habit of practicing six days a week for a half hour or more. After telling them that I expect to maintain this routine for the next eight to ten years to gain a modest level of proficiency, I pause briefly before asking them how much time they plan to commit to their chosen vocational practice over the course of this semester, year, and their professional lives.

Taking this kind of a "long view" approach to teaching and learning preaching also helps instructors prioritize what happens in the classroom. Rather than trying to teach students "everything they need to know" about preaching, teachers can instead design a course that not only introduces them to the practice and trains them in "the basics" of the discipline, but also equips them to continue learning once they have graduated.

A final point regarding lifelong learning: If as teachers of preaching we sincerely believe that cultivating in our students a commitment to disciplined habits and continuing education is integral to training excellent preachers, then it is not enough simply to encourage lifelong learning on the part of students. Seminaries must increasingly furnish such opportunities and produce resources of high quality to assist learners who practice at a distance. It may, perhaps, help us commit more fully to this task if we can imagine and believe that the educational experience we give our students during their seminary career may serve as their initial training, but is certainly not their primary training, as that inevitably comes through their experience of preaching in an actual congregation and via whatever continuing education opportunities they avail themselves of after several years at the craft. Just as we encourage other students to continue their training in their vocational practice throughout their careers, so also must seminaries realize that their commitment to students does not end at commencement.

THE TELOS OF PREACHING

Much of the rest of this volume will discuss the distinct elements of the practice of preaching, both describing the distinct knowledge, skills, and attitudes that together constitute preaching as well as suggesting methods and strategies by which to engage students in developing proficiency in them. Before doing so, it will be helpful to describe the goal, end, or telos of preaching more fully—this for several reasons.

First, and as we discussed in the preceding chapter, practices are inherently teleological; that is, they are strategic and purposeful actions executed in order to achieve certain intrinsic ends, goods, or goals. When one plays the violin well one participates in the internal and intrinsic end, or good, of musical performance—experiencing the joy, even rapture, that music can bring—that is distinct from whatever external ends such as monetary compensation or audience appreciation may also be involved. Similarly, by playing baseball one participates in the internal end or goal of baseball—being caught up in the excitement and joy of playing this particular sport. In the same way, when one preaches one seeks to participate in the distinct end the practice has been cultivated to achieve: participating in God's active, saving, and electing word of grace.

Second, all of the constituent parts or elements we consider are themselves intended to contribute toward reaching this goal. Keeping this in mind helps us to conceive and define the discrete parts of the practice in service toward this end. That is, biblical exegesis when employed as a part of preparing to preach is not ultimately about determining what the text meant in a certain time and place, but rather is about enabling us to perceive through our work with the biblical witness how God is at work in the world today. Further, a clear sense of the telos toward which the various component parts of preaching point will also assist us in evaluating and prioritizing our teaching of the constituent elements in relation to how we believe they will best contribute to realizing preaching's distinct teleological aim. We may choose to begin an introductory preaching class, for instance, with a presentation on biblical exegesis, theological analysis, or the importance of studying our context, depending on how we believe such an ordering will assist us in training students to reach the telos of the practice of preaching. Such decisions about how to begin and proceed through our courses are governed, implicitly or explicitly, by our convictions about the end toward which we strive.

Third, it is by realizing (or failing to realize) the intrinsic goal or good of preaching that we receive the clearest indication of whether we have developed proficiency in the practice. In this way, a clear sense of preaching's telos will serve as the basis for assessing our development in the practice. Failure to realize our goals, from this point of view, is therefore not a tragedy, but rather an opportunity to reflect on our understanding and execution of the component elements of preaching in order to assess the performance and increase the likelihood of achieving our desired end the next time. If the feedback loop is to succeed, there must be a clear sense of the teleological goal of the practice.

Finally, we should note the contextual nature of any propositions about the telos of preaching. That is, even as the practice aims to achieve—and therefore is governed by—a particular telos, that very goal is conceptualized in light of the practice itself. That is, because the goal is an internal good, arising from the practice and serving the aims of the participating community, the telos itself is neither universal nor permanent, but is affected by changes in the practice over time as well as by the needs and demands of particular Christian communities.

It will be helpful, then, to sketch a preliminary description of the Christian practice of preaching with a particular view toward its teleological goal. Others may wish to modify, extend, or formulate an alternative confession of preaching's goal, purpose, or telos, and these formulations (implicit or explicit) will have significant implications for their teaching. At this point, therefore, I want to (a) assert the importance of identifying one's sense of the telos of preaching and (b) put mine on the table as a working "good faith" example of what I am advocating.

In brief, therefore, I describe the telos of preaching as *drawing people into an encounter with the crucified and risen Christ that they may come to new life and be caught up into the present and ongoing work and story of God.* Two brief forays into the biblical witness will help to flesh this definition out. The first passage I want to consider is the formal conclusion to John's Gospel, paying specific attention to its relationship to the overarching rhetorical function of the Fourth Gospel. In John 20:30–31, the Fourth Evangelist seems finally to "come clean" on his intentions regarding his work: "Now Jesus did many other signs in the presence of his disciples, which are not written in this book. But these are written so that you may come to believe that Jesus is the Messiah, the Son of God, and that through believing you may have life in his name." Strikingly, John admits that he self-consciously exercises authorial intention. That is, he includes some narratives while excluding others. Why? Because he has a rhetorical goal in mind: persuading listeners that Jesus is the Christ, the Son of God, so that they may believe in him.

This, in turn, sheds light on John's larger work, as one may view the Fourth Gospel as structured around a series of encounters between different characters and Jesus. Each character offers the reader a distinct potential response to Jesus, ranging from the confusion of Nicodemus to the faith of the Samaritan woman, and from the openness of the man born blind to Peter's denial. This panoply of reactions culminates in the scene with Thomas just prior to John's formal conclusion (John 20:19–29), where Thomas first doubts the proclamation of Christ's resurrection but ultimately responds in faith by making the great confession of John's Gospel (echoing and amplifying the parallel confession in the prologue) that Jesus is God.[18] Significantly, immediately after this model response by Thomas, Jesus offers his blessing to all those who will make a similar confession without the benefit of seeing Jesus face to face.

While John at no point speaks directly about preaching, this brief reading of the evangelical thrust of this Gospel invites our assertion that the goal or telos of all Christian witness and proclamation is to facilitate, even create, an encounter between the hearer and the risen Christ so that he or she may come to faith. Preaching, therefore, cannot afford to be simply talk "about" what God has done in Jesus but rather must re-present the resurrected and living Christ as God's ongoing presence and work in the world, thereby inviting the hearer to participate in the new reality God has created and continues to sustain through our life in Christ.[19]

Luke's account of Jesus' encounter with two disciples on the road to Emmaus (Luke 24:13–35) offers a second biblical touchstone for our discussion of the telos of preaching. Meeting two hitherto unmentioned disciples in the midst of their grief over the death of their Lord, Jesus first interprets Scripture in order to make sense of the cross and then breaks bread with the disciples so that they may recognize him. Unable to contain their excitement, the two depart and make the dangerous evening journey back to Jerusalem in order to tell the others what they have witnessed. Unique to Luke, this narrative seems to point the hearer to the Sunday gathering of the faithful around the interpretation of Scripture and the sharing of the Communion meal as the primary location for encountering the resurrected Christ. Further, it seems to promise that once encountered by the risen Christ, disciples—then and now—will be propelled to witness to their experience.

Again, there is a clear conviction that Jesus continues to be available to those who believe in him through the proclamation of the gospel in the spoken and visible words of Christian worship. Preaching therefore cannot be mere instruction, exhortation, or even kerygmatic announcement, but must always seek to prompt an encounter with the living Christ.

This lends a distinct edge to Christian proclamation, as we acknowledge that we are not simply reporting on past deeds of God but, rather, are participating in God's ongoing work of redemption, re-creation, and election. As Paul Scott Wilson writes, "When we preach we participate in a unique way in God's salvation history. We break open the biblical text and allow God's Word to move out into today's world with the same transformative power and freshness as it held for the original hearers. We preach as though someone's life depended on it because someone's life does!"[20] Christian preaching extends the act of Christ's resurrection into the present, where it continues to raise the dead to life.

Such a view of preaching privileges direct address and relational forms of speech as the primary means by which to witness, confess, proclaim, and pronounce in such a way as to confront hearers with God's ongoing and immediate work in the resurrected Christ present in the world.[21] It also demands that teachers of preaching attend to the presence or absence of a preacher's sense that God is truly present and active in the preaching of the gospel. That is, there are theological and rhetorical criteria that, while varying in degree from one tradition to another, are inescapably present and demand the attention of both teacher and preacher. While it may be difficult at times to pinpoint exactly what contributed to or hindered the success of a particular effort, the sermon that is both successful and faithful will leave hearers with a sense that they have been caught up into God's present and ongoing work to redeem the world.

NOTES

1. Shinichi Suzuki, *Nurtured by Love: The Classic Approach to Talent Education*, 2nd ed., trans. Waltraud Suzuki (Miami, FL: Warner Bros. Publications, 1983), 1–2.

2. For example, Jane Vella promotes a "dialogical" approach to adult education that has been applied across numerous disciplines and practices and that overlaps with Suzuki's principles at many points. See her *Learning to Listen, Learning to Teach: The Power of Dialogue in Educating Adults* (San Francisco: Jossey-Bass, 1994). See also, Mark E. Quirk, *How to Teach and Learn in Medical School: A Learner-Centered Approach* (Springfield, IL: Charles C. Thomas, Publisher, 1996), and *Immersion Education: International Perspectives*, ed. Robert Keith Johnson et al. (Cambridge: Cambridge University Press, 1997).

3. In addition to Vella, see Chet Myers and Thomas B. Jones, *Promoting Active Learning: Strategies for the College Classroom* (San Francisco: Jossey-Bass, 1993), which surveys and builds on much literature on active and transformative learning.

4. See, for instance, Stephen D. Brookfield, *The Skillful Teacher* (San Francisco:

Jossey-Bass, 1990), and Stephen D. Brookfield and Stephen Preskill, *Discussion as a Way of Teaching: Tools and Techniques for Democratic Classrooms* (San Francisco: Jossey-Bass, 1999).

5. See, for example, Rena M. Palloff and Keith Pratt, *Building Learning Communities in Cyberspace* (San Francisco: Jossey-Bass, 1999).

6. See, among many titles, Patricia Cranton's *Understanding and Promoting Transformative Learning: A Guide for Educators of Adults* (San Francisco: Jossey-Bass, 1994).

7. See also Alasdair MacIntyre, *After Virtue: A Study in Moral Theory*, 2nd ed. (Notre Dame, IN: University of Notre Dame Press, 1984), esp. 181–203; Miroslav Volf and Dorothy C. Bass, eds., *Practicing Theology: Beliefs and Practices in Christian Life* (Grand Rapids: Wm. B. Eerdmans Publishing Co., 2001); and Charles L. Campbell, *The Word before the Powers* (Louisville, KY: Westminster John Knox Press, 2002), esp. 128–39.

8. See Jim Trelease's *The Read-Aloud Handbook*, 5th ed. (New York: Viking Penguin, 2001), which documents numerous studies about relationships between being read to, literacy, and academic success.

9. The term "mentor," in fact, comes from Homer's *Odyssey*, where the character Mentor serves as a guide to Telemachus, Odysseus's young son, during his absence.

10. See Suzuki, *Ability Development from Age Zero*, trans. Mary Louise Nagata (Miami, FL: Warner Bros. Publications, 1981), 7–8.

11. See Vella, *Learning to Listen*, 53–77, and Brookfield, *The Skillful Teacher*, 163–76.

12. See Vella, *Learning to Listen*, 78–86. In addition to Suzuki, Maria Montessori also adopted this approach; see her *The Absorbent Mind* (New York: Holt, Rinehart & Winston, 1967), and Paula Polk Lillard, *Montessori Today: A Comprehensive Approach to Education from Birth to Adulthood* (New York: Random House, 1996).

13. See Alvin C. Rueter's *Making Good Preaching Better* (Collegeville, MN: Liturgical Press, 1997) for an example of the first, and Thomas G. Long's *The Witness of Preaching* (Louisville, KY: Westminster/John Knox Press, 1989) for the second.

14. See Donald A. Schön, *Educating the Reflective Practitioner* (San Francisco: Jossey-Bass, 1987), 9.

15. See Donald A. Schön, *The Reflective Practitioner* (New York: Basic Books, 1983), 21–69.

16. Vella advocates repeating something 1,142 times!

17. See John S. McClure, *The Round-Table Pulpit* (Nashville: Abingdon Press, 1995), and Craig A. Loscalzo, "Feedback," in *Best Advice for Preachers*, ed. John S. McClure (Minneapolis: Fortress Press, 1998), for counsel regarding gaining feedback through congregational sermon groups and other means.

18. My view of the rhetorical goal of John's Gospel has been influenced deeply by R. Alan Culpepper's *Anatomy of the Fourth Gospel: A Study in Literary Design* (Philadelphia: Fortress Press, 1983).

19. See James F. Kay's *Christus Praesens: A Reconsideration of Rudolf Bultmann's Christology* (Grand Rapids: Wm. B. Eerdmans Publishing Co., 1994) for a helpful exploration of how Christ is present in the preaching of the gospel.

20. Paul Scott Wilson, *Imagination of the Heart: New Understandings in Preaching* (Nashville: Abingdon Press, 1988).

21. For more on the kinds of language appropriate to such preaching, see David J. Lose, *Confessing Jesus Christ: Preaching in a Postmodern World* (Grand Rapids: Wm. B. Eerdmans Publishing Co., 2003), 220–31.

SECTION TWO

The Components of the Practice of Preaching

4

Interpreting Texts for Preaching

JAMES W. THOMPSON

In the oldest extant sermon to a Christian audience, the author of Hebrews announces to his community that the God who spoke "to our ancestors in many and various ways by the prophets," has now "spoken to us by a Son."[1] The unknown preacher suggests that his own community lives in continuity with previous generations insofar as they have all heard the voice of God. Although God has spoken "in many and various ways," and ultimately through the Christ event, the community now hears the voice of God through ancient texts that speak directly to the community. Indeed, the author's role as the interpreter of texts is evident in the striking way that he moves between the past and present tense when he cites Scripture; God "has said," "speaks" (4:3, 4), and "testified" (2:6) in Scripture; at the same time God also speaks to and encourages the church through ancient texts (3:7ff; 12:5–6). The "today" of the ancient text is also the "today" of the author's sermon (3:13), for Scripture continues to speak as a voice that is "living and active" (4:12).

This ancient sermon, with its many predecessors in Judaism and successors in the Christian tradition, reflects the Christian understanding of the telos of preaching. To preach the word of God is to interpret texts through which God speaks, to offer good news to the community, and to invite the listeners to participate in God's story. If Hebrews is a model, the preacher is an interpreter of Scripture. Just as the ancient author and his community lived in continuity with their ancestors, the modern preacher and church live in continuity with predecessors who assembled to hear the word of God mediated through Scripture.

The fact that the preacher is an interpreter of Scripture makes the disciplined study of Scripture an essential aspect of preparation for preaching. However, few homiletics textbooks actually offer guidelines for students in the art of biblical interpretation. In our brief survey of homiletics textbooks, we found that Fred Craddock's *Preaching*,[2] Thomas Long's *The Witness of Preaching*,[3] and Paul Scott Wilson's *God Sense: Reading the Bible for Preaching*[4] offer thorough treatments of exegetical and hermeneutical strategies for preaching. The absence of chapters in many other textbooks guiding students from text to sermon probably reflects the homiletics teacher's desire to leave biblical interpretation to scholars in New Testament and Old Testament/Hebrew Bible and to assume that courses in exegesis prepare students to interpret the Bible for preaching.

One cannot assume, however, that students who have taken the basic courses in Bible are equipped to make the journey from text to sermon, inasmuch as the seminary curriculum has divided biblical interpretation into separate disciplines. Thus students have rarely seen models of the integration of exegesis and preaching. The preacher may become impatient with the biblical scholar's fascination with the world behind the text. The energy that the exegete devotes to identifying the opponents in Philippians or the earliest layers of the Q tradition is daunting to the nonspecialist who preaches each Sunday. The amount of useful information may appear meager for the preacher who knows that, just as few come eagerly wanting to know "what happened to the Jebusites,"[5] not many come to hear about the status of biblical scholarship on the united monarchy or the Synoptic problem. Much of the critical information, if presented to the congregation, would be boring and irrelevant for their needs. Moreover, the biblical scholar commonly answers the questions of the academic guild rather than those of the church, treating the biblical text not as a voice addressing the believing community, but as an artifact of the past. Without the guidance of either biblical scholars or homileticians in appropriating biblical scholarship for preaching, students will face the temptation to compartmentalize biblical exegesis and preaching, omitting any disciplined study of Scripture in the preparation of the sermon.

Interpretation involves the interaction between the author(s), the text, and the reader(s). Interpreters have often focused on one of these aspects to the exclusion of the others. Prior to the Enlightenment, they rarely expressed an interest in authorial intent, but focused on the meaning of the text for the reader. They recognized the authority of texts transmitted by earlier generations, but assumed that passages took on new meaning as communities read them in new situations. Prophets appealed to Israel's ancient traditions to interpret their own situation.[6] New Testament writers found entirely new meanings in Scripture as their experience of the cross and resurrection elicited a rereading of sacred Scripture that would make sense of these events. Modern exegetes are often amused and perplexed by the interpretive methods of the author of Hebrews and of all premodern interpreters who recognized no historical distance between themselves and the ancient text. The author of Hebrews belonged to the world of premodern exegesis in which interpreters studied Scripture to see what it *says* to the church. Although ancient approaches to interpretation varied, almost all were united in the merged horizons between the author, the text, and the community. The ancient commentaries were indistinguishable from the sermons. The fourfold interpretation of Scripture that dominated the Middle Ages was based on the assumption that Scripture speaks to the church in order to be interpreted for the church. Paul's approach to interpretation, according to which all Scripture "was written for our instruction" (Rom. 15:4), was the basic premise for interpreters and preachers for centuries. The interpreter's horizon was scarcely distinguishable from the horizon of the text.

If premodern readings of Scripture were intended to serve the church, holding together the horizon of author, text, and reader, the historical-critical reading of Scripture that accompanied the Enlightenment became the wedge to liberate the interpreter from the church and even to challenge church teaching. With its emphasis on authorial intent, historical-critical interpretation attempted to place controls on the possible meanings of a passage by stripping away the layers of traditional readings in order to recover the *real* meaning of the passage. This understanding has dominated commentaries since the nineteenth century, when H. A. W. Meyer stated that his commentary, the premier series in Germany for more than a century, would bracket all confessional issues and answer only historical and philological questions. The objective and scientific analysis of Scripture remains the dominant paradigm for the analysis of biblical texts in most commentaries. This attempt to place limits on the meaning of texts has been, for many people, a welcome alternative to the focus on the subjective reader-centered interpretation. However, in separating the horizon of the original author from that of the believing community, it created a special challenge for preachers who have received a calling to interpret Scripture for the community of faith.

Because biblical studies and homiletics commonly ask different questions, the practice of interpretation should be a vital part of the homiletics class. This practice is not an alternative to critical scholarship in biblical studies, but the incorporation of new dimensions in biblical study that will ensure that the Bible is the possession not only of the academy, but also of the church. Arthur Koestler offered an analogy to our insistence on reading in more than one dimension:

> As children we used to be given a curious kind of puzzle to play with. It was a paper with a tangle of very thin blue and red lines. If you just looked at it you couldn't make out anything. But if you covered it with a piece of transparent red tissue-paper, the red lines of the drawing disappeared and the blue lines formed a picture—it was a clown in a circus holding a hoop and a little dog jumping through it. And if you covered the same drawing with a blue tissue-paper, a roaring lion appeared chasing the clown across the ring. You can do the same thing with every mortal, living or dead. You can look at him through Sonia's tissue-paper and write a biography of Napoleon in terms of his pituitary gland as has been done: the fact that he incidentally conquered Europe will appear as a mere symptom of the activities of those two tiny lobes, the size of a pea. You can explain the message of the Prophets as epileptic foam and the Sistine Madonna as the projection of an incestuous dream. The method is correct and the picture in itself complete. But beware of the arrogant error of believing that it is the only one. The picture you get through the blue tissue-paper will be no less true and complete. The clown and the lion are both there, interwoven in the same pattern.[7]

As the homiletics class incorporates the discoveries and analytic tools from biblical studies, it adds new dimensions to the study of Scripture. The class will conduct its own conversation with biblical studies, asking the questions of the text that are rarely asked in the exegesis class while appropriating the skills that are developed in the critical study of the Bible. In some institutions, professors in homiletics and biblical studies may team-teach courses in preaching biblical texts and model the conversation between the disciplines. Assignments in preaching classes may involve exegetical working papers that require the students to describe the exegetical and hermeneutical moves that accompany preparation of the sermon.

Scripture can only be "living and active" for the church if the preacher overcomes the distance between exegesis and homiletics. Thus the class will be the occasion for learning to merge the horizons of the author, the text, and the contemporary audience. The class will move beyond the older paradigm of exegesis–application to a conversation involving the interpreter, the text, and the contemporary audience. Interpreters will ask the questions of the text that arise from the church as it attempts to bear faithful witness in the world, enter into the new world of Scripture, and envision the church's continuity with its predecessors who also listened for the word of God.

REMEMBERING OUR PREDECESSORS:
THE "FIRST NAÏVETÉ"

Contrary to the Enlightenment interpreters, who sought to rescue Scripture from premodern ecclesiastical readings, the preacher will recognize the value of ancient interpretation for the church. James Sanders has suggested that we can learn from the hermeneutics of our predecessors as they approached ancient traditions with the questions that were determined by their own place in history.[8] In the hermeneutical work of the author of Hebrews, for example, we recognize an ecclesiastical hermeneutic that focuses on the continuity between the ancient and modern readers, as the author finds in the ancient text both a word of exhortation and a sharp warning for his own audience. David Steinmetz argued for the importance of the medieval fourfold interpretation of Scripture, noting that interpretation originated in the church for the benefit of the church.[9] Ancient allegorical exegesis existed within the framework of the church's rule of faith. Because preachers interpret for the church, the ancient practice provides a welcome model of the importance of merging the horizons between the ancient author and the modern text.[10]

Students who first learn historical-critical exegesis often comment on the "naïveté" of the premodern reading, which does not ask the modern questions of historical context. The preacher will benefit by sharing this naïveté, which does not regard the text as an object to be dissected, but as a voice to be heard and a word to be incorporated into the memory. Like ancient writers, the preachers will speak with the intertextual echoes of Scriptures that have formed their imagination. Paul Ricoeur's image of the "first naïveté" is an appropriate description of the preacher's original encounter with the text. One reads the passage as an address to the church, joining ancient writers as they offer praise, listening as they tell stories, and entering into the "strange new world within the Bible."[11] A dimension of the practice of interpretation is the development of the habitus of listening to Scripture.

Historical Criticism and the Loss of Naïveté

Although the preacher employs more than one dimension in interpretation, traditional historical criticism remains an essential foundation for biblical interpretation. Indeed, homiletics will benefit from the biblical scholar's distance from the text, even if this distance separates the horizon of the text from that of the reader and contributes to the loss of the original naïveté. Without this "otherness" of the text, familiar passages become useful platitudes and proof texts to use for our own purposes. Disciplined study may take away our favorite passages by placing them within their historical contexts, but it will also give depth to our interpretation. While historical, linguistic, and social-scientific observations do not appear directly in the sermon, the critical distance provided by these disciplines provides new insights that challenge our original naive reading. Thus the steps for writing an exegesis are indispensable in biblical interpretation for preaching. Preachers who develop the habitus of disciplined study will be liberated from the Scylla of the overreliance on commentaries and the Charybdis of the inability to develop the capacity for interpretation. In the following reflections on Philippians and other texts, we see the value of historical-critical exegesis for preaching. While these steps need not be followed in a strictly linear fashion, they constitute indispensable components in the interpretation for preaching. These tasks are not only important for asking the questions of historical criticism, but also guide preachers as they prepare for preaching.

1. *Selection of the text.* Although some students work consistently from the lectionary while others choose their own texts, careful selection of the text is an important dimension of preaching. An appropriate exercise for a class member is to explore the boundaries of the passage, realizing that such boundaries are not self-evident but are vital to the task of interpretation. A comparison of translations and of the passage in the original languages will indicate the variety of possibilities for interpreting the text. Decisions will be judgment calls, and class

members may reach different conclusions about the appropriate reading. For example, according to the Revised Common Lectionary, the reading for Proper 20 is Philippians 1:21–30. According to the Nestle Text, 1:21–26 is a part of Paul's autobiography that extends from 1:12–26; at 1:27–30 Paul begins the exhortation to the readers. In preparing the sermon, several options are possible. If one (a) follows the RCL, the passage juxtaposes Paul's own outlook and conduct with that which he instructs the Philippians to adopt. One may (b) extend the passage to include 1:12–30, with its larger juxtaposition of Pauline conduct with Philippian conduct. Finally, one may (c) select a smaller unit for proclamation (i.e., 1:12–26 or 1:27–30). The preacher's decision about the limits of the text will determine the essential focus of the sermon.

2. *Recognition of genre.* The recent emphasis on preaching in the form of the text requires preachers to understand what the biblical genres actually do. One examines not only the genre of the document in question, but the subgenre (or form) of the passage, recognizing that genre recognition involves knowing the "rules of the game." For example, Philippians 1 has three specific subgenres: thanksgiving (1:3–11), autobiography (1:12–26), and paraenesis (1:27–30), each with its own communicative impact. In preparing a sermon on the autobiographical section in 1:12–26, one will want to ask, "What do the autobiographical sections in Paul's letters actually do?" In some instances, Paul's autobiographical units answer charges against him, while in others he presents himself as a model for the conduct that he expects of his listeners. The latter function is most likely in this passage, as a reading of the entire letter suggests. Because what genres do is not self-evident, the preacher will benefit from the genre studies in biblical scholarship. The recognition of the generic characteristics of the unit should assist preachers in locating the essential communicative focus of the passage and prevent them from emphasizing minor issues within the passage.

3. *The world behind the text.* For many, historical criticism not only provides much irrelevant information, but reduces passages to "little stories which mean nothing to our own existence, which affect us less than the Greek or Teutonic myths and contain less wisdom than Grimm's Fairy Tales"[12]—scarcely a promising venture for one who seeks a word from the Lord. Despite its limitations, the study of the world behind the text is an indispensable task for the preacher, for biblical texts speak to people in concrete situations. To ask what lies behind the text, therefore, is to acknowledge that the Bible does not contain timeless

truths, but witnesses to community in the context of the dilemmas and crises of their lives. We can address communities in their concrete circumstances if we are able to draw analogies between the situation of our communities and those to whom the texts were addressed. The force of the passage becomes clear when we recognize the world behind the text. With the discipline of historical criticism, we recognize that Paul's advice, "Rejoice in the Lord" (Phil. 3:1; 4:4) and "Do not worry about anything" (Phil. 4:6)—favorite passages in American piety—are not timeless platitudes, but words spoken to people in great duress. An examination of the world behind these passages reveals that Paul wrote the letter from prison to a community that experienced the inevitable suffering (1:28) that accompanied those who converted to a minority group. Although the ancient community probably did not suffer from state-sponsored persecution, they suffered the loss of family, close relationships, and economic security as a result of Paul's preaching. This loss of status undoubtedly created a crisis among the readers, leading Paul to reassure them of the advance of the gospel (1:12). This historical information, gained from a careful reading of the letter and ancient sources that recall the shame associated with the rejection of familial religious practices, provide the necessary background for recognizing that our favorite passages in Philippians were addressed, not to well-fed Western people to instruct them in positive thinking, but to ancient people who struggled with the consequences of their Christian commitment in a hostile environment.

One may augment the historical-critical analysis with additional social-scientific and anthropological insights that describe the insecurity faced by groups that are alienated from the larger society and the strategies for maintaining their loyalty. Numerous commentaries now employ contemporary sociological models in order to recognize the situation and the strategy of the biblical author.

The task of historical criticism is not only to reveal interesting background information, but to bring our own congregation into dialogue with our predecessors. We recognize that we hear texts in our communal context, just as the ancient community heard Paul's message. Paul's attempt to maintain community solidarity in the context of a pre-Christian and hostile climate is the occasion for our own communities to hear his voice in our own post-Christian atmosphere. The homiletics class is the occasion for students to reflect on the parallels between the situation of Christians who lived in a pre-Christian society and those who live in a post-Christian society.

4. *The world within the text.* The lectionary's division of passages into small units provides a manageable text for the sermon, but may tempt the reader to conclude that texts can be interpreted in isolation from their literary contexts. However, recent advances in literary and rhetorical criticism demonstrate that the meaning of pericope is to be found in the careful analysis of the world within the text. Ancient texts were meant for communal hearing, as audiences listened to entire books at one setting. Consequently, one may assume that the ancient listener followed the narrative or letter, recognizing the development of plot and theme. Shakespearean actor Alex McCowen's oral interpretation of Mark offers a graphic illustration of the power of the world within the text. Through the experience of hearing the entire text of Mark in one setting, the listener recognizes how each passage contributes to the plot and characterization that the ancient author intended. For example, the feeding of the four thousand (Mark 8:1–10), an apparent repetition of the earlier feeding of the five thousand (Mark 6:30–44), is at first puzzling to the interpreter, especially when the disciples ask in the second narrative, "How can one feed these people with bread here in the desert?" (Mark 8:4). Earlier interpreters considered the dual feeding stories to be evidence of the carelessness of the author in combining alternate sources. The significance of the passage is evident only when one places it within Mark's consistent theme of the blindness of disciples, who continue to worry that they have no bread (8:16) even after the second feeding story. Only by hearing the entire narrative can we see the force of individual units as they are linked to the entire narrative. These insights assist the preacher in focusing the center of gravity for the passage.

The rhetorical criticism of the epistles also provides the means for the interpretation of specific units. With careful literary and rhetorical analysis of the letter, the preacher sees each unit in the light of the whole, recalling that the letters are actually sermons that Paul delivered in absentia and sent to congregations for public reading. For example, much of the literature on Philippians in the past has focused on the problem of literary integrity of the book. For many interpreters, the radical break between 3:1 ("rejoice in the Lord . . .") and 3:2 ("beware of the dogs, beware of the evil workers . . .") indicates the incoherence of the book in its present form and indicates that Philippians is a composite of two or more separate letters. Other interpreters, including most rhetorical critics, have recognized that the focus of Philippians 3 is not the evil workers, but Paul's autobiographical demonstration that his own personal story has been shaped by the story of Christ in the "hymn" recorded in 2:6–11. That is, just as the preexistent Christ "emptied himself" (2:7) at the incarnation and "humbled himself" at the cross (2:8), Paul has emptied himself of his own personal privileges. The references to opponents in 3:2, 18 are actually rhetorical foils for Paul's self-presentation. This recognition of the world within the text determines the focus of the preaching text. Paul's narration of his own life in Christ provides the opportunity for preachers to describe their own stories in Christ and to invite the community to tell their own story within the framework of the story of Christ.

A vital exercise for the student of preaching is to read (or hear) a Gospel or letter in its entirety and then consult secondary references to note the alternative approaches to the structure of the book. For books that are especially lengthy, the students may note the major blocks of material in order to place their own studied passage within its literary context.

5. *The analysis of the text.* Disciplined preparation involves the careful examination of the dynamics of the passage, which the student can ascertain in both word usage and the structure of the textual unit. Those who work with the original languages will recognize the particular force of words that is lost in the English translation, which preachers can develop in the sermon without obtrusive references to the Greek or Hebrew text. For example, Paul uses vivid imagery in Philippians 1:27–30 that is lost in translation. In the first place, the instruction to "live your life in a manner worthy of the gospel" (1:27) employs a political image. The verb *politeuesthe* ("live your life" in the NRSV) means literally "live out your citizenship." The word, addressed to a minority community in the house church, suggests the political implications of the gospel. It was commonly used by Jews who lived as a minority group in cities like Alexandria to express their loyalty to the divine laws. Paul indicates that the community in Philippi recognizes Jesus Christ, not Caesar, as Lord, and that it lives by its own traditions. His instruction to "[strive] side by side with one mind" (*synathlountes*, 1:27) and his description of his own struggle (*agon*, 1:30) employ vivid athletic images for evoking the memory of athletes who struggle to the point of exhaustion. The athletic image was common in Jewish literature for the martyrs whose heroic struggle was compared to an athletic contest. These political and athletic images vividly describe the plight of Paul's converts as they faced the hostility of their own culture, and they remain evocative for the preacher who reflects on the meaning of Christian existence in a post-Christian culture.

Although we do not slavishly follow the sequence of the passage in sermon preparation, a recognition of the structure of the passage is important for recognizing its center of gravity and focus. For example, narrative passages normally move from difficulty to resolution, providing the normal plot for the sermon. Epistolary and legal passages follow a logical sequence that contains the main idea combined with supporting clauses that elaborate and support the central focus. For example, Philippians 1:27–30, like many textual units in Paul, is only one sentence in the Greek text, and thus the central idea is to be seen in the main clause ("live out your citizenship worthily of the gospel"). The remainder of the passage elaborates on this instruction, first by adding the specific examples of this conduct in the clause introduced by "so that" (Greek *hoti*, 1:27) and then by providing a reason for the conduct, introduced by "for" (Greek *hoti*, 1:29). Thus the logical sequence provides focus for the text and the sermon, and it can be the basis for the movement of the sermon.

Students may demonstrate their development of the habitus of disciplined study by submitting a brief paper accompanying the manuscript in which they describe the specific exegetical procedure they employed in the development of the sermon. This paper should indicate how they included dimensions of reading that both incorporate historical-critical questions and transcend these questions in reading the text for the church.

THE SECOND NAÏVETÉ AND THE WORLD IN FRONT OF THE TEXT

Recent interpreters have challenged the dominance of historical criticism, arguing persuasively that it does not disclose the *only* meaning of the text. Indeed, while we learn much from historical criticism, the task of interpretation is not complete when we discover the original meaning of a text, as anyone knows who has tried to preach an exegesis. As Robert Morgan has observed,[13] the meaning of texts depends on the questions that we are asking. Postmodern interpreters, like their premodern predecessors, insist that our own circumstances influence the reading of the text. In our own interpretation, we are open to the contributions of those who come to the text with insights and questions that are shaped by their experience. Similarly, the church is a reading community that discovers meaning in the merging of its horizons with that of the text. Thus we ask questions that extend beyond the original meaning of the pericope and lead us to reflect on the significance of this text for our own reading community. As we merge our own horizon with that of the text, we discover the "second naivete" described by Ricoeur in which the Bible again becomes a living voice.

Reading in Canonical Context

Although we have learned from historical criticism to examine a specific passage with care without superimposing other texts on it, interpretation for preaching involves placing our passage in conversation with other passages, recognizing the multiple voices of Scripture. Careful exegesis for preaching should not result in the myopia of seeing only the perspective of one textual unit, but should result in a conversation between texts. We learn from canonical criticism to listen to the text as it is placed within the context of the entire canon and to recognize that, in giving shape to the canon, the church acknowledged the multiple voices of Scripture.

Reading in a Theological Context

Edward Farley's distinction between preaching the Bible and preaching the gospel[14] is a reminder that the aim of the sermon is to preach the gospel, not a fragment of Scripture. Although one's reflection on the gospel begins with the reading of Scripture, the interpretation of specific passages should lead the preacher to ask larger questions about the relationship between the text and the Christian message. Paul Scott Wilson's insistence that the interpreter move from exegesis to ask what the passage says about the major doctrines of the Christian faith is an appropriate consideration.[15] To ask what the text says about God or the human condition is to recover the theological dimensions that historical criticism ignores.

Discovering the Impact of the Passage

Some commentaries now offer, in addition to the historical-critical comments, a unit on the impact of the passage in the history of Christian thought. Other commentaries focus entirely on the history of the interpretation of biblical books. The contemporary church, therefore, is the heir of centuries of reading communities that have encountered biblical passages. Whereas historical critics, with their insistence on the singular meaning of texts, denied the importance of the history of interpretation, contemporary interpreters recognize that the church maintains a conversation with its predecessors.

This habitus appears daunting for the preacher for whom the Sunday sermon is one of many duties to perform during the week. However, the fact that this practice involves a rigorous discipline argues for the development of this habitus. Like other practices that we develop through repetition, this practice becomes less daunting as the preacher participates in the process on a regular basis. The accumulation of facility with exegesis and knowledge of the associated disciplines provides the preacher with a background that enables the preacher to engage in this discipline on a regular basis.

HELPFUL READINGS

Bartlett, David L. *Between the Bible and the Church*. Nashville: Abingdon Press, 1999.

Davis, Ellen F., and Richard B. Hays. *The Art of Reading Scripture*. Grand Rapids: Wm. B. Eerdmans Publishing Co., 2003.

Fowl, Stephen E. *Engaging Scripture: A Model for Theological Interpretation*. Oxford: Basil Blackwell Publisher, 1998.

González, Justo L. *Santa Biblia: The Bible through Hispanic Eyes*. Nashville: Abingdon Press, 1996.

Ukpong, Justin, et al. *Reading the Bible in the Global Village*. Atlanta: Society of Biblical Literature, 2002.

Wilson, Paul Scott. *God Sense: Reading the Bible for Preaching*. Nashville: Abingdon Press, 2001.

NOTES

1. The term "word of exhortation" (Heb. 13:22) is used for the synagogue homily in Acts 13:15.

2. Fred B. Craddock, *Preaching* (Nashville: Abingdon Press, 1985).

3. Thomas G. Long, *The Witness of Preaching*, 2nd ed. (Louisville, KY: Westminster John Knox Press, 2005).

4. Paul Scott Wilson, *God Sense: Reading the Bible for Preaching* (Nashville: Abingdon Press, 2001).

5. Harry Emerson Fosdick, "What Is the Matter with Preaching Today?" reprinted in Mike Graves, *What's the Matter with Preaching Today?* (Louisville, KY: Westminster John Knox Press, 2004), 10.

6. See James L. Kugel and Rowan A. Greer, *Early Biblical Interpretation* (Philadelphia: Westminster Press, 1986), 52–59. See also James Sanders, *From Sacred Story to Sacred Text* (Philadelphia: Fortress Press, 1987), 25.

7. Arthur Koestler, *Arrival and Departure* (New York: Macmillan & Co., 1944), 17–18. I am indebted to Karl Plank, *Irony and Affliction* (Atlanta: Scholars Press, 1987), 38, for this reference.

8. James Sanders, "Hermeneutics," *Interpreter's Dictionary of the Bible Supplement*, 1993.

9. David Steinmetz, "The Superiority of Pre-Critical Exegesis," in *A Guide to Contemporary Hermeneutics,* ed. Donald K. McKim (Grand Rapids: Wm. B. Eerdmans Publishing Co., 1986), 65–77.

10. See Brian E. Daley, S. J., "Is Patristic Exegesis Still Usable? Some Reflections on Early Christian Interpretation of the Psalms," in Ellen F. Davis and Richard B. Hays, *The Art of Reading Scripture* (Grand Rapids: Wm. B. Eerdmans Publishing Co., 2003), 69–88.

11. Cf. Karl Barth, *The Word of God and the Word of Man* (New York: Harper & Brothers, 1957), 28–50. For the "first naiveté" within the Catholic homiletic tradition, see Gregory Heille's article, chap. 15 in this volume.

12. The phrase is taken from K. Miskotte, *When the Gods Are Silent* (New York: Harper & Row, 1967), 199.

13. Robert Morgan with John Barton, *Biblical Interpretation* (Oxford: Oxford University Press, 1989), 16.

14. Edward Farley, "Preaching the Bible and Preaching the Gospel," *Theology Today* 51 (1994): 90–103.

15. Paul Scott Wilson, *God Sense: Reading the Bible for Preaching*, 69–82.

5

Exegeting the Congregation

LEONORA TUBBS TISDALE

Preaching not only requires students to have facility in exegeting and interpreting biblical texts, it also requires of them the ability to "exegete" the various congregational contexts within which preaching takes place, and to speak a word that is both fitting and transformative for a particular people in a particular place and time. While students may come into the seminary classroom fully aware that biblical exegesis requires a certain set of skills and practices in order to be done well, congregational exegesis is another matter altogether. Knowledge of the congregation, it is often assumed, is something the preacher will pick up by intuition and osmosis—simply by living with a group of people and coming to know them over time.

While it is true that a deeper understanding of a congregation is ultimately born out of the kind of long-term commitment that fosters genuine "knowing" in any human relationship, it is also true that students of preaching can acquire knowledge and skills in the classroom that make congregational exegesis a more intentional and disciplined practice. Like anthropologists who go into a strange new culture equipped with tools for studying it from multiple angles and "thickening" their descriptions of it, so students of preaching need to be better equipped to enter the strange new worlds of local congregations and to thicken their own understandings of congregational worldview, values, and ethos.

Such knowledge is critical for preaching on several fronts. First, if students are going to preach to people with respect and understanding,

75

it is important to address them as they are, and not as the student assumes or imagines them to be. A thicker understanding of the congregation leads to a more complex appreciation of hearers in all their multidimensional reality, and also helps preachers avoid those "false stumbling blocks" that can impede the hearing of the gospel.[1]

Second, if preachers are to bring a fitting and relevant word from the pulpit, it is imperative that they first become aware of the concerns, questions, heartaches, and dreams that members of particular faith communities bring to the preaching event. The U.S. Catholic Bishops Conference asserts: "Unless a preacher knows what a congregation needs, wants or is able to hear, there is every possibility that the message offered in a homily will not meet the needs of the people who hear it."[2] Whether preparation for preaching begins with a biblical text or with a life issue, relevancy in preaching is a worthy goal. However, the very definition of relevancy is also context-dependent.

Third, preaching is at heart a theological act. If pastors are going to proclaim theology that is transformative for local congregations, it is important that they first become aware of what their people already believe and value. Sometimes the most effective strategies for theological transformation in preaching involve stretching the edges from within, rather than bombarding belief from without. But to do so requires insider knowledge of the local theologies a congregation holds dear.

Finally, preaching—like all theological discourse—should be "seriously imaginable"[3] to a particular people in a particular time and place. That is, people should be able to envision their own daily lives lived in accordance with the gospel. In order to assist people in this task, however, students of preaching must first gain a deeper awareness of how the world and life are actually viewed from the vantage point of their hearers. They cannot always assume that what they themselves find seriously imaginable is equally imaginable to their congregations.

Fortunately for students of preaching (as well as for students of other ministerial practices), there has been a renewed emphasis on the study of congregations in theological literature of recent decades. The field of congregational studies now offers many valuable resources that can assist students in their exegetical task. However, not all of these resources are equally geared toward the preaching task. While some focus on the study of the organizational dynamics and processes of congregations, it is often those approaches which focus on understanding congregational identity and culture that prove to be most helpful for the preaching task.[4]

Furthermore, there is also a readiness-for-learning factor among students that should be taken into account when approaching this topic in the classroom—especially in an introductory preaching course. My own teaching experience tells me that there is a continuum of interest in congregational exegesis that begins to be tapped in an introductory preaching class, but which is not yet fully appreciated—especially by students who have little prior preaching experience. That interest escalates significantly as students undertake field education, so that an entire upper-level preaching class can fruitfully be devoted to the practices of congregational exegesis and contextual sermon preparation—especially if the student's field-education congregation is the arena for undertaking a congregational study. Interest often reaches its zenith, however, with pastors in a Doctor of Ministry program—most of whom have already been preaching for several years and are eager to supplement their intuitive knowledge of congregations with more focused and disciplined study. Consequently, the goal in an introductory class is often to whet the appetite of students for what, hopefully, will become with time a valued set of practices that can benefit them not only in preaching, but also in other areas of ministerial practice.

TO WHAT CONGREGATION DO WE PREACH?

One of the first contextual challenges for teachers of introductory preaching classes lies in identifying the congregation(s) for whom students are to prepare their classroom sermons. Do students design sermons for their seminary peers? for congregations of their acquaintance? for an imagined congregation (described by the teacher)? or for some alternative context that takes them out of their own comfort zones (e.g., preaching in a prison, on a street corner, or at a nursing home)?

Students, of course, have their own divergent opinions on the matter. While some are eager to prepare sermons that can also be preached in contexts where they are serving as a pastor, chaplain, or intern, others have a difficult time even imagining designing a sermon for anyone other than the people to whom they will literally be preaching: their classroom peers. The tensions are real, and also point to the significance of contextuality in preaching. While, on the one hand, there is an immediacy and relevancy involved in preaching to the classroom congregation that cannot be underestimated, students who preach only to their peers can also get away with using theological jargon, seminary buzzwords, insider humor, and references to shared experiences that cannot be used when preaching in another context.

One constructive way to deal with this tension might be to have students preach their first sermons for their peers, and then to use that experience both as a case study in the positives of contextuality in preaching (What is it that makes you want to preach to your peers? What can you do in sermons with your peers that you can't do in sermons preached to strangers? What connections do you observe between preaching and your knowledge of the seminary community? How did you attain that knowledge?), and also as an incentive to identify, develop, and build upon their own intuitive skills as congregational exegetes. Local congregations, like seminary communities, tend to have their own distinctive cultures—each with its own unique history, corpus of shared experiences, and internal language and symbol system. By helping students first become more cognizant of the distinctive marks of the seminary culture, we can also assist them in identifying the distinctive marks of congregational cultures.

But it is also important that students be required to prepare sermons for congregations other than their seminary peers. Such practice not only presses them to begin thinking in earnest about the task of congregational exegesis, it also helps prepare them for the inevitable "crossing of the boundary" that will occur when they graduate from seminary and are faced with the challenge of preaching to people whose life experiences, beliefs, and perspectives may be very different from their own.

UNIVERSALS, PARTICULARS, AND CULTURAL TRAITS

When introducing preaching students to congregational exegesis I frequently begin by putting the following statement (by a cultural anthropologist) on the board: "All people are, in certain respects, like *all* others (sharing certain universals with the whole human race), like *no* others (having distinctive traits that mark them as individuals), and like *some* others (sharing cultural traits with a particular group of people)."[5] Faithful congregational exegesis (I go on to tell them) requires preachers to give attention to all three realities—and frequently to all three at the same time.

The Universals of Human Experience
(All people are, in certain respects, like *all* others.)

In recent decades, when much of the focus on the hearers in homiletical literature has centered on issues related to multiculturalism and pluralism, preaching has sometimes lost sight of the fact that there are still basic universal human needs that sermons can and should address. James A. Wallace identifies three hungers that homilies seek to satisfy: a hunger for wholeness, a hunger for meaning, and a hunger for community and belonging.[6] Fred Craddock contends that all listeners long to be brought into the presence of God, long to be reminded that they are "the crowning achievement of God's creation," and long to find a place to stand that "that feels like home."[7] While scholars may differ on what the universals for preaching are (or whether they even exist), it is helpful for students to begin reflecting on those basic human existential longings, desires, and needs that many people share, and how preaching might address them.

Certainly one of the factors that makes some of the sermons of great preachers of previous eras timeless is their ability to tap into the universals of human experience that transcend space and time. When Harry Emerson Fosdick rails against the inanities of war in his sermon "The Unknown Soldier,"[8] when Martin Luther King Jr. gives voice to his dream for a new and equal society, or when William Sloane Coffin questions any theology that would maintain that the accidental death of his teenage son was the "will of God,"[9] they voice human themes as timeless as the ages: war and peace, the struggle for human community, and the search for meaning in the face of a seemingly senseless tragedy.

The fact that there are universals for preaching can actually be a great comfort to students of preaching. First, it assures students that they *can* preach to very diverse congregations, across cultures, and even to strangers, because they share a common humanity with their hearers. Indeed (and paradoxically), it may well be within a context of postmodern pluralism—a time in which many in our midst would question whether there *are* any universals—that the common longings of the human spirit become most significant for preaching. Universals give beginning preachers, as well as seasoned pastors, a starting point for hermeneutical reflection when addressing diverse audiences.

Second, attention to shared human experience encourages students to recognize that one of the most valuable resources they bring to the preaching event is their own existential wrestling with a biblical text, a burning theological question, or a tough social issue. William Sloane Coffin names a basic preaching truth when he says, "Finally, you preach for yourself but, if you go down deep enough, you touch enough common humanity so that everyone's involved."[10]

While students of preaching should certainly not assume that all their life experiences are universal experiences, they should nevertheless be encouraged to recognize that it is often at the point at which their own existential hungers and deepest needs intersect with the biblical text that they will also discover the heartbeat of a sermon that resonates with their hearers. As Gardner Taylor so aptly stated in his 100th Anniversary Lyman Beecher Lectures at Yale:

> The power and pathos of the preacher are to be found not in the volume of voice nor those patently contrived tremors of tone preachers sometimes affect, but in passionate avowals which are passionate because they have gotten out of the written word into the preacher's heart, have been filtered and colored by the preacher's own experiences of joy and sorrow, and then are presented to and pressed upon the hearts and minds of those who hear.[11]

Finally, paying attention to the universals of human experience reminds students that people through the ages have come to the preaching event with profound existential human questions and needs, and that preaching should be equally profound in addressing them. Frederick Buechner's classic description of what is at stake in the preaching act, though somewhat dated and culture bound, still has a ring of authenticity about it—especially regarding the basic human needs of the hearers in Christian worship:

> So the sermon hymn comes to a close with a somewhat unsteady amen, and the organist gestures the choir to sit down. . . .
>
> In the front pew the old ladies turn up their hearing aids, and a young lady slips her six year old a Lifesaver and a Magic Marker. A college sophomore home for vacation, who is there because he was dragged there, slumps forward with his chin in his hand. The vice-

president of a bank who twice that week has seriously contemplated suicide places his hymnal in the rack. A pregnant girl feels the life stir inside her. A high-school math teacher, who for twenty years has managed to keep his homosexuality a secret for the most part even from himself, creases his order of service down the center with his thumbnail and tucks it under his knee. . . .

The preacher pulls the little cord that turns on the lectern light and deals out his note cards like a riverboat gambler. The stakes have never been higher.[12]

What are practices through which teachers of homiletics might encourage students to identify some of the "universals" of human experience? We might begin by describing a very diverse congregation (ethnically, theologically, in terms of class, etc.), and asking our students to reflect on the question: Are there any common traits or characteristics that these very diverse hearers share, and, if so, what might they be? While the initial conversation might focus on traits that are *biological* ("All people are born, age, and will eventually die"), *psychological* ("All people hunger for belonging and affirmation"), or *existential* ("All people have fears, anxieties, and big life questions"), it is also important for students to reflect *theologically* on what it is the gospel itself would say about all humanity ("All human beings are created in the image of God"; "All people are loved by God, no matter what they've done"; "All have sinned and fallen short of God"; "All are in need of the redeeming grace of Jesus Christ and the regenerative power of the Holy Spirit").

Fred Craddock contends that all humans, despite the fall, share a "faint recollection of Eden."[13] It might be interesting to press students to debate whether or not they think this is true, and, if so, how that memory manifests itself universally in the lives of congregants they know.

Individual Hearers and the Particulars of Human Experience
(All people are, in certain respects, like *no* others.)

As every pastor knows, there is an intimate and reciprocal relationship between preaching and pastoral care. Local pastors are called to be priestly listeners who attend to the particular needs of the individual parishioners entrusted to their care as they seek to bring a biblical and theological word to bear in their contexts. Consequently, in the course of a preaching ministry, preachers should frequently expect to address pastoral themes such as illness (physical and mental), death, divorce, abuse, doubt, addiction, despair, anger, fear, loneliness, and the like. But the inverse is also true. Preachers are also called to be pastors, embodying the compassion they proclaim on Sundays in their daily care for their flocks. As Phillips Brooks said long ago, "The preacher who is not a pastor grows remote. The pastor who is not a preacher grows petty."[14]

To say that preaching should attend to the needs of individuals does not necessarily mean that sermons become subjective in tone or therapeutic in concern. Indeed we teachers of preaching need to help our students see that the dividing line frequently drawn between "pastoral" and "prophetic" preaching is a false and misleading one. If we care deeply and genuinely about individuals, we will also care about all the sociocultural forces that impinge on their lives for good or for ill.

Furthermore, "care-full" preaching, as Lee Ramsey reminds us, is not just about addressing the pastoral concerns of individuals; it is also about building up the body of Christ into a community of mutual care and support.[15] As we do so, we also equip the church for its ministry of care for and transformation of the larger world.

There are many different pastoral practices that can help students of preaching become more cognizant of the needs of the individuals to whom they will preach. Among them are the following:

Visiting parishioners at homes, hospitals, their places of work or schools;

Pastoral counseling of various kinds;

Praying with and for members of the congregation;

Keeping the names of representative congregants of various ages, ethnic backgrounds, social classes, genders, sexual orientations, and so on, visibly before us while preparing sermons.

All students of preaching also need to hone their "empathetic imaginations." In this regard, Fred Craddock suggests that students take a blank sheet of paper, write at the top "What's It like to Be . . . ?" and then respond to phrases such as: "facing surgery," "living alone," "suddenly wealthy," "rejected by a sorority," "arrested for burglary," "going into the military," "fired from one's position," "graduating," "getting one's own apartment," "unable to read," "extremely poor," "fourteen years old."[16]

Cultural Realities within Congregations
(All people are, in certain respects, like *some* others.)

In recent decades there has been a renewed focus in homiletical literature on exegeting and attending to the sociocultural realities of congregational life, and on shaping sermons that are theologically and
communicationally "fitting" for various congregations and their subcultures or cohorts (as related to race, ethnicity, class, age, gender, learning
styles, and theology).

THE CONGREGATION AS CULTURE

In my book *Preaching as Local Theology and Folk Art*, I contend that the
local congregation itself might be considered a culture with an intricate
web of symbolic communication that gives witness to its distinctive
worldview, ethos, and values. I encourage beginning preachers to
approach the study of a new congregation much as an ethnographer
might study an unknown culture: namely, by attending to the various
signs and symbols of its corporate life.

In order to facilitate this process, I identify seven symbols of congregational life that have proven to be particularly fertile ground for congregational exegesis: history and archival materials, demographics,
stories and guided interviews, ritual and liturgical patterns, church
architecture and the visual arts, people (including the "sages" and those
on the margins), and congregational events and activities. In each
instance I provide leading questions that the exegete of congregational
culture might ask in order to deepen and thicken her or his understanding of a church's culture.[17] For example, when interpreting congregational stories, the preacher might ask questions such as:

*Who are identified as heroes in the stories of congregational life, and
what are the qualities that have made them so? . . .*

*Where are the silences in the storytelling of the congregation—the
things everyone knows (or at least all the insiders), but no one talks
about? . . .*

*Are there any recurring images or metaphors in the congregational
story that give you insight into how they perceive themselves and their
world? . . .*

Is there any common dream or vision that seems to unite this people as they move toward their common future?

If you were to plot the story of this congregation like the plot of a novel, what would that plot line look like?[18]

The goal of these exercises is not only that students might become more cognizant of congregational worldview, values, and ethos from a sociocultural perspective, but that they might also be able to identify the "local theologies" that are already extant in the life of the congregation. To that end, I encourage students to ask questions like the following:

What is the operative view of God within the congregation? (Which person of the Trinity is most emphasized in congregational life? least emphasized? Is God viewed primarily as immanent or transcendent? as judge and giver of law, or as merciful and forgiving parent? as miracle worker, or as one who works primarily through the natural processes?)

What is the operative view of human beings? (Are people primarily viewed as sinners without hope, save in God's redemption of them through Christ? as children of God, created in God's own image and re-created in Christ? or as fallible yet perfectible through the inner workings of the Holy Spirit? What is valued more in human nature: being, doing, or becoming/growing?)

What is the operative view of the church and its mission? (Is the church primarily understood to be a hospital for sinners, or a holy community of saints? Would the congregation's mission orientation best be characterized as: activist, civic, evangelistic, or sanctuary?)[19]

Knowledge of a congregation's own "local theologies" then assists students in discerning appropriate strategies for addressing them in their own preaching. For example, when bringing the worlds of the biblical text and the congregation together in one's sermons, the preacher might adopt any of the following strategies:

1. Preaching can affirm and confirm what the congregation already believes, values, and practices.
2. Preaching can stretch the limits of the congregation's theological imagination.
3. Preaching can invert the assumed ordering of the congregation's imagined worldview.

4. Preaching can challenge and judge the false imaginings of the congregational heart.
5. Preaching can help congregations envision worlds they have not yet begun to imagine.[20]

Having students undertake some of these exercises with a field-education congregation or with a congregation where a student regularly worships or preaches could provide them with needed practice in exegeting congregations for preaching. In addition, the sharing in class of their exegeses could enhance students' awareness of the diverse congregational contexts in which preaching takes place.

Brian K. Blount and Gary W. Charles's volume *Preaching Mark in Two Voices*[21] might also be used in the classroom as a case study regarding the significant differences sociocultural location makes for sermons preached on the same biblical texts. Blount, a New Testament professor who preaches out of his own African American church heritage of slavery and oppression, and Charles, a pastor who struggles with how to make Mark's disturbing Gospel "good news" for well-educated white suburbanites living on the outskirts of Washington, D.C., model for students how to be faithful to their own preaching contexts while, at the same time, openly engaging and learning from the perspectives of others.

Homiletical scholars have also produced a number of texts that can help students gain a deeper understanding of preaching in a particular sociocultural context—whether it be a culture that is distinguished by race and ethnicity (such as African American or Korean American congregations[22]), by class (preaching to street people or to blue-collar congregations[23]), or by other distinguishing factors (e.g., preaching to people with disabilities[24]). Giving students in an introductory preaching class a choice of reading and reflecting on one of these books (rather than assuming that in textbooks "one size fits all") is a way of respecting and celebrating cultural diversity.

Another text that might be used as a multicultural "wake-up" call for homiletics classrooms (and especially those where white students are in the majority) is *Preaching Justice: Ethnic and Cultural Perspectives*, edited by Christine Smith. The authors in this volume provide a helpful overview of the ways in which the concerns, theology, and preaching of justice differ significantly when viewed from a Native American, Filipino, Korean American, African American womanist, or lesbian perspective. In the introduction to this volume, Smith reminds us that "Euro-American voices still dominate every aspect of homiletics," and that radical change is needed to break this impasse.[25] Her text offers a way to do just that in the homiletics classroom.

The Subcultures (or Cohorts) *Within* a Congregation

While it is helpful to view the congregation itself as a culture, it is also important to note that almost every congregation has within it a diversity of subcultures (or cohorts), and preachers also need help identifying and addressing a multiplicity of hearers in their sermons. In *Preaching to Every Pew: Cross-Cultural Strategies,* James Nieman and Thomas Rogers suggest that the "cross-cultural challenge to preaching is neither exotic nor rare, but can be found virtually anywhere in our society. Whether urban or rural, large church or small, on the coasts or in the heartland, congregations and their leaders are realizing that ethnic, class, and religious diversity are as close as next door."[26] These homileticians identify four different "frames" through which preachers can view a congregation: ethnicity, class, displacement (such as that known by immigrant communities), and beliefs. They also provide characteristics and helpful preaching strategies for each frame.

In *One Gospel, Many Ears,* Joseph Jeter and Ronald Allen address similar frames (especially as related to ethnicity, class, and theology), but also expand the list to include differences occasioned by gender, age (including generational cohorts[27]), and learning styles. This book and Nieman and Rogers's book encourage students to become more cognizant of the diverse cultures they will regularly address in their preaching, and also to become more intentional about avoiding a "one style fits all" approach in their own preaching. Jeter and Allen also push students to move outside their own comfort zones in parish ministry in order to enter more fully into the diverse worlds of their hearers. They write:

> [T]he wise pastor will spend some time every week stepping out of his or her world and into the worlds of the people, learning more about their generations, the ways they perceive the world, the ways they use language, the movies and TV shows they watch, the music they listen to, the books they read. Only by doing that can the pastor get a sense of the nuances of the listening community and of how to relate with people in settings beyond the sermon.[28]

In addition, they offer four different approaches preachers might take in addressing the wide variety of listening patterns within a congregation:

1. By preparing a particular message (or series of messages) to speak to a single cohort of listeners;
2. By conscientiously integrating several distinct qualities in the sermon that enhance receptivity for a range of listeners;
3. By integrating approaches designed for a diversity of listeners over a season of sermons; or
4. By concentrating on the biblical passage (or topic) for the occasion and then asking yourself questions such as: *How will the listening groups at the assembly hear (or not hear) the sermon? How can I adapt the sermon to give an optimum opportunity for the configuration of listeners present to hear the sermon on their own wavelengths?*[29]

THE CONTINUING NATURE OF THE TASK

Finally, students of contextual preaching should be reminded that congregations are living bodies that are constantly in flux. Thus the task of congregational exegesis is never a static or finished endeavor. The exegetical process is more like going on a treasure hunt in a perpetually changing terrain, and finding fresh and startling discoveries around every bend. When the insights and understandings gained from this adventure are brought into a critical and constructive dialogue with the fruits of weekly biblical exegesis, the results for preaching can also be surprisingly fresh. Indeed, through the power of God's Holy Spirit, preaching can become an act of constructing local theologies, capable of changing lives and transforming congregations.

NOTES

1. Paul Tillich in *Theology of Culture* (New York: Oxford University Press, 1959) draws a distinction between genuine and wrong (or false) stumbling blocks in proclamation. While genuine stumbling blocks (such as a crucified Messiah or Jesus' call to us to love our enemies) are an integral part of our Christian faith and cannot be removed in preaching lest we truncate the gospel itself, false stumbling blocks are those things that we humans do communicationally that block a full and fair hearing of the gospel on the part of our congregations. Examples might include the use of unintelligible theological jargon, failure to use inclusive

language, or illustrations that fail to embody the gospel in a believable way for members of a particular faith community.

2. Bishops' Committee on Priestly Life and Ministry, *Fulfilled in Your Hearing: The Homily in the Sunday Assembly* (Washington, DC: U.S. Conference of Catholic Bishops, 1982), 4.

3. I have borrowed this phrase from David Kelsey, who first used it in his book *The Uses of Scripture in Recent Theology* (Philadelphia: Fortress Press, 1975), 170–74. Kelsey contends that one of three yardsticks by which to judge the adequacy of any theological construction is whether or not it is "seriously imaginable" for a particular people in a particular time and place. For a fuller discussion in relation to preaching, see Leonora T. Tisdale, *Preaching as Local Theology and Folk Art* (Minneapolis: Fortress Press, 1997), 43–45.

4. One very practical resource for students and pastors is *Studying Congregations: A New Handbook* (Nashville: Abingdon Press, 1998), ed. Nancy T. Ammerman, Jackson W. Carroll, Carl S. Dudley, and William McKinney. Chapter 2, "Culture and Identity in the Congregation," is especially helpful for addressing the concerns of this chapter.

5. Clyde Kluckhohn and Henry Murray, *Personality in Nature, Society and Culture* (New York: Alfred A. Knopf, 1948), as quoted in Tisdale, *Preaching as Local Theology and Folk Art*, 11.

6. James A. Wallace, *Preaching to the Hungers of the Heart: The Homily on the Feasts and within the Rites* (Collegeville, MN: Liturgical Press, 2002), x.

7. Fred B. Craddock, *Preaching* (Nashville: Abingdon Press, 1985), 88–89.

8. Harry Emerson Fosdick, "The Unknown Soldier," *Riverside Sermons* (New York: Harper, 1958).

9. William Sloane Coffin Jr., "Alex's Death," in *A Chorus of Witnesses: Model Sermons for Today's Preacher*, ed. Thomas G. Long and Cornelius Plantinga Jr. (Grand Rapids: Wm. B. Eerdmans Publishing Co., 1994), 262–65.

10. William Sloane Coffin Jr. as quoted in *The Riverside Preachers*, ed. Paul H. Sherry (New York: Pilgrim Press, 1978), 143.

11. Gardner C. Taylor, *How Shall They Preach* (Elgin, IL: Progressive Baptist Publishing House, 1977), 51.

12. Frederick Buechner, *Telling the Truth: The Gospel as Tragedy, Comedy & Fairy Tale* (New York: Harper & Row, 1977), 22–23.

13. Craddock, *Preaching*, 88.

14. Phillips Brooks, *Lectures on Preaching* (New York: E. P. Dutton, 1877), 77.

15. G. Lee Ramsey Jr., *Care-full Preaching: From Sermon to Caring Community* (St. Louis: Chalice Press, 2000).

16. Craddock, *Preaching*, 97.

17. Tisdale, *Preaching as Local Theology*. See especially chap. 3, "Exegeting the Congregation," 56–90. See also Ammerman et al., *Studying Congregations*, for additional exercises for deepening the understanding of congregations.

18. Tisdale, *Preaching as Local Theology*, 66–67.

19. For a fuller explication of these and other theological questions that can thicken congregational understanding, see Tisdale, *Preaching,* 80–86.

20. For a fuller explication of these strategies and sermonic examples of each, see Tisdale, *Preaching as Local Theology,* chap. 4, pp. 110–21.

21. Brian K. Blount and Gary W. Charles, *Preaching Mark in Two Voices* (Louisville, KY: Westminster John Knox Press, 2002).

22. For African American congregational preaching, see works by Cleophus J. LaRue, *The Heart of Black Preaching* (Louisville, KY: Westminster John Knox Press, 2000); Frank Thomas, *They Never Like to Quit Praisin God* (Cleveland: United Church Press, 1997); James H. Harris, *Preaching Liberation* (Minneapolis: Augsburg, 1995); Henry Mitchell, *Black Preaching: The Recovery of a Powerful Art* (Nashville: Abingdon Press, 1990), and *Celebration and Experience in Preaching* (Nashville: Abingdon Press, 1990); Evans Crawford, *The Hum: Call and Response in African American Preaching* (Nashville: Abingdon Press, 1995); and Samuel Proctor, *The Certain Sound of the Trumpet: Crafting a Sermon with Authority* (Valley Forge, PA: Judson Press, 1995). For Korean American preaching, see Eunjoo Mary Kim, *Preaching the Presence of God: A Homiletic from an Asian American Perspective* (Valley Forge, PA: Judson Press, 1999), and Jung Young Lee, *Korean Preaching: An Interpretation* (Nashville: Abingdon Press, 1997).

23. For homiletical reflection on preaching to street people, see Stanley P. Saunders and Charles L. Campbell, *The Word on the Street: Performing the Scriptures in the Urban Context* (Grand Rapids: Wm. B. Eerdmans Publishing Co., 2000). For reflection on the particular needs of blue-collar congregations, see Tex Sample, *Hard Living People & Mainstream Christians* (Nashville: Abingdon Press, 1993).

24. See Kathy Black, *A Healing Homiletic: Preaching and Disability* (Nashville: Abingdon Press, 1996).

25. Christine Marie Smith, *Preaching Justice: Ethnic and Cultural Perspectives* (Cleveland: United Church Press, 1998), 1.

26. James R. Nieman and Thomas G. Rogers, *Preaching to Every Pew: Cross-Cultural Strategies* (Minneapolis: Fortress Press, 2001), 6.

27. See also Andrew Carl Wisdom, *Preaching to a Multi-generational Assembly* (Collegeville, MN: Liturgical Press, 2004).

28. Joseph R. Jeter Jr. and Ronald J. Allen, *One Gospel, Many Ears: Preaching for Different Listeners in the Congregation* (St. Louis: Chalice Press, 2002), 175.

29. Ibid., 15–18, 176.

6

Interpreting the Larger Social Context

JAMES HENRY HARRIS

Congregations that understand their context often make choices to
attempt to alter it.[1]
          —Nancy Ammerman, Jackson W. Carroll, et al.,
                                    Studying Congregations

This chapter is concerned with practical, theoretical, and theological
understandings of the preaching context. In part 1, I focus on a sociological method for analyzing the congregation, seen as a part of the
global nature of our society. Congregations (and their preachers) are
placed in a global, transnational, social, political, economic, and cultural context. In part 2, I focus on the theory of interpreting congregations as texts in the larger context of church and world.

I

Congregations are not isolated units. They exist in the contexts of the
neighborhood, the city, the state, the nation, and the world. These
demographic settings ultimately mean that the social world of the
preacher and the congregation is both global and local. Airline travel
and the ubiquitous presence of the media, symbolized by CNN, and
perhaps to a lesser extent by the big three network news divisions, have
made the world much smaller and created a reality that some theorists
are now calling "glocalization." Glocalization has to do with what
Eduardo Mendieta describes as the result of an understanding of religion in an age of secularization, scientization,

> . . . an age of accelerating homogenization and simultaneous manu-
> facturing of difference, what sociologists of globalization have called

90

glocalization, . . . the last refuge of unadulterated difference, the last reservoir of cultural autonomy.[2]

Ultimately, a congregation can best be described as a system set into the context of its ecology or environment, which is not only geographical, but economic, political, social, and cultural:

> The ecology with which you are concerned may begin with the particular neighborhood in which you are located, but it will also extend outward to include the larger region from which you likely draw members and participants, as well as the economic and political institutions that create the jobs and build the roads that bring people to your door step (or take them away). In addition, congregations are part of even larger ecologies of religious institutions—denominations, networks, and ecumenical coalitions—that define and shape local mission and identity. Indeed, events in every corner of our global village can have an impact on local congregational life.[3]

Interpreting the global village provides the preacher with the necessary depth of understanding that will enable him or her to relate the national and international issues to the ministries of the local congregation. Nancy Eiesland and R. Stephen Warner in the book *Studying Congregations*, in the chapter "Ecology: Seeing the Congregation in Context," provide significant elements of ecological analysis or analysis of the environment that is external to the congregation as wide in *scope*.[4] They state:

> By wide in scope, we mean the open-ended character of the congregation's environment—its extension from the local neighborhood to the global community, and from the immediate present to the past and future. A congregation is linked to networks and events across geographic and temporal space. . . . These conversations, practices, and structures often connect communities and congregations in what some have called a "global village."[5]

Because technological innovations have made the world so accessible, the separation between the local and the global has essentially been obliterated, enabling both a "movement back and forth among communities around the world" and "transnational circuits of relationships."[6] The wide scope of things external to the congregation is not confined to that which is religious, but extends to the "economic, political, and educational contexts within which congregations exist."[7] Moreover,

Eiesland and Warner indicate that ecological analysis is not just wide in scope, but this scope has several layers. They indicate that "to speak of several *layers* refers to the fact that the interaction between a congregation, or any institution, and its environment occurs at different levels."[8] These layers are constituted by *demography*, *culture*, and *organization*. They state:

> The first layer is *demography*, or the characteristics of the people in the community, described in terms of number, age, and sex distribution; ethnic and racial profile; and changes in these data over time. The second layer is *culture*, or the systems of meaning, values, and practices shared by (and constitutive of) members of the community and groups within the community. The third layer is *organization*, or the systems of roles and relationships that structure the interactions of people in the community. These three levels—demography, culture, and organization—will help us understand the complex dynamics of the community.[9]

These aspects of the congregation's larger context are indeed very complex, such that each aspect when properly interpreted will provide the preacher and the people with a better understanding of themselves and their larger environment. The congregation's context can now be interpreted vis-à-vis an understanding of the aforesaid variables—demographics, culture, and organization. Culture is probably the most complex layer in this ecology of contextual environmental analysis because it is so inclusive and comprehensive, that is, encompassing elements of identity such as race, language, ethnicity, class, gender, sexual orientation, social and political beliefs, and practices, and so on. Culture is a comprehensive term that reflects almost everything that a congregation does and claims to value, even what the anthropologist Robert Redfield calls "style of life."[10]

In focusing on the larger social context, Joe Holland and Peter Henriot, S.J., have provided a valuable resource, *Social Analysis: Linking Faith and Justice*. This little book provides a method of doing social analysis that will benefit the preacher and the congregation. Their chapter titled "Industrialization and Pastoral Responses" is as timely today as it was twenty years ago. The authors discuss industrial capitalism from the perspective of "three historical structural stages or periods": *laissez-faire*, *social welfare*, and *national security* industrial capitalism. This third and final stage seems prophetic and very appropriate and applicable to the current economic, social, and political environment. The nation is obsessed with national security, and since the 9/11 attacks the terminology has expanded to include "Homeland Security" which is now a cabinet-level position appointed by the president. National security and homeland security are both grounded in the language and spirit of fear and have obviated any and all concerns about the poor, the disenfranchised, the oppressed within the cities and states of the United States, and the national deficit while coming dangerously close to superseding personal and individual rights. We live in a transnational world where "global capital will flow wherever the return is greatest. Returns will be greatest where wages are restrained and taxes low (hence, where social services are curtailed)."[11] The preacher and the church are compelled to recognize the relationship between their ministry and the larger social, political, economic, and cultural context. The church can no longer hide behind its local address and remain isolated from events in the region, state, nation, and world. For example, plant closings in Mechanicsville, Virginia, may be caused by a management decision that transcends local concerns, namely, the desire to reduce labor costs, and move the operations to another country where labor costs are far less. Human marginalization, domestic streamlining, and other economic realities are tied to forces beyond the local demographics. We are operating in a multinational and transnational economic and political system. Holland and Henriot state:

> It is in the *political* system, however, that one sees some of the most frightening changes; it is this system that is the source of the period's name—"national security" industrial capitalism. Social welfare considerations have yielded to national security's imperatives. . . . The domain of national security has expanded to include cultural, political, and economic as well as military dimensions—in both domestic and foreign policies.[12]

In response to this new reality, the preacher and the congregation have to understand that they are caught in this web of globalization and preoccupation with national and homeland security vis-à-vis war in Iraq and other parts of the world. Joe Holland calls for a radical strategy by the pastors of congregations that is transformative, such that it will serve human needs and human rights. He states:

> This principle, the transformation of capital and technology to serve basic human needs and fundamental human rights, is accountable to community at every level, from the local to the global. If the social

style of the pastoral response is transformative, the faith problematic in which it is grounded is *justice*. Justice, in this case, is set over against the dominant theme of national security. . . . In this new style, justice is no longer a subdivision of moral theology, but a reconstituting vision for faith and theology. Because this new strategy digs to the root of the problem, it can be called a "radical strategy."[13]

The main insight here is that dealing with the larger context of preaching gestures toward transformation theologically and programmatically. Social analysis provides the tools for analyzing the local congregation's context in relation to the larger world. This analysis involves social, economic, political, and cultural understandings of people and practices beyond the often introverted interior psyche of the particular congregation. This means that particularity must take on a universal or global vision mediated by the quest for justice. In practice, then, congregations black, white, yellow, and brown now have an opportunity to embody the gospel through their radical actions of transformation. Preaching now takes on a new urgency where the principle of conforming to the status quo is replaced by the principle and practice of transformation: "Do not be conformed . . . but be transformed."[14]

Holland and Henriot provide a method for social analysis that is constituted by questions or statements that deal with the following areas: social, economic, political, and ecclesial dimensions of the congregation (see below).[15] Preachers and congregations can adapt the specifics of the questionnaire to their own denominational affiliation and their specific needs.

II

In this section, I am concerned that students of preaching learn to avoid parochialism and an introverted mentality as it relates to congregational preaching. In this connection, Martin Luther King Jr. said in his book *Strength to Love* that "it has always been the responsibility of the church to broaden horizons and challenge the status quo."

It seems to be a law that the local congregation cannot afford to be parochial and introverted in its theology and practices. The only hope for escaping this comfort zone rests in the preacher's ability to expand the horizon of the congregation through the sermon. Preachers will have to be taught how to be cognizant of the world, that is, developing a worldview that is expansive and comprehensive as it relates to issues of freedom, justice, race, gender, and culture and such, as discussed in the previous section. The local context cannot exclude the "other" in its understanding and practices. Justo and Catherine González have asserted quite clearly that exegeting the larger context is crucial to the preaching enterprise. They write:

> Concretely, this means that preaching should always take into account, not only the immediate context of the congregation, but also that wider context of the community of faith throughout the world. . . . Preaching must be addressed to the needs of a parish; but it must not be parochial, for one of the needs of every parish is to be connected to the church universal.[16]

This connection to what the Gonzálezes call the "church universal" is critical, but there is also a need to be connected to others who may or may not be a part of any church.

The fact that congregations seem to be culturally, socially, economically, and racially homogeneous translates into a type of narrowness that can only be challenged by the preacher who is broadly concerned about theological and contextual interpretation in the hopes of transforming the congregation into one that hears the cries and feels the pain and hurt of the poor, the dispossessed, the oppressed—the other. Conversely, the preacher in the poor and oppressed congregation is compelled to expand the horizon of his or her context by imagining a new world beyond the boundaries of the particular local congregation, where the bounteous glory and blessings of God abound. In his sermon "The Good News and the Quest for Community," Samuel DeWitt Proctor helps us to understand the meaning of community in the larger context in his discussion of community and the worth of persons. He writes:

> What do we find in the good news that we can share with a pluralistic, secular society that may bring it closer to real community? First, the good news stamps God's unique sign of worth and dignity upon each person in so indelible a way that no other person can claim the right to use anyone for his or her own purposes. This affirmation changed the direction of history. A lonely Simon, with sores covering his body, his toes and fingers eaten away by invading infections and his nerves numbed by leprosy, with no one allowed to be near him, nevertheless was good enough, clean enough, safe enough for Jesus to find room and board at his house in Bethany during Jesus' last week on earth. Jesus did not lodge with the high priest or the ruler of the Sanhedrin, not with any of the mighty and powerful, but

with Simon the leper. There is our signal that every soul is precious in God's sight and that genuine community begins here.[17]

Unless the preacher and the congregation are open to a radical under-standing of Jesus and the meaning of the gospel, there can be no broad and expansive interpretation of the social and political world of the con-gregation. David Buttrick is correct when he says that "homiletic instruction must begin with hermeneutic issues."[18]

What follows is a questionnaire designed to be used by a preacher in assessing the social context of a congregation:

QUESTIONNAIRE

Beginning Social Analysis

Beginning social analysis in a local situation can be simple. First, we must ask ourselves what we know about the various sectors of our social reality. What we already know—and what we don't know—will push us to further study. Below are several questions that may help us to determine the areas upon which to focus our attention.[19]

I. SOCIAL
    A. What is the *demographic* character of the locality?
        present population
        growth rate (decline/increase)
        projections toward year 20__
        present geographic concentration
        projected shifts in concentration
        urban/rural differences
    B. What is its *racial/ethnic* character?
        European ethnic groups
        Hispanics
        Blacks
        Native Americans
        Asians
        Other
    C. What is the *cultural* character of the locality?
        ethnic heritages of population
        character or "stamp" of the people

level of education
strength of community ties
state of the arts
D. What is the *class structure* in the locality?
underclass
low-income service workers
blue-collar workers
white-collar workers
managerial class
superrich
E. What are the dominant *social problems* in the area? Are they related to:
race
migratory labor
the aging
women
families
youth
abortion
schools
drugs; alcohol
health care
leisure activities
crime
other
F. What is the *social-psychological "temper"* of the area?
predominant values
class divisions and conflicts
general outlook on life: satisfaction/malaise

II. ECONOMIC

A. What is the general economic *profile* of the locality?
major industries
agricultural situation
natural resources
new technologies
relationship to defense/military industries
role of business and labor groups in community
B. What is the economic *situation*?
self-reliance vs. dependency

growth rate

inflation; cost of living

unemployment

income distribution

strength of unions

labor-management relations

C. **What is the *environmental* situation?**

pollution—air, water, land

energy prospects, present and future

effectiveness of environmental regulations

D. **What are the key economic *problems*?**

flight of capital

urban gentrification and displacement

housing

tax bases

public services

other

E. **What is the relationship between the *local* economy and the *international* economy?**

imports/exports

offices of multinational corporations

foreign-owned local businesses

runaway shops

III. POLITICAL

A. **What is the political *profile* of the locality?**

relationship of political parties

existence of party "machines"

liberal-conservative divisions

voting registration/election turnout

church-state relationship

B. **What is the nature of its political *leadership*?**

record of senators, representatives in Congress

record of state legislature, governor

record of local officials

C. **What is the nature of its *informal* leadership?**

names of "influential" people

socioeconomic background of leaders

connections (business, family, etc.) with other influential groups or individuals

        nature of power concentration
        active interest groups and lobbies
   D. **What *nonpolitical* factors have influence on political life?**
        churches and synagogues
        media
        business groups
        labor unions

IV. ECCLESIAL

   A. **What is the *religious climate* in the locality?**
        percentages of Catholics, Protestants, Jews, etc.
        percentage of religiously nonaffiliated
        presence of religions/traditions/movements of other than
           Judeo-Christian origin
        degree of ecumenical cooperation
        religious affection/disaffection (provide reasons)
   B. **What is the health of the *local church*?**
        state of dioceses and other church jurisdictions
        character of bishops, church leadership
        pastoral councils; participation of laity
        morale/style of clergy and religious professionals
        vocations (clergy, religious)
        institutions—hospitals and schools, for example

NOTES

1. Nancy Ammerman, Jackson W. Carroll, et al., *Studying Congregations: A New Handbook* (Nashville: Abingdon Press, 1998), 41.

2. Jurgen Habermas, *Religion and Rationality: Essays on Reason, God, and Modernity,* ed. with introduction by Eduardo Mendieta (Cambridge, MA: MIT Press, 2002), 1.

3. Ammerman and Carroll, *Studying Congregations*, 15–16.

4. Ibid., 41.

5. Ibid.

6. Ibid.

7. Ibid., 42.

8. Ibid.

9. Ibid.

10. See Lawrence W. Levine, *Black Culture and Black Consciousness* (Oxford: Oxford University Press, 1977), 4.

11. Joe Holland and Peter Henriot, S.J., *Social Analysis: Linking Faith and Justice* (Maryknoll, NY: Orbis Books, and Washington, DC: Center of Concern, 1980), 78.

12. Ibid., 81.

13. Ibid., 84.

14. Romans 12:2, NRSV.

15. Joe Holland and Peter Henriot, *Social Analysis: Linking Faith and Justice* (Washington: Center of Concern, 1980), 42–43.

16. Justo González and Catherine González, "The Larger Context," in *Preaching as a Social Act: Theology and Practice,* ed. Arthur Van Seters (Nashville: Abingdon Press, 1988), 31–32.

17. Samuel D. Proctor, *Preaching about Crises in the Community* (Philadelphia: Westminster Press, 1988), 96–97.

18. David Buttrick in *Preaching on the Brink*, ed. Martha J. Simmons (Nashville: Abingdon Press, 1996), 79.

19. Reprinted from *Social Analysis: Linking Faith and Justice* by Joe Holland and Peter Henriot (Washington: Center of Concern, 1980), 42–43, with permission from the Center of Concern www.coc.org.

7

The Use of Language

TERESA FRY BROWN

Church sanctuaries, office parking lots, Sunday restaurant tables, Internet chat rooms, public television programs, academic gatherings, and seminary classrooms are replete with conversations, critiques, and clichés about what the preacher said in the latest sermon. Seemingly, religious rhetoric bleeds over into political, social, and private engagements, regarding what life is or should be, who believes what, and who the greatest preachers are today. At some point discussions may lead to queries about the clarity and intent of the preaching moment: "What did the preacher mean?" "How did she say it?" "Did you understand that point?" At other times, the analysis may lead to statements of boredom, disbelief, satisfaction, pride, or apathy.

Preaching is one of the most vulnerable occupations in which a person can engage. One's gifts and talents are on public exhibition. One's faith and theology are laid bare before the masses. One's idiosyncrasies are revealed. One's linguistic agility is on open display. And the proclaimer's love or disdain for the congregation is more than circumstantially evident. Consequently, the preacher has an obligation to craft sermons that clearly communicate what she or he wants to say.

The purpose of this chapter is to provide an overview of the effects of language and oral competence during the preaching moment, and to examine methods for maintaining connectedness with the listeners during the preaching event. I will review basic principles of language, hearing, and listening, and will examine sociocultural considerations for language usage. I will also attend to issues related to nonverbal communication in preaching. Standard research in homiletical and communication theory, as well as my own research, experience, and praxis as a homiletics professor, speech language pathologist, and voice coach are foundational to the development of this overview.

HOW SHALL THEY HEAR . . . ?
ACTIVE HEARING AND LISTENING

Speech communication includes sounds, gestures, events, and people. One of the primary complaints about sermons is that they are boring, flat, uninspired, or irrelevant. One of the contributing factors to this reaction is the manner in which persons listen to sermons.

Hearing involves the mechanical and neurological reception of sensory impulses of sound in the outer ear, middle ear, and inner ear. It is the reception of sound through sensory fluctuations of air pressure. Hearing is the process of translating these fluctuations into an electrical signal that our brains can understand and interpret as distinct sounds arranged into an auditory amalgamation of syllables, words, phrases, sentences, and paragraphs.

Listening is active hearing. The elements of listening include not only hearing the message, but also understanding what is said, evaluating the information, and responding to what is heard by doing something or by storing information for future use.[1] We spend approximately 45 percent of our time in active listening. However, 70 percent of oral communication is misunderstood, ignored, or quickly forgotten.

Craig Loscalzo speaks of identification with the listener as one of the primary means by which the preacher attains linguistic unity with the congregation.[2] Preaching out of relationality developed over time "distinguishes one as prophet and priest." The mutual evolution of communication is a head and heart experience transcending stereotypes developed in initial encounters.

In addition to identifying with the preacher, the listeners should be able to recognize the sermon's premise, associate it to past experience, identify the premise by references to the historical or invented examples, and draw conclusions from presented information. The listener evaluates the preacher's effectiveness through emphatic or deliberative listening. Emphatic listening provides maximum understanding of the speaker's intent and content. The emphatic listener recalls critical issues, agreements, or disagreements with the speaker, and draws conclusions. This listener is more likely to have studied the text previously or heard other sermons using the focused text, or is able to relate to the flow or the sermon's ideas. The deliberative listener, on the other hand, may have minimal understanding of the sermon and is predisposed to criticize, summarize, conclude, agree, or disagree. This listener may have little or no background with the text, have preconceived notions about either the preacher or the text itself, or simply have a different interpretation of the sermon.[3]

COMMUNICATION AND PREACHING

Basic Communication Paradigm

Figure 1.

In basic communication theory there is a sender (preacher/proclaimer/ speaker) and a receiver (congregant/listener). There are also oral and written communication channels or conveyances of the message. Preaching is informational and dialogical, melding the call and response of preacher and congregant.

In order for the paradigm to work properly there must be a sense of mutuality. Both parties send and receive information in a feedback loop, or two-way communicative flow. The preacher (sender) initiates the communication, understanding that the congregant (receiver) is ready to listen. The congregant, in turn, trusts the preacher to impart information without force, manipulation, prejudice, offense. The preacher awaits feedback from the receiver, which may come through nonverbal cues (such as a nod, a turn of the body, or a facial expression), or through verbal cues (such as an "*Amen*," or some other sort of vocalized assent). These cues let the speaker know that the message was received, affirmed, and understood.[4]

Language is manifest through channels of communication that employ the encoding and decoding of symbols and signs. Language can be either "denotative," effecting clarity and precision, or "connotative," effecting ambiguity through the use of metaphor, image, or other symbolic speech forms. Language is socially shaped through traditional or contemporary values and usage. It has the power to shape human consciousness and to bring about changes in human perspectives or worldviews.[5]

Barriers to Communication

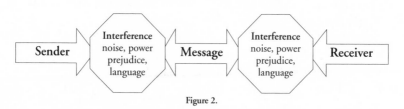

Figure 2.

In the preaching event, communicational interference can come from a variety of sources. It may come, for instance, from something as minor as the hum of a heater, or the feedback given by a microphone, or from the more serious "noise" that comes when a preacher conveys a condescending mood, tone, or presence in the pulpit, or uses language that is difficult for the congregants to understand. Power and authority disparities between the preacher and the congregation often hamper both the preacher's ability to speak and the congregation's ability to hear the sermon. Preconceived notions about the preacher's oratorical skill, reputation, personhood, or faith can also obscure the communication channel. While the preacher has little power to control some of these obstacles to hearing, others are more easily addressed.

I developed the following paradigm of amplified communication factors through a combination of research and years of observations of the preachers and listeners in the preaching moment in churches, classrooms, and other settings (see figure 3, p. 105). The factors are representative rather than exhaustive. Theological position is a factor in all three areas.

Amplified Preaching Communication Factors

As a way of heightening student awareness of the complexity of these communication factors, I ask each student in my Introduction to Preaching class to exegete themselves, exegete the congregation, and exegete the text in that order. Each stage begins and ends with prayer. After jotting down notes or items for consideration in each area, the

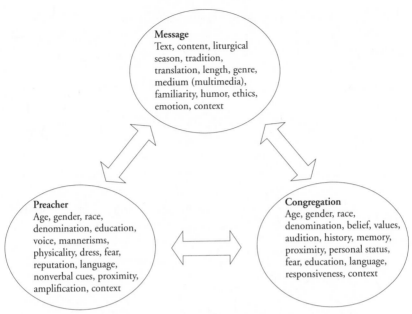

Figure 3.

student then continues formal sermon preparation. The sermon goal or purpose is derailed if the preacher ignores any one of the areas.

I emphasize that as the audience for preaching changes, so also the sermon needs to change as an exercise in communicational engagement. For instance, at times students preach in class a sermon they have preached in another context. The communicational disconnect is often immediately evident, particularly in a class that is more ethnically, racially, or denominationally diverse than their home congregation. At other times, the model for preaching is set using the class demographics as the context for the sermon. This allows for sermons tailored to a specific congregation. And at still others the students are assigned a choice of text to be preached in a context that is distinctively different from their "home" congregation. This is an exercise in the portability of communication.

What Is the Message?

The initial consideration for students is the choice of the text. Aware that many students are not lectionary preachers, each class provides an opportunity for students to preach from diverse genres of biblical literature. The descriptors used in giving expression to the text depend on the liturgical season. Generally students use terms such as "joy" and "peace" more often during Advent than during Lent, where "love" and "pain" are more the norm. In like manner, they often use "should" and "must" more often in social justice/prophetic sermons, while terms like "neighbor" and "community" are more frequently used in pastoral sermons.

Communication issues are also a factor in selecting the translation of the text to be read in worship. The seventeenth-century language of the King James Version is at times confusing for persons living in the "message age," and there can be cognitive dissonance when the language of Bible times conflicts with community vernacular. The congregation's and preacher's own familiarity with a narrative or biblical text may also mute its effectiveness, so that the sermon has a "been there, done that" feel to it. And the twenty-first-century move to multimedia sermons may also influence the clarity of communication—particularly when PowerPoint projections do not work, or when there is an awkward move from the oral preached word to the audiovisual stimuli.

The "content" of the sermon means what the preacher means to say and what he or she hopes the congregation ultimately hears. There are, of course, as many interpretations of the message as there are of a specific text.

Who Is the Preacher?

I am a member of a denomination that introduces the preacher a few moments before she or he begins to preach. This is the one moment I dread most in worship. If the introduction, with accompanying biographical flourishes and every line of my curriculum vitae, is lengthy, the congregation has been likely to expect that I am going to be stiff, aloof, too academic, boring, or too old to wheeze out the title before I sit down. On the other hand, on one occasion the congregation began to rejoice as the senior pastor "preached" my biographical information, because they were proud that I had done so much. In either case, the preacher can be set up for success or failure before making it to the podium.

The preacher also contributes to the communication cycle with his or her mere presence—exuding humility, confidence, boldness, apathy, or fear. Often one's reputation precedes him or her, for better or worse, and analysis of the preacher's dress, mannerisms, voice and diction, hair, jewelry, facial expressions, gestures, mobility, and projection can all be fodder for the Sunday lunch conversation.

The important factor is: Does the preacher connect with the listener?

In my preaching classes, student peer evaluations are filled with comments like: "I disagree with your theology, but you were very conversational." "You used such passion when you talked about your family." "I have never heard anyone explain the text that way." "The last time you preached you . . ." "I did not understand what you meant when you said. . . ." Regardless of the method used, the students accept peer comments with a bit more calm than those of the professor. I have observed more acceptance of comments made by males and older more experienced students than by women and younger less experienced students, regardless of the commentator's preaching ability. There is also a deference to comments made by African American and Korean students, depending on the demographics of the classroom. This underscores how authority or power also affects the communication channels.

Who Is the Congregation?

The congregation's contribution to the communication or preaching event is similar to that of the preacher. Persons of like ethnicities, values, denominations, ages, and beliefs are often more accepting of the preacher than are hearers who are distinctively different. Congregations also have a collective memory, and may compare one preacher to another in terms of voice, physicality, education, and handling of the text.

The collective body language of the congregation is a strong signifier of acceptance or rejection of a message. Shrugging of shoulders, yawning, walking, throat clearing, facial contortions, smiling, laughing, nodding, clapping, and sleeping are all cues or signs related to interference or clearance of the communication channel.

Joseph Webb, in *Preaching and the Challenge of Pluralism*, identifies a number of symbols that can have positive or negative meaning in the communication *between* the preacher and the congregation. One must remember that there is no "communication" unless there is a sender and a receiver of the message. Among Webb's symbols are: diversity of language responses, the traits and idiosyncrasies of the speaker and listener, objects in the environment context, the text itself, and insignias and clothing.[6] I would add to Webb's list: voice volume and quality, ritual actions, race, gender, age, denomination, geography, level of language, intellectual capacity, appearance, and perceived preaching ability. In the preaching moment orality, aurality, semiotics (symbols and signs), and nonverbal language or metalanguage combine in a communicative channel with or without distractions and interference.

Religious Language

> If the language of faith ceases to be in dialogue with the experience
> of the world, it has effectively become a language of unbelief.[7]

Religious language is a distinct discourse. Theologian Paul van Buren
describes religious language as a fruitful source of rule breaking. It is a
means of attempting to describe God and faith issues in imperfect yet
creative ways. The speaker bends language to express a sense of reality
that exists beyond it. She walks the edge of meaning to talk insightfully
about spiritual realities. She understands that word meaning changes
with the setting, context, or community.[8]

Religious language is consciously retrospective as persons strive to relate
their beliefs or faith stance. It is prescriptive in its orthodoxy and identity
as exemplified in prayers, invocations, sermons, and songs. It is imaginative and exploratory as the speaker responds to claims of belief.[9] It may be
groundbreaking as new words are created in the delivery of homiletical
material or monotonous due to obscure, inert, elitist, or canned linguistic
rudiments. It may also be filled with sound and fury signifying nothing,
when the verbosity of the speaker overshadows the message intent.

Preachers encounter life issues with a depth of spirituality and pathos
that few others have the opportunity to do. They are called on to rekin-
dle the vitality of lives; to call people to Christlike living; and to refocus
on the distinctiveness of faith. Preachers are to stem the "everybody is
doing it" mentality with a "because God said do it" lifestyle. In a 1987
study by the Commission on Theology, Education and Electronic
Media, the National Council of Churches stated that the preacher, like
the media, has the power to mold the worldview (ethos) of the listener
(viewer). The main effect is enculturation. Dull preaching, slick pro-
gramming, and viewer experience of low involvement and passivity
decrease the desire to hear and do. When preaching is disconnected
from the life of the listener, manipulatively condemning, or dispassion-
ately delivered it is irrelevant. Consequently preachers need to pay close
attention to the cultural realities of their hearers.

During the act of preaching there is a genuine identity of preacher
with people's lives, personal involvement, and emotions. Preaching is
communication in the concrete, filled with language and images from
day-to-day details, dynamics, sights, sounds, smells, tastes, texture, and
life scenes. Preaching revisits the familiar through recognition of the
frame of reference of listeners and identity with their environment. One

delivers the sermon in a manner in which the hearers are able to see and hear themselves within it.[10]

One exercise that has been particularly helpful in bringing the senses into preaching is assigning specific texts to small groups of three to four persons, and then asking them to discuss the multisensory imagery in the text. How does the text sound? How does it look? What do you hear? How does the text feel? Act out the text. What are the smells, textures, sizes, colors, or shadows in the text? The students then preach a minisermon using the new imagery discovered in the text.

Power of Language

Language has power. The adage "Sticks and stones may break my bones, but words will never hurt me" is false. As a child of the modern civil rights movement and a contemporary woman preacher, I am well aware of the damage inflicted on the psyche of the listener from pulpits. The exclusionary language that denies full personhood to women, children, elders, homosexuals, the poor, the homeless, or the disabled in particular, and others in general, is alive and well in preaching. At times, those who are called to speak about love and power perpetuate an ethos of "*in-powerment*" (my word, meaning that those who have power dictate what is acceptable language).

The social-political nature of language means that those with actual power dictate what is academic/intellectual language, what is "proper"/ standard language, what meanings/descriptors are acceptable, or whose sentences/grammatical structures are correct. Those who are not privileged to the "in language" or "theo-speak" are unable to understand or deliver sermonic material. These power dynamics are inculcated by one group in order to control or limit another's participation in the communicative encounter. Consequently, the preacher needs to seriously consider words in common use, vernacular, or culture that may have a negative effect or insult certain groups of persons during the preaching encounter. Bigoted gender or racial names and labels, use of color symbolism indicating black is bad and white is good, ethnocentric representations of one perspective or race over another, or sociopolitical designations of persons as "credit to race," "at risk," "well dressed," or "primitive" are examples of linguistic land mines. Students can exchange their manuscripts with a small group in order to filter and discuss derogatory language.

Inclusive Language

> Like an incessant dripping on the head, the words come: man, men, he, his, him, father, son, brethren, brotherhood. Instead of joining in the intercession, one begins to count the times the pastor uses "Father" in a prayer. One begins to lose the points of sermons while fuming over statements like "Christ died for all men" and "God in Christ became man." The pain and anger become excruciating.[11]

In this quotation, Nancy Hardesty witnesses to the power of exclusive speech from the perspective of women who have heard years of sermons dominated by male preachers and male language. I hear male and female students, however, using exclusive language in preaching. When challenged to use balance in language, they state: "You know what I mean." "My Bible says men." "God is not a woman." "This politically correct stuff is what is killing the church today." Every semester I retort, "This is not about being politically correct, it is about justice." Inclusive language is a means of relief for the violence of sociolinguistic prejudicial language. It provides a reassessment of how we give expression to gender, class, race, age, education, ethnicity, denomination, and God talk. It is not about political correctness, but about speaking in the fullness of the gospel message about all being equal before God.

Occasionally entire groups are demonized or damned in order to promote a particular political agenda or ideology. Students should be encouraged to review who is being left out of sermons, who is demeaned, who is ridiculed, or who is stereotypically labeled. Since "naming" is a depiction of one's essence or being, students should be urged to develop a "justice thesaurus" that includes alternative words that are less offensive and more comprehensive of the fullness of God's creation.

Cultural Imperatives

In the African American preaching culture there is a decided love for the beauty of language.[12] Elements contained in most traditional African American preaching styles are currently evident in evangelical, charismatic, and neo-Pentecostal preaching styles. These elements are used by men and women, across ethnicities, ages, and cultures:

> Intonation—described as having a musical quality using sustained tones. It is a carryover from traditional African culture, where

impromptu songs, folktales, wisdom fables, and inspirational sayings are intoned in a natural, free-flowing voice.

Use of rhythm breaks (breaths) that make room for congregational response.

Call and response—an exchange of information between preacher and people that takes place in the preaching moment. The congregation's response is meant to encourage or guide the preacher.

Repetition—restatement of a sound, word, or phrase for emphasis. It is useful for sermonic impact or effect, and for instilling something into people's memory.

Stammer—repetition of part of a word or a blocking sound production that builds intensity and causes people to attend to what comes next.

Speed of delivery—dependent on soloist and the listener's response.

The increasing popularity of televangelism, webcasts, religious conferences, international evangelistic crusades, and the sale of sermonic audio- and videotapes has led to linguistic patterns that have pushed traditional cultural, ethnic, denominational, and sexual "sound like" boundaries.

Televangelism

Televangelism or electronic preaching began in 1954 when Everett C. Parker founded the Office of Communication of the United Church of Christ to facilitate increased communication skills of ministers, to highlight activities of local churches, and to use television for educational purposes. Its predecessor, religious radio, dates back to 1927. Televangelism has today morphed into a multibillion-dollar, twenty-four-hour-per-day webcast, tape, and DVD distribution of preaching with its own distinctive language.

Students assigned to view televangelists describe their experience with adjectives as diverse as "flat," "distant," "loud," "energetic," "techno-enhanced," "evangelical," "prejudiced," "theologically weak," "colorful," and "exciting." Critiques and entertainment value notwithstanding, television and webcast sermons provide immediate and easy access to faith language. Pulpits, robed choirs, crosses, altars, organs, the Bible, hymn singing, responsive interracial congregations, and powerful convicted preachers are also readily evidenced. William A. Fore, media expert, states that the robe and Bible of the preacher indicates the authority held by that person. Many, however, no longer wear robes but substitute colorful suits and dresses with diamonds and other symbols of wealth for traditional pulpit garb. Some celebrity preachers speak of being "favored by God" to be wealthy, and their churches attract thousands of members. Entertainers, athletes, and politicians make guest appearances to discuss how their faith has elevated them.

Topics for preaching include healing, wealth, faithfulness, obedience, patriotism, and family values. Pentecostals and charismatics spend considerable time on the gifts of the Holy Spirit, fundamentalists on doctrine, and evangelicals on winning converts around the globe. The preacher usually uses one or more proof texts to substantiate his or her point. Frequently repeated theological mantras include: "The Bible says," "Name it and claim it," "Stepping into your season," "Live into your purpose," and "What He's done for others, He'll do for you." Personal testimonies abound.[13] The Bible is the principal authority. The preacher is the prophet.

More needs to be written on the effect of televangelism on the local church and the future of preaching—especially given that some of our students are mirroring the televangelists in their own preaching language, style, and pulpit demeanor.

Nonverbal Language

Hands waving without any connection to the text, frowning while preaching about joy, gripping the podium as if it were the railing of the Titanic, pacing like a ball in a tennis match—these are just a few common examples of the ways in which nonverbal language can impact the preaching event. Negatively, nonverbal communication may become a basis for judgments, prejudices, stereotypes, and barriers to "hearing the preacher" or attending to the spoken word. Positively, nonverbal communication can also enhance and expand the meaning of the verbal message, extend grace or hospitality toward the hearers, or help listeners visualize what the preacher is verbally describing.

In his listing of the major elements of nonverbal language, Peter Anderson includes the following; physicality (attire, body type, hair, and clothing), oculesics (eye contact and usage), kinesics (body movement, gestures, and posture), vocalics (speech tempo, rhythm, resonance, control), chronemics (structure and use of time), haptics (physical contact with listeners), and proxemics (space, distance between preacher and listener).[14] Thomas Troeger refers to the combination of Word and movement in preaching as "logosomatic language." Experiencing the "full bodily weight of truth" is one of the strategies he recommends preachers employ when interpreting biblical texts in sermons. In an age replete with cyberspace, vivid media, shorter attention spans, and a maturing population, the preacher must also use all the senses to undergird the spoken word.

One exercise I have used to encourage the incorporation of the body in preaching is to ask students first to read a biblical text aloud, and then to nonverbally interpret the passage to group members utilizing the nonverbal elements listed in Anderson's work. The listeners/observers then assess the effectiveness of the presentation in terms of fluidity of movement, "comfortable" or purposeful actions utilized, adherence to possibilities within the text, and the expression of emotion through facial expressions. The preacher must also review his or her own sermon tape with and without sound to assess the appropriateness of gestures and other nonverbal cues.

CONCLUSION

Preaching is an opportunity to use language to its fullest. Words affect the heart, soul, and mind. The preacher must be committed to oral communication, keeping words simple, clear, and appropriate. Using vivid, attractive, and engaging language, the preacher strives to join intellect and emotion as persons reconsider their faith.[15]

In a preaching class I took in seminary, Dr. Charles G. Adams, Senior Pastor of Hartford Memorial Baptist Church in Detroit, Michigan, summed up his ten commandments for effective communication in preaching:

Don't be dull, tedious, or laborious.

Don't apologize for the sermon.

Don't be inaudible—reach the farthest person from the pulpit.

Don't be monotone.

Don't preach at, under, or over, but to, with, and for the people.

Do not steal other people's sermons, no matter how good it feels. This will rob the preacher of his/her own integrity, authority, creativity, character, and spirituality.

Don't repeat a sermon unless it has been refiltered.

Don't imitate others—be yourself.

Don't preach too long.

Prepare your own heart and spirit before preaching for adoration, confession, thanksgiving, and supplication.[16]

I have found these principles invaluable both in the development of my own preaching voice, and also in the maintenance of relevant and purposeful connection with the listeners.

NOTES

1. Lyman Steil, "Your Listening Profile (Sperry Corporation), Toward Better Listening," excerpt from Sperry Corporation Listening Program, Lyman K. Steil, Communication Development, Inc., 1979, in Robert Cathcart and Larry Samovar, *Small Group Communication*, 4th ed. (Dubuque, IA: William C. Brown Publishers, 1984), 305.

2. Craig Loscalzo, *Preaching Sermons That Connect: Effective Communication through Identification* (Downers Grove, IL: InterVarsity Press, 1993), 23–29.

3. Charles Kelly, "Emphatic Listening," in Robert S. Cathcart and Larry A. Samovar, *Small Group Communication* (Madison, WI: Brown and Benchmark, 1995), 296–97.

4. Richard Johannesen, "The Emerging Concept of Communication as Dialogue," in *The Quarterly Journal of Speech* 57 (December 1971): 373–82. See also classic discussions of communication by Reuel L. Howe, "The Miracle of Dialogue," in *The Human Dialogue*, ed. Floyd W. Matson and Ashley Montagu (New York: Free Press, 1967); and Martin Buber, *I and Thou*, trans. R. G. Smith (Charles Scribner's Sons, 1958).

5. Lucy Rose, *Sharing the Word: Preaching in the Roundtable Church* (Louisville, KY: Westminster John Knox Press, 1997), 76–78.

6. Joseph Webb, *Preaching and the Challenge of Pluralism* (St. Louis: Chalice Press, 2001), 17–30.

7. Gerhard Ebeling, *Introduction to a Theological Theory of Language* (London: William Collins Sons & Co., 1972), 192.

8. Paul van Buren, *The Edges of Language* (London: SCM Press, 1972), 368–95.

9. David Crystal, ed., *Cambridge Encyclopedia of the English Language* (New York: Cambridge University Press, 1995), 371.

10. Henry Mitchell, *Celebration and Experience in Preaching* (Nashville: Abingdon Press, 1990), 79–84.

11. Nancy A. Hardesty, *Inclusive Language in the Church* (Atlanta: John Knox Press, 1987), 2.

12. See Teresa Fry Brown, *Weary Throats and New Songs: Black Women Proclaiming God's Word* (Nashville: Abingdon Press, 2003), 157–70.

13. Erling Jorstad, *Popular Religion in America: The Evangelical Voice* (Westport, CT: Greenwood Press, 1993), 113–15. See also Jeffery K. Hadden and Anson Shupe, *Televangelism* (New York: Henry Holt, 1988), and Quentin Schultze, *Habits of a High-Tech Heart* (Grand Rapids: Baker Book House, 2002).

14. Peter A. Anderson, " Nonverbal Communication in the Small Group," in Cathcart and Samovar, *Small Group Communication,* 258–70. See also my chapter on attire and delivery in *Weary Throats and New Songs.*

15. Mark Gallie and Craig Brian Larson, *Preaching That Connects: Using the Techniques of Journalists to Add Impact to Your Sermons* (Grand Rapids: Zondervan Publishing House, 1994), 16–21.

16. Charles G. Adams, lecture in "Preaching in Black and White," summer school class at Iliff School of Theology, Denver, Colorado, 1987.

8

The Preaching Imagination

ANNA CARTER FLORENCE

You walk into the preaching classroom, ready to teach, and immediately sense that something is different. Is it just you, or is there a heightened anxiety in the air? Your students are watching you perhaps a bit more carefully than usual, and you scan their faces for a clue before it hits you: *Of course—they've read the syllabus.* The topic for today is "The Preaching Imagination." And *now* you have a pretty good idea about the thick emotional smog hovering over the classroom, because the word "imagination" tends to elicit strong reactions.

Some of the students are visibly nervous. Among them are the woman who has never taken a creative writing class, the man whose only experience of art is making construction paper turkeys, and half a dozen souls who failed miserably to color inside the lines in first grade and now will seriously tell you that they have no creative talent. They see "The Preaching Imagination" on the syllabus and fear that you are about to subject them to guided imagery, haiku, and finger paint, any of which makes them break out into a cold sweat.

Other students are visibly suspicious. They include the former engineer who was trained to value logic over intuition, the youth minister who wants to give young people the truth about Jesus rather than any made-up stories, and a few budding exegetes who have fallen in love with biblical-historical criticism. They are concerned that "imaginative sermons" will lead a congregation straight into sin, and that human creativity has no place in biblical preaching that proclaims the Word of God.

Still other students are visibly excited. They include the computer experts itching to experiment with technology in sermons, the closet poets and writers who love words in any form, and the musician in the front row who is planning to ask you, at the break, if he can write songs instead of sermons and perform them for credit. These students are hoping that "imaginative preaching" will give them license to try anything and everything in the pulpit, and they are inspired and raring to go.

Nerves, suspicion, excitement: no wonder the atmosphere feels tense. When the topic is "imagination," your students are literally all over the emotional map. Your first job, as a teacher, is to gather them together by meeting them where they are. So before you do anything else, take time to clear the air. As a tension diffuser, ask the students to shout out anything that comes to mind when they hear the word "imagination," positive words (ideas, creativity, childhood, Albert Einstein) as well as negative ones (fanciful, unreal, head in the clouds, idolatry). Write these words on the board; talk about them. Clearly, the word "imagination" triggers a wide range of responses! Why is that? Invite the students to comment. Reassure them that you are not out to make them into something they are not, nor will you force them to *do* anything they cannot; an "imaginative preacher" is not required to be artsy, heretical, or currently at work on a brilliant finger-paint translation of the parables. Instead, ask them to consider another starting point for thinking about imagination: faith. *An imaginative preacher is a person who lives by faith . . . and in faith.*

FAITH: A PECULIARLY *CHRISTIAN* FORM OF IMAGINATION

"Faith," writes the author of Hebrews, "is the assurance of things hoped for, the conviction of things not seen" (Heb. 11:1). What a marvelous paradox!

To believe in something that is invisible

To be sure of a promise that has yet to be fulfilled

To keep hoping, beyond reason and well past the expiration date

This is faith, the author of Hebrews tells us, and God's people have *always* lived this way. They have lived *as if* the promises of God are true. They have traveled *as if* they knew where they were going. They have waved at the promises *as if* they were right next door. None of this is reasonable behavior, nor is it even remotely practical—but it *is* faithful, for one who trusts and hopes in the faithfulness of God. It just happens also to be an excellent illustration of the word "imagination," which the *Oxford English Dictionary* defines as "the action of . . . forming a mental concept of what is not actually present to the senses . . . [and] not yet in existence," as well as "[an] impression as to what is likely; expectation, anticipation."[1] Lay ·the Hebrews verse next to the dictionary definition, and you might come up with something like this: *Faith is the imagination of things hoped for. Faith is a peculiarly Christian form of imagination.*

Historically, religion has long been linked with imagination, and the association has often been a happy one. But with the rise of the Enlightenment, with its emphasis on empirical data and foundational theories, the association soured. Western Enlightenment thought was deeply suspicious of imagination, which it viewed as a dangerously subjective, metaphorical, and speculative enterprise; religious truth, since it was an act of the imagination, was deemed equally subjective, and therefore an *un*-scientific, inferior form of knowledge. Science was grounded in *fact;* religion was grounded in *fiction.* Science offered indisputable proof; religion offered none. Obviously this resulted in deeply contentious dualisms that persist to this day. Furthermore, since a dualism implies that two things (in this case, science and religion) are irreconcilably opposed, it insists that we choose between them. It forces us to take sides:

Is he a man of science, or a man of faith?

Should our school system teach evolution or creationism?

Will I trust my body to the power of medicine or the power of prayer?

For a person living within a positivist framework, these are perfectly normal questions to ask. It is simply assumed: You can't have it both ways. You have to choose one and reject the other.

In the postmodern world, however, scholars are more and more critical of Enlightenment ideals and the dualisms and universalisms we once took for granted. Garrett Green, in his book *Imagining God,* suggests that perhaps there is a way to redeem the tarnished role of imagination in Christian theology without resorting either to Enlightenment absolutes or fanciful woolgathering. "Imagination," Green writes, "turns out to be not the opposite of reality but rather the means by which manifold forms of both reality and illusion are mediated to us."[2] We might put it this way: Imagination is not the truth itself (revelation, gospel, Word), but the *point of contact* between God and human beings, the place where we meet God. Furthermore, since every human experience requires some sort of process for meaning making, imagination takes the form of *interpretation:* it is how we see, receive, and make meaning of our experiences of God in this world.

Imagination works like metaphor: it brings near something that is far away. It makes recognizable something that is new and strange to us. If we say, "God is our light and our salvation," "the Lord is my shepherd," or "God is a rock and a shield," those images and associations for God give us access to realities that might have remained beyond our reach. Jesus knew this quality of imagination well: it is what allowed him to take something as simple as a handful of seeds and see *more* than seeds: a truth, perhaps, about God's Word, alive and scattered and growing in the world. Imagination—as Jesus knew, as Moses knew, as the people of God have always known—can lift us up and out of the everydayness of our world into the coming realm of God . . . if, of course, we have learned to see and interpret in this way. And that is a big "if."

So what is it, exactly, that makes us hear the voice of God in a bush that burns? What is it that persuades us to buy a field just as the city is evacuating? What is it that shows us the hope of liberation in our own chains? Can *any* form of imagination prompt us to believe the promises of God, even when our everyday experience shows us otherwise? Not by a long stretch! Garrett Green is careful to remind us that imagination is, by definition, ambiguous. It can be a vehicle for truth as well as for lies, for God as well as for Eden's serpent. But the *faithful imagination*—that is, one that has been shaped by Christian hope and God's vision given to us in the Bible—guides us toward God's truth, so that we see as well as interpret with the eyes of faith. The faithful imagination, for example, encounters a wilderness . . . and, remembering the stories of Abraham and Sarah and Moses and Jeremiah and John the Baptist and Jesus, starts looking for the pillar of fire to guide it by night...and enough manna for one day . . . and a voice crying, "Prepare the way of the Lord!" *Other* voices (the serpent, the Adversary, the Tempter, the Censor) will urge us to give up, break down, cave in, sell out—but they are the imaginations that try to kill hope, insisting that wilderness and captivity always signal death. The faithful imagination, therefore, has a monumental task: to keep on believing in the promises of God. To look at a handful of seeds, and see more than seeds.

INTERPRETATION: A PECULIARLY *HUMAN* ACT

There is one more important assumption we need to highlight. *For human beings, imagination is not a question or a luxury. It is a given; it is part of our hardwiring. And it is how we interpret life.* This may be a bit of a shock, for those of us who have prided ourselves on being the sort of straightforward, down-to-earth, logical interpreters who don't *need* to "use our imaginations" to get at the plain sense of God's Word. Yet the shock does not need to be faith- or life-threatening. Remember: we are not condoning an "anything goes" approach to interpreting life and Scripture. We are simply relocating imagination from a nonessential part of human being to an essential part, and redefining it as the interpretive, meaning-making function. We have experiences in life, and those experiences will have to be interpreted by some sort of imaginative process. This means that we don't have a choice about using our imaginations—but we *do* have a choice about *what kind* of imagination to use. For example, once we reach a certain level of maturity, awareness, and agency, we can decide whose voice (God? the Tempter?) we are hearing out there in the desert. If we have been steeped in the biblical narratives, so that a faithful imagination has been nurtured within us, we will have had some practice "learn[ing] to hear the melody of revelation in the polyphony of scripture," and so are more apt to recognize the tune.[3] A faithful imagination is better equipped and therefore more likely to distinguish the voice of the Tempter from the voice of God (*stones into bread, stones into bread . . . Where have I heard that before?!*).

One of the most encouraging things about the faithful imagination is that it has a definite shape, a discernable rhythm. It can be learned. It can be taught. It can be recognized. This is not to say that it takes the form of only *one* shape or *one* rhythm; it is not nearly so uniform or limited as that. It would be more accurate to say that the faithful imagination *provides* a shape and a rhythm—maybe even a genre, or a key—from which the Christian community takes off in joyful improvisation. But note well: we may take off, but we cannot float away, up into the stratosphere of way-out interpretation. There are boundaries to this imaginative process. They are generous and fluid boundaries, to be sure, but they delineate clear spaces, they point toward borders, beyond which are other sorts of imagination, other ways to see and interpret the world. Every Christian community's faithful imagination has its own built-in tethers to keep it in shape, in rhythm, and in character as distinctively *Christian*.

Who, then, decides where those boundaries are? Who decides what a particular community's faithful imagination looks like? In one sense, the task of Christian theology is to critically articulate those shapes and rhythms within a particular context of human life and faith; in another sense, the task of a particular Christian community is to decide how those shapes and rhythms will take form within its context. Yet there are built-in tensions to these decisions. Theologians and communities are fallible. Sometimes they make interpretive mistakes. What looks like a faithful imagination in one time and context (as expertly reasoned, broadly informed, contextually relevant, and passionately framed as the theologian or community can make it) may look quite different with the passage of time, or after other theologians and other communities have offered their perspectives. For this reason, it is essential to remember that every attempt to define the faithful imagination is always *provisional*. We can never decide, once and for all, where the lines of "faithful" are and will be. We can only interpret the best we can, hoping and leaving room for the Spirit to make itself heard in the voice of the community as well as in the questions—and new musical rhythms—of outsiders.

PREACHING: A PECULIARLY *CHRISTIAN* APPEAL TO THE FAITHFUL IMAGINATION

We come, now, to preaching. If the task of theology is to *articulate* the music of revelation, the task of proclamation is to *sing* it. Preachers are therefore theologians, but at a precise moment of the task. A sermon (I would argue) is not the place for preachers to *explain* or *teach* an interpretation of the biblical text through the lens of the faithful imagination; that work needs to happen earlier in the week, when preachers are preparing the sermon, and deeply immersed in the articulating mode of the theologian's task. This interpretive, descriptive work—we might call it "local theology"—is essential, to be sure.[4] It will orient and ground the sermon within the boundaries of the faithful imagination, so that it doesn't float off into the ether. It will give the sermon its shape and its own distinctive metaphors and language. But the preaching moment is something else, and so calls for something different, a different moment of the theological task.

Again, Garrett Green is helpful here. The task of proclamation, he says, is to *appeal* to the faithful imagination of the congregation. Yet the principal player in this event is not the preacher, as we might expect, but God. Green shifts the focus from what the preacher does to what God does. "To save sinners," he writes, "God seizes them by the imagination: the preacher places [himself or herself] at the service of this saving act by the obedient and lucid engagement of [his or her] own imagination."[5] In preaching, then, the imagination is a point of contact between God and God's people, but also something far more: it is where God meets us *and saves us*. There is a purpose to the interpretive act, a promised land on the other side of the wilderness. Interpretation is more than wandering, and preaching is more than wondering. Through the grace of God, it is ultimately a saving act. The preacher becomes a part of this process when she allows her *own* imagination to serve as another point of contact, a place where God can confront and transform the listener.

This is a theological emphasis that many preachers profess to believe, although few manage to trust. The preaching life can be so demanding that sometimes we forget who is really in control. We begin to think that *our* words, *our* creativity, *our* imaginative (even excellent) work is the thing: each sermon becomes fraught with anxiety, because *everything* depends on *us*! Yet preachers and sermons do not save congregations. Only God can do that. Preachers, of all people, need to remember where the emphasis is: *preaching is not all about us*. Certainly that does not excuse us from taking appropriate ethical responsibility for what we say or do in the pulpit, but perhaps it does prevent us from falling into traps of overwork or self-congratulatory pride. If something amazing happens in a sermon, . . . praise God, not the preacher!

So what exactly does a "faithfully imaginative" sermon *look* like? This is hard to say; it may be easier to start with what it *doesn't* look like. A sermon that has arisen out of the preacher's faithful imagination doesn't look like a dressed-up version of a regular old, workaday sermon. It isn't a sermon in party clothes. It probably looks like an invitation to go and *live* somewhere. It probably looks like a person (the preacher) who has agreed, for a few transparent moments, to show us what it might look like to actually *accept* that invitation. Most of all, I think it looks like a moment when we *know*, for *sure*, that we are in the presence of grace and truth—and the world we thought we knew seems different, somehow. It has movement. It has possibility. It has a place where we fit, each one of us. In those moments, the preacher disappears. The focus is on another realm, another place; we leave that sort of sermon saying, "I saw something completely new today!" instead of, "What a star that preacher is!" The reason, of course, is that the preacher has stopped obsessing about the actual artifact of the sermon, and has turned his attention to keeping his imagination as supple and limber as a dancer's body. He has figured out that before he can *see* anything in the text to dance, he has to *practice* seeing, which is going to translate into a lot of barre exercises while he learns to *pay attention to the world and the text with new and faithful eyes.*

Obviously, we are following Green's shift in focus, from the preacher as star of the show (the one who saves as well as the one who shines) to the preacher as "point of contact" for the divine-human encounter—which I am suggesting entails an emphasis on staying in shape (imaginatively speaking) over time, rather than scrambling for a message on Saturday night. Green's work encourages us to aim for transparency on the part of the preacher (What do we see through and beyond this person?) rather than brilliance. Preachers who are imaginatively in shape will find it easier to make their way into the text, and easier to get out of the way during the sermon—primarily, I think, because preaching becomes a *spiritual* exercise, a way of praying.

If we cannot be as precise as we might like about what imagination *looks* like in a sermon, at least we can be precise about its *location* within the act of preaching. I suggest that there are at least two moments when the imagination figures prominently in the act of preaching.

1. The preacher's engagement, as a local theologian of a particular congregation, with the biblical text and the listening context, **as she or he prepares the sermon**

2. The congregation's engagement with the biblical text, **as the preacher preaches the sermon.**

Both moments rely on God to provide the spark that lights the faithful imagination, allowing first the preacher and then the congregation to see and interpret Word and world differently. But they are two separate moments, and the first precedes the second. As teachers of preaching, our job is primarily concerned with the *first* moment: **to help our students develop and strengthen faithful imaginations, *so that* they will be better equipped to prepare sermons that will, through God's grace and the Spirit's help, facilitate the congregation's engagement with the biblical text.**

This is a simple pedagogical goal, but a deceptive one. There are many preachers and teachers of preaching who assume imagination has to do with learning fancy new methods or techniques, or adding some special ingredient: master the latest contortions, sprinkle on a few poetic illustrations, stir, and *presto!*—a sermon with imagination! In my view, nothing could be farther from the truth, or worse for preaching. Imagination is not an ingredient you add. It is a muscle you develop, and it doesn't happen overnight. You cannot simply wake up one day and decide, "Today, I will be imaginative!" You have to work at it, to exercise it, to get in the habit of using it, living by it, seeing through it, every day. This takes no particular skill or creativity on the preacher's part, but it *does* take sweat and discipline and a commitment to routine. It also takes time. It takes the pain of going to the edge and beyond, to see what is at the margins of self and community. It takes an insistence on limits, both setting them and (when faithfully interpreted) breaking them. You have to be open. You have to pay attention. You have to stay engaged. And, as the cloud of scriptural witnesses constantly shows us, you have to live subjunctively: *as if* holding onto God's vision were possible, even when the opposite seems true. All these things, working slowly and together, will shape a preacher's imagination along the contours of the biblical witness—*although exactly what the resulting sermon may look and sound like will be as varied and diverse as the preachers themselves.* There is no such thing as an "imaginative" sermon. There are only preachers and listeners who choose to engage their imaginations.

Our students will probably feel deflated by this news, especially if they were hoping that a preaching class would induct them into all the trade secrets. It's a lot less glamorous (and even, frankly, a little *disappointing*) to hear that a preaching imagination has to do with ordinary fitness rather than extraordinary knowledge. It's a lot less exciting to work out every day than to run the race. Yet if we teachers set our preaching students down the path to fitness and well-being, as far as the faithful imagination is concerned, they will never want for more or better nourishment. The manna will fall, because God has promised that it will fall; it will be easy to gather, and it will be easy to gather (hoard) too much of it. Our job is to teach our students how to recognize manna—and then to recognize *enough* manna.

GETTING READY TO TEACH:
PRELIMINARY ASSESSMENTS AND GUIDELINES

The first pedagogical task is to assess the "state of the nation," as it were, concerning the students and their own "faithful imaginations." How do their denominational authorities and seminaries define the faithful imagination? How does their seminary curriculum cultivate and nurture it? How do you see that faithful imagination at work in them, when they are *not* in the pulpit? (How, for example, are they taught to interpret biblical texts? congregations? culture? society?

believers? the "Other"? the larger world?) You will likely have to teach them to interpret biblical texts and cultural contexts *for preaching*. But what do they already know and believe about the act of interpretation in many different venues? Do you sense an imaginative freedom in them, when it comes to the act of interpretation? Or are they tentative and reserved, believing, perhaps, that interpretation is a privilege reserved for people of a certain age, education, gender, class, race, creed, culture, or religion (and that *they* do not share or deserve that privilege)? Another way to get at this is to ask the students who ought to have *access* to the pulpit: what gives a preacher the authority to preach, imaginatively or otherwise?

The reason this is such critical preliminary work is that we cannot teach students to *use* their faithful imaginations if they do not believe they are *allowed* to use them. Most pastors who come to workshops seeking solutions for "preacher's block" and so-called unimaginative sermons don't need a creative jump start. They need a hacksaw, to cut through their own chains. They need a paradigm shift from the myth of scarcity (*not enough time, not enough skill, not enough answers, not enough imagination*) to the promise of God's abundance: that there is bread enough, and daily bread, for everyone. They probably also need permission to begin *receiving* the biblical text, instead of trying to *solve* it (through special knowledge, or contortions) every week. A preacher who has been liberated into the daily practice of the faithful imagination isn't worried about finding out what the biblical passage *means*. He knows that if he asks, "What is this biblical passage *saying* to me?" he will *discover* meaning. The difference is one of emphasis, but it is also one of order: knowing which practices come first, and which lead to insight. A preaching imagination is not born. It is lived.

That said (and I realize I have said little in the way of the concrete and practically helpful!), let me suggest five guidelines for the preaching student's imaginative life, as it pertains to reading and interpreting the biblical text:

1. **Know the difference between what is *right* and what is *possible*.** The person who best expressed this for me is my friend and colleague, the Rev. Dr. Margaret Aymer Oget. Professor Aymer Oget teaches New Testament at the Interdenominational Theological Seminary; she routinely has students representing a host of denominations in her classes. And, in this richly pluralistic context (which is another way of saying that her students do not always agree with one another, at all—even remotely), her job is to teach interpretation of the New

Testament. Other teachers might dread such an environment, but Dr. Aymer Oget finds it a marvelous opportunity, both for her and for her students. "We will be looking at many different ways to interpret these texts," she tells them, right up front; "but I am not going to answer questions about which interpretation is *right*. If you want to know which interpretation is *right*, ask your denominational authorities. In this class, I am going to show you what is *possible* in the text." I echo Dr. Aymer Oget. Know the difference between what is right and what is possible in a text—and suspend judgment for as long as you can. Sometimes, the most amazing insights come from entertaining possibilities rather than rushing to conclusions.

2. **Go for the subjunctive.** The subjunctive is the "as if" mood: what if we behaved *as if* this were possible? What if we lived *as if* our captivity were not permanent and *as if* we really believed we would return home to Jerusalem one day? I tell my students that it is not their job to be *right* about a text, it is their job to be *true* to it—but that this is actually *much harder!* To stand in the middle of a text and *live* in it for a while—not as an intellectual exercise in allegory (to find out what *a*, *b*, and *c* in the text stand for) but as a living exercise in the subjunctive (How is it to live *as if* this text were true, both for me and for my community?)—is demanding and even dangerous. It keeps us from holding the Scripture at a distance (allegory), insisting that we bring it near (metaphor) and then up close (subjunctive). It forces us to ask questions and entertain possibilities (see above) that we might never have dared to explore. And in so doing, we may find that our boundaries—for what is real, what is true, what is possible, what is permissible—get blurred or even enlarged. We may happen upon *new* lands of meaning.

3. **Don't isolate yourself.** This is an important addendum to the "subjunctive" exercise. Students are often accustomed to writing papers and assignments in isolation, and many of them think sermon preparation, too, is something that happens alone in the study: the preacher puts a "Do Not Disturb" sign on the door and retreats into isolation until the sermon is done. But in an increasingly pluralistic and complex world, this splendid isolation no longer seems appropriate or even responsible. No matter how skilled the preacher may be with the subjunctive (imagining various *as if* scenarios for various persons), it is no substitute for communication with a real, live human being—and an opportunity to encounter and learn from the *Other* among us. In our classes, we attempt to kick the isolation habit right away by getting intentional about our interpretive practices, and incorporating those

practices into our already existing lives and schedules. For example, just as a pastor might bring the sermon text along to the hospital, the youth group meeting, the local night shelter, the child-care center, the session meeting, and the women's Bible study—each stop along the way becoming an occasion for fresh and deeper reflection and discussion—so our students are asked to bring their sermon texts along with them to the dining hall, the Laundromat, the soccer game, or wherever their week happens to bring them. We ask them to pull those texts out, invite others to read with them, solicit opinions, invite reactions. The purpose is to create yet another atmosphere of possibility where the subjunctive might come into play. But, in a deeper sense, the students become aware of their own limitations, their own need for others to engage with them in the process. Invariably, they are astounded to find that even the Mom standing next to them at the soccer game has a perspective on the text that they had never anticipated . . . and that leads them, on further reflection, to some remarkable insights. And these are insights they would never have found in isolation.

4. **Be patient. This is slow work.** "Be patient toward everything that is unsolved in your heart," wrote the poet Rilke, "and one day you may live into the answer." The words are almost cliché, but they are true nonetheless. It is the nature of a practice to take time. If the practice is to become a habit, it will require of us even more time, not to mention countless repetitions. This is when we, as preachers who would exercise and develop our faithful imaginations, are most vulnerable: the everydayness of routine can easily slide into monotony, boredom, or (most crippling) the sense that we are absolutely on the wrong track. It is hard to have perspective, let alone patience. We need friends and companions and teachers who will remind us—when the pace is maddeningly slow—that we *are* on the right track, and that we have even come a distance.

5. **Don't call www.desperatepreachers.com. Call a therapist.** There are two reasons for this. The first is that desperate preachers (on a Saturday night) can get into the very bad habit of piecing together sermons from the Internet—which, in the heat of the moment and at the end of an insanely busy week, can look like an excellent just-this-once, save-your-neck option. The trouble, however, is that the Internet can be heroin: powerful, fast, and amazingly addictive. Abused over the long term, it prevents preachers from flexing and toning their own imaginative muscles, until very soon they are out of shape and out of touch with sermon preparation. They have forgotten how to read a text and really

see anything. My advice to students is to set a clear boundary about never using Internet sermons—and not cross it.

The second reason for this guideline is that preachers are so busy that there are *always* good excuses to skimp on sermon preparation in favor of some other ministerial deed. A preacher who has not been putting in the imaginative muscle workout time, and who is feeling a little flabby around the interpretive edges, quickly discovers that sermon preparation is actually taking *longer* than it used to; out-of-shape muscles hurt more and stretch less. The temptation, at this point, will be to assume that the preacher's busy schedule is to blame—which then excuses another Internet visit and perpetuates the cycle. Yet it isn't the schedule. It's the preacher's priorities. My counsel to students and colleagues (and myself!) is that if you find yourself drowning in your own sermon preparation, and wallowing in practices that do not and cannot nourish you, it is time to ask for help. Don't assume that you are out of luck, out of talent, or out of your league. Call a therapist to help you get at the root of the problem.

And now, on to the actual practices themselves.

Cultivating a Faithful Imagination for Preaching: Practices and Exercises

When I was young, I had an artist friend who lived across the street. I spent many hours in her studio, watching her melt plastic, paint canvases, assemble fake fruit in wooden boxes, or whatever else she happened to be working on at the time; her media were as diverse as her creative stages. She was always welcoming, as long as I could sit on a stool quietly and work on my own version of *l'art du jour* without disturbing her train of thought. Once, though, after watching her mash a plastic doll's head into a rusty tin can, I forgot myself and burst out, "Alex, *I* could have done that!" To which she replied with a smile, "Yes. But you didn't."

That was my most important lesson about art.

There was a time when I would have rolled my eyes at the following exercises, none of which is particularly unique or original or earthshaking. I would have told you that I could predict exactly what would result if I tried any one of them (which would have been my grown-up version of "Alex, *I* could have done that!"). But that was before I

actually did them. So now, I smile at my world-weary and sophisti-
cated students (as they prepare to tell me how *childish* it is of me to
expect them to *color* with *crayons!*—etc., etc.), and tell them to come
back and talk after they have done the exercises. The only difference
between *thinking* about them and *doing* them . . . is doing them, and
seeing a whole new world.

I have used each of these exercises with my own students. Some of
them we developed together, and some of them we have adapted from
other sources. Depending on the class, I will let the students choose
between a number of options or assign particular exercises for particular days (the "Dislocate it" exercise is an excellent one to begin a discussion on interpretation, since it gets at issues of context and subjectivity).
Often we will try nearly all the exercises over the span of a course, and
students will find themselves resonating with particular ones. I also use
the exercises as diagnostic tools for students who need to work on specific things (for example, if you sense that a student is spending too
much time reading the text in isolation, assign him or her the "Soccer
mom it," "*Other* it," or "Push it" exercise, all of which require the student to actually leave a desk and talk with other persons).

One final suggestion: I heartily recommend that you do the exercises along with your students. Your discussions will be much richer if
you do.[6] And you will have the joy of being surprised, together, by
gospel imagination.

1. **Write it.** By hand. In a journal—preferably one that is bigger than
the standard 8½ by 11 inch page, and definitely one that is unlined. We
all need help getting out of the box and off the computer screen. As you
write out the text, notice how you are forced to slow down and really
see it, *notice* it, *hear* it. If something grabs your attention, make a note
to follow up on it.

2. **Pocket it.** Now write out a copy of the Scripture on a small piece
of paper, small enough to fold and fit in your pocket. Get in the habit
of carrying it around with you. You are going to be using it a lot. For
example . . .

3. **Memorize it.** My students always balk at first when I tell them
we are going to memorize our Scripture texts—but that's before they
try it, and become converts to the practice. The first rule is never to sit
down at a desk and tell yourself, "Now, I will memorize." This is work
that happens best when you are doing other things, mundane things,
preferably with your hands. So take that Scripture text out of your

pocket as you go about your weekly chores. Take it out when you're folding laundry, doing dishes, taking a walk, rocking a baby. Say the text aloud, over and over, until you've memorized it. Now live with it. (Note: Remember, you don't have to read the text as a memorized piece in worship. You aren't doing this for anyone but you, the preacher; you don't even have to advertise that you are doing it! The point is just to make sure that you turn your Scripture into the toddler that follows you around everywhere you go and never leaves you alone for even a single moment.)

4. **Underline it.** Read the text you've written out in your journal. Without stopping to edit yourself, underline/circle/mark words and phrases that stand out to you. Now look at the words or phrases you've underlined, and write them out separately. Spend some time pondering and praying about those words. What do they suggest to you? What questions are you asking? Translate the underlined words into Greek or Hebrew. Keep asking: Where are these words leading you?

5. **Image it.** Do the above exercise until you have a list of underlined words. Close your eyes, and say aloud the first word on your list. Because the mind "translates" abstract ideas into pictures or images, you will probably "see" a string of images (for example, *FIRE: truck, poppies, marshmallows roasting, lights, wineglass*). After a moment, open your eyes, and write down everything you "saw." Don't edit; just write rapidly, no matter how bizarre the image; your mind is telling you something, making a connection that isn't readily apparent to you. When you have gone through all the words or phrases on your list, reflect on the images you wrote down. What connections do you see?

6. **"Soccer mom" it.** I call this practice "soccer momming the text" because I *am* a soccer mom; it's how I spend a lot of time. So I have learned to read texts where I already am. If you aren't a soccer mom yourself, think about where you do spend your time (the dining hall, the coffee shop, the office, the car pool), and begin pulling your text out of your pocket as you frequent those places. Invite friends (strangers, if you're brave) to sit down and read the text with you. If they feel unqualified (you know, because you're the expert; you're a seminarian), tell them you aren't trying to *solve* the text, you're just trying to *hear* it through many other ears. You'll be amazed at what they *do* hear.

7. **Dislocate it.** Take your text someplace that you wouldn't ordinarily go, someplace where you feel "dislocated"—either because of yourself (being among others who are different from you) or because of what you are doing (reading Scripture in a place where such a thing isn't ordi-

narily done). It's best if the dislocation makes you feel odd, marginalized, or even nervous. Dislocate your self/body, and read the text from your journal (aloud, if you dare!). Now pay attention. How does the text look and sound different in this location? What do you notice that you might have missed before?

8. **Block it.** "Blocking" is a theater phrase used to describe the physical movement and placement of actors in a scene: where they stand, when they are to cross downstage, when they are to drink from a glass, whether they say a line kneeling or lying down, and so on. Block your Scripture scene, first in your mind, then on paper in your journal, then (best of all) with some agreeable volunteers. Look at the physical movements of the characters; notice where they are in relation to one another. Are they facing each other? Is there eye contact? What does their physical placement communicate about their status, their feelings, and the like?

9. **Subtext it.** Subtext is nonverbal communication, and we all do it, all the time. Subtext is what we are *thinking* when we actually speak words aloud. (Example: to the question, "How are you, honey?" try saying the word, "Fine," while *thinking*, "I am having a miserable day," "I just aced that test!" and "Sometimes you make me so mad I could just spit.") One of the simplest and most evocative interpretive practices for a Scripture text is to play around with subtexts. Don't let yourself dwell on what the characters or narrators were *really* thinking when they said or wrote those words (Who knows, anyway?!). Ask yourself the Dr. Aymer Oget question: What is possible? Then try some subtexts that actually sound *im*possible. You might be surprised at what you see.

10. **Push it.** Try the ancient rabbinical practice of *havruta,* which gives you a way to explore the limits of interpretation. You need a partner for this. Sit down facing each other, each with a copy of the text in front of you. Take turns reading the text aloud, while your partner listens. Then take turns reacting to the text: what do you each see and hear in it? Now get extreme: push your ideas and images as far as they will go, even to the point of the absurd or heretical, just to see what happens. If the listening partner feels the speaking partner has gone too far, the listener should communicate it calmly and nonjudgmentally. The point of this exercise is to find the limits of the text by crossing them, secure in the knowledge that your partner won't leave you stranded. Spend fifteen minutes engaging in *havruta,* then stop and reflect. Did the exercise give you freedom to push the boundaries of the text? Where are the limits of interpretation for you, now?

11. **"Other" it.** If you're a woman, read your text with a man. If you're a man, read it with a woman. Ask the other person to reflect particularly from the perspective of the person's gender (which you don't share). What do you each see differently? Talk about it. Now "other" the text for different races, ages, sexual orientations, nationalities, income levels, religions, or anything you can think of.

12. **Counter it.** Every text is a response to some other text, somewhere, in Scripture; they work together, talk to each other, agree with each other, challenge each other. What text is *your* text responding to? Which text do you imagine it might be countering? Another way to go at this is to ask yourself what question your text is trying to answer.

13. **Dream it.** Keep that journal near your bed. Read the text before you go to sleep; pray in its words and images. In the morning, as soon as you wake up, write down what you can remember of your dreams, without editing. Don't worry if you forget parts; that's fine (this isn't psychotherapy). You will begin to notice two things: (1) how easily our unconscious minds free-associate, jumping around between scenes and characters and not bothering with the gaps; and (2) that dreams are powered by emotions, not logical narratives. The conscious mind constructs a narrative to *evoke* an emotion; the unconscious mind constructs a narrative *around* an emotion. Reflect on your dreams; ponder them; pray about them. They probably won't hand you your finished sermon on a platter, but they may (and often do) contribute, in surprising ways. Think of this as an experiment; be grateful for what comes.

14. **Create it.** Take your journal to a quiet place outside. Bring paints, pastels, charcoal, crayons, pencils, fountain pens, Magic Markers, or whatever else makes you feel like an artist. (You might bring one medium you know, and one you've never tried before.) Read your text aloud several times. Draw whatever comes to mind, giving yourself time limits of two, five, ten, or fifteen minutes (to keep you from staring at the paper all afternoon). You can do one drawing or several. This works especially well with a group, since others often see things in our own art that we are blind to ourselves.

15. **Study it.** Yes, it *is* important to remember the world of scholarship! But now that you've had time to really *live* with the text, how do you hear the words of our biblical and theological colleagues? What insights seem especially truthful to you? What subtexts do you hear in *their* words? How might you continue this dialogue with them in the body of the sermon?

HELPFUL READINGS

Buechner, Frederick. *Telling the Truth*. San Francisco: Harper & Row, 1977.
Brueggemann, Walter. *The Prophetic Imagination*. Philadelphia: Fortress Press, 1978.
———. *Finally Comes the Poet*. Minneapolis: Fortress Press, 1989.
Cameron, Julia. *The Artist's Way*. New York: Penguin, 2002.
Dillard, Annie. *The Writing Life*. New York: Harper & Row, 1989.
Green, Garrett. *Imagining God*. San Francisco: Harper & Row, 1989.
King, Martin Luther, Jr. *Strength to Love*. New York: Harper & Row, 1963.
Lamott, Anne. *Bird by Bird*. New York: Anchor, 1994.
LaRue, Cleophus. *The Heart of Black Preaching*. Louisville: Westminster John Knox, 1999.
McClure, John. *The Roundtable Pulpit*. Nashville: Abingdon Press, 1995.
Mitchell, Henry. *Celebration and Experience in Preaching*. Nashville: Abingdon Press, 1990.
———. *The Recovery of Preaching*. New York: Harper & Row, 1977.
Saunders, Stanley, and Charles Campbell Jr. *The Word on the Street*. Eugene, OR: Wipt & Stock, 2006.
Smith, Christine. *Preaching as Weeping, Confession, and Resistance*. Louisville: Westminster John Knox, 1992.
Taylor, Barbara Brown. *The Preaching Life*. Boston: Cowley, 1993.
Tharp, Twyla. *The Creative Habit*. New York: Simon & Schuster, 2005.
Troeger, Thomas. *Imagining a Sermon*. Nashville: Abingdon, 1990.
Wilson, Paul Scott. *Imagination of the Heart*. Nashville: Abingdon, 1988.

NOTES

1. *The Compact Edition of the Oxford English Dictionary*, vol. 5 (Oxford: Clarendon Press, 1933), 53.

2. Garrett Green, *Imagining God: Theology and the Religious Imagination* (New York: Harper & Row, 1989), 83.

3. Ibid., 151.

4. The term "local theologian" is Leonora Tubbs Tisdale's; see her book *Preaching as Local Theology and Folk Art* (Nashville: Augsburg Fortress Press, 1997), as well as her chapter in this book, for an excellent discussion on this particular role of the preacher.

5. Green, *Imagining God*, 149.

6. This list of exercises was first published in my book *Preaching as Testimony* (Louisville, KY: Westminster John Knox Press, 2007). For more ideas, see that book, chap. 7.

9

Creation of Form

LUCY HOGAN

To watch the television program *Law and Order* once is to have watched nearly all of the episodes that have aired throughout its ten-year history. The producers have found a form and arrangement that the audience loves, and a pattern that apparently allows for infinite variations.

The victim, murderer, and modus operandi may change each week, but the regular viewer knows exactly how each program will unfold. The program always begins with two people walking down or working in a street in New York City. They are totally engrossed in an animated conversation, or, for a slight variation, they may be arguing. Suddenly, one person will be distracted and, on discovering the current week's dead body, will tell the other person to "call the police." Then two lead detectives will arrive on the scene, learn from the police officer who the victim is and what has happened, and then the opening scene will fade to the commercial as one of the detectives wisecracks. As the show unfolds, the suspect is arrested, tried, and, unlike *Perry Mason*, may or may not be found guilty. When you find a format that works, you stay with it.

The apostle Paul also knew that he had found a form that worked. Paul had, no doubt, learned the classical letter form when he was in the Roman *litterator*, or primary school. While he had been taught the form in order to conduct his private correspondence, he discovered that he was able to adapt the form: salutation, introduction, narration, argument, and conclusion, to communicate his encouragement, his clarification, as well as directions to his sisters and brothers in Christ from whom he was separated. The form was so reproducible that later members of the Pauline school were able to write letters that are easily confused with the originals.

Deciding the form and arrangement of a sermon is as crucial a part of preaching as deciding the content of the sermon. Unfortunately, many preachers, and most listeners, are unaware of the presence or the importance of form and arrangement. They tend to think of form as neutral, an empty vessel into which one "pours" the content. Consequently, many preachers rely on a "default" preaching form, that is, what they have "always heard." Therefore, an essential dimension of teaching preaching must be to introduce the new preacher to the concepts of form and arrangement, and perhaps to the variety of options available to today's preacher. We have come a long way from "three points and a poem." Given the multiplicity of service types and the diversity of our listeners, the ability not only to utilize a variety of sermon patterns, but to know of the aptness or appropriateness of various forms, will be crucial to the practice of preaching in the future.

As we move into an examination of the various questions pertinent to the teaching of this component of the practice of preaching, it might be helpful to note that, in discussions with teaching veterans, many of them groan when it comes to teaching form. Yes, they say, we know that it is crucial in preaching, but it is one of the most difficult dimensions of teaching. We have gathered here some of their suggestions for teaching this competency.

QUESTION ONE: FORM OR NO FORM?

Classical Roots

Although the students may not need to know the history of form and arrangement, it might help those who are teaching this dimension of preaching if they are familiar with the conversation that has gone before.

In the classical canon of rhetoric, once one had decided what one was going to say, *inventione*, one needed to decide how one would set forth those ideas, *dispositio,* or the orderly arrangement of what had been found. The Greek word for arrangement, *taxis,* usually appeared in works on military strategy to describe the arrangement of one's troops for battle. In other words, after marshaling one's troops, or arguments, one had to decide what would be the most appropriate order in which to "march" them out.

For some speakers there was the understanding that, if you "dealt with your subject, the words will fall into place." There was a sense that the subject would dictate the order; the speaker only had to follow that natural order. Plato, for example, identified the parts of a speech as the definition, collection, and division, but preferred a more biological description—the head, the body, and the legs of a speech. Aristotle essentially agreed with this "natural" approach and devoted very little time to taxis. In the thirteenth chapter of Book 3 of *Rhetorica*, he states quite simply, "There are two parts to a speech; for it is necessary to state the subject [*prothesis*] and to demonstrate it [*pistis*]."[1] But for others, the parts of a speech were complex and carefully prescribed. According to Cicero, in *De inventione*, there are six parts of a speech that must be "arranged in proper order": exordium, narrative, partition, confirmation, refutation, peroration.[2]

You will notice that we have been discussing arrangement, the sequence in which items appear in a speech. But we might also discuss form. Teachers of rhetoric began to notice that different kinds of occasions called for different kinds of speeches. Traditionally, rhetorical scholars identified three types of speeches: judicial or forensic, the speeches of the courtroom; deliberative, political speeches; and finally, *epideictic* or ceremonial speeches. Each type of speech was directed to a very different audience and sought to do very different things, so they needed different forms.

If we think back to Paul's choosing to write a letter, that was the form he felt was most appropriate for what he wanted to do. Decisions of arrangement are about what will appear when. Classical rhetorical theorists helped us to understand that form and arrangement matter. We are not preaching to ourselves—we are preaching to others, and we need to make our sermons clear, understandable, and engaging. How we arrange our sermon makes a difference in how it is received and how successful we will be in achieving our goal.

Another Voice

While it is helpful for students to be aware of the classical roots of arrangement theory, they should also be aware of the tension that has marked the relationship between rhetoric and homiletics. Practical considerations about rhetoric will appear later in this work (section 2, chapter 11), but suffice it to say at this point in our discussion that not all preachers and teachers of preaching believed preaching to be a rhetorical art; consequently questions of form and arrangement were not just ignored, they were to be discouraged.

Many of the early church fathers, who had been teachers of rhetoric before their conversions, rejected rhetoric and the rhetorical forms. They equated rhetoric with human philosophy and human wisdom, and understood that the words spoken by the preacher were to be supplied by God, not human knowledge. It was the Holy Spirit who persuaded, not the preacher. Therefore, one should not be concerned about crafting an introduction or conclusion because, in doing so, one replaced the appropriate theological orientation with a rhetorical one. As George Kennedy notes in his discussion of preaching in the early church, it "was basically 'a projection of the eloquence of Scripture' and not an achievement of the eloquence of the preacher."[3]

With his text *De doctrina christiana*, Augustine forged an uneasy truce between Christian preaching and classical rhetoric. As a bishop, Augustine had the opportunity to hear all his priests preach and, in light of those experiences, the former teacher of rhetoric realized that he could no longer eschew his former profession. Why, he wonders:

> Should they [secular orators] speak briefly, clearly, and plausibly while the defenders of truth [Christian preachers] speak so that they tire their listeners, make themselves difficult to understand and what they have to say dubious?[4]

Ironically, stating that he will not "give the rules of rhetoric," Augustine does discuss some of those "rules," and in doing so creates a way for preachers to apply those rules to their preaching so that they may "teach, delight, and move" their listeners.

Many were persuaded by Augustine's armistice, but periodically, throughout the history of Christian preaching, there appeared those individuals who continued, not only to question, but totally to reject any appeal to rhetoric and its precepts. We do not have to go very far back in our history to find one who "gladly drove a stake into the heart of rhetoric and called upon the newly widowed homiletics not to mourn but to dance on the grave."[5] Karl Barth rejected rhetoric because it replaced God's Word with human word. He argued, for example, that a sermon must not have an introduction. Not only does an introduction, according to Barth, suggest that a "point of contact" between humans and God is possible, but introductions are also a "waste of time" that distract the listeners.

It must be noted, however, that whether he would admit it or not, Barth was making rhetorical judgments. When one decides what will and what will not be included in a sermon, what will have priority and what is to be rejected, one is making decisions about form or arrangement. Nevertheless, his position challenges us to think about who or what drives our decisions about sermon content and form.

Therefore, before one moves into a discussion of sermon forms and their use, the first question to be addressed by a preacher is whether or not he or she believes, for theological reasons, that sermons should have a specific form or arrangement at all. However, it is the understanding of this author that all sermons employ a form and arrangement, whether one intentionally applies one or not, and therefore it is to the preacher's, and listener's, advantage that the preacher apply that form thoughtfully and carefully, lest the form work against, rather than for, the purpose of the preacher and the sermon. What is essential for students to understand is that sermons take listeners on a journey, and the preacher is responsible for moving people through that journey.

QUESTION TWO: WHY ONE FORM AND NOT ANOTHER?

In chapter 1 of this volume, Thomas Long observes that some recent homiletical shifts have placed a greater emphasis on the listener, and that, in doing so, those shifts have brought with them attendant shifts in the construction of sermons, from the logical and propositional to the dynamic and narrative. Recent preaching, therefore, has called for a move from the deductive to the inductive, and in that move has returned arrangement and form to the forefront. Form is not something that preachers can either ignore or reject. The second question then becomes: What are the possible sermon forms that are available, and why does one choose one particular form over another?

However, as we move into the discussion of choosing different forms and sequences of arrangement, it might be important to discuss with students two ideas. First, there is no magic form that will make every sermon a success. Form and arrangement are very important, but they are not the end-all and be-all of preaching. Second, many preachers do not set out to use a particular form. They take more of an Aristotelian approach, getting people into their sermon with some sort of introduction or statement, and off they go. Examination of different sermon forms, therefore, might be better done after the fact—helping students to see what they did, plotting out their sermon and linking it to a particular sermon form. This might also be done by listening to or viewing the sermon of an accomplished preacher and working with the class to discern the form and arrangement strategies chosen by the preacher.

"How One Preaches": A Look at One Solution

As noted earlier, Bishop Augustine, having completed his episcopal visitations, was prompted to return to his work *On Christian Doctrine* to add one final chapter. Boring, dull, confusing sermons convinced him that it was not possible for the church to completely reject the use of rhetoric in preaching. Similarly, when, in the mid-'60s, Fred Craddock joined the faculty of the Graduate School of Phillips University as Professor of New Testament and Preaching, he began to realize that preaching was "an anachronism." Craddock observed, in his work *As One without Authority,* that "on an average corner on an average Sunday, preaching has been tolerated and the ministers have given sermons that were tolerable. Where the expectation is low, the fulfillment is usually lower."[6] Craddock believed that preachers and the church had lost respect for words. But the solution was not accomplished "simply by turning up the volume." In today's cultural context, a world of flexibility and change, where the relationship between preacher and listener has also changed dramatically, symmetrical forms would no longer work.

When Augustine recognized that preaching was in trouble, he turned to style. A significant portion of Book 4 of *De doctrina christiana* examines the description of and directions for use of the grand, subdued, moderate, and plain manners. Craddock, on the other hand, saw preaching's rescue in arrangement. While he first qualifies his proposal, "forms of preaching should be as varied as the forms of rhetoric in the New Testament, or as the purposes of preaching or as the situation of those who listen,"[7] Craddock goes on to advocate that what is needed is the inductive form of preaching: "Perhaps the alternative sought is induction. In an inductive form, thought moves from the particulars of experience that have a familiar ring in the listener's ear to a general truth or conclusion."[8] Craddock believed that traditional forms of preaching had ignored, at best, or dominated, at worst, the listeners and that the time has come to "invite the hearer to participate in the sermon."[9]

What Craddock appreciated, and hoped to communicate to preachers, was not only that form mattered, but that arrangement is crucial to the listener's involvement. If one preached what he identified as the "deductive" form, "There is no democracy . . . no dialogue, no listening by the speaker, no contributing by the hearer."[10] The "general truth" or "conclusion" is presented at the outset and the remainder of the sermon consists of demonstrating or reproducing how the preacher arrived at that conclusion. If one employs this form, according to Craddock, the expectation is that all responsibility for the sermon lies with the preacher, who is the knowledgeable expert. The congregation is expected to be the ignorant, passive recipient of the preacher's superior knowledge. To revive preaching, Craddock argued, one needed to change the form of the sermon. We need to choose the inductive form because that form involves our listeners—it is the way they think, it captures their imaginations and connects with their concrete experiences. It is better to invite the listeners into a story about a man who welcomed home his wayward son than simply to tell them that "God loves us."

Satisfying an Appetite

Different forms demand different things from the listener and produce different results. Think about milk and eggs, combine them in different proportions with different ingredients and in different orders, and one is able to make cakes, cookies, pancakes, or even a soufflé. Crucial to understanding and employing form, then, is developing the awareness, first, that form is not a neutral player in the preaching enterprise and, second, that one cannot separate content from form.

Rhetorician and literary critic Kenneth Burke claimed that form is neither a skeleton nor a container designed merely to hold the content. Form, he argued, is linked to the psychology (*pathos*) of the listener; it is "the creation of an appetite in the mind of the auditor, and the adequate satisfying of that appetite."[11] If one has been prepared by the cook to expect a huge, four-layer cake with plenty of frosting, then discovering that one is going to be getting only a plain square of cake with just a little frosting will be disappointing. If we return to the image with which we opened this chapter, if the viewers tuned in to *Law and Order* and, in the opening segment, the detective kneeling over the body looked up and pointed to a bystander and exclaimed, "Look, there's the murderer!" the viewers would be disappointed. They have settled in to watch the slow development of the case, trying to see if they can guess the murderer before the detectives. Similarly, if a preacher whets the congregation's appetite for narrative, that is, a story sermon, they will be disappointed if the sermon that follows is recitation of "three points and a poem."

Burke argued that the scientific age has driven everyone—not only scientists, but poets, playwrights, and perhaps we could add preachers as well—away from the joy of form and arrangement to an "emphasis on the giving of information."[12] We are so focused on transmitting information and explaining Gospel texts or church doctrines that form, or how we convey the content, becomes secondary, "a luxury, or, as some feel, a downright affectation."[13] Consequently, as Burke observes, form "remains . . . sluggish . . . its true vigor is gone, since it is no longer organically required."[14] And, as Craddock had also observed, this concentration on information (deduction), according to Burke, satisfies the appetite of the preacher, not the listener.

Milk or Solids

People come to the preaching table with different appetites and different needs. As Paul observed when he preached to the Christians in Corinth, "I fed you with milk, not solid food, for you were not ready for solid food. Even now you are still not ready, for you are still of the flesh" (1 Cor. 3:2–3). On some Sundays the preacher will need to carefully nurture those who, because of illness and tragedy, need soft food. There will be others in the congregation, each week, who need the "milk" of the gospel, things laid out clearly and simply, while others will need the solid food of a more complicated, complex sermon. This reality makes preaching a challenge, and it is important for the new preacher to be aware of the arrangement options available. As Edward Corbett observes in his work *Classical Rhetoric for the Modern Student*:

> Disposition [arrangement] then becomes something more than the conventional system for organizing a discourse, something more than just a system of outlining the composition; it becomes a discipline that trains writers in the judicious selection and use of available means to the desired end.[15]

Thinking about form and arrangement demands that the preacher think about who are the listeners, what is the context in which they and the preacher find themselves, how God is acting in this moment, and what should be the "desired end."

While we will later examine the resources that are available specifically for the preaching student, it is helpful, at this point, to turn back to rhetoric that has identified the general organization options that are available, and some of the understandings of when to employ some of these options.

In general, one might discuss the pattern of all pieces as introduction, body, conclusion, or beginning, middle, and ending. While this seems rather simplistic, experience would seem to demonstrate that beginning preachers are not even aware of this fundamental option for identifying the parts of a sermon. It is also important for the new preacher to understand that preachers often work backward. That is, they start at the end and plot backward, thinking about their various building blocks and then making decisions about the clearest, most informative, and engaging arrangement of those building blocks.

Preachers and Arrangement

Over the past fifty years, preaching has turned its attention to form in a variety of ways. It is helpful for the student of preaching to take a moment and listen to the conversation that has taken place since the middle of the last century. A few voices come to the fore. We have already mentioned the contribution that Fred Craddock made in the mid-1960s to that conversation, that of the inductive sermon. But there have been others. While we cannot look at all, it is important to single out two, Grady Davis and Eugene Lowry.

Grady Davis's *Design for Preaching*, in the late 1950s, argued that one cannot separate substance from form, in fact, as his opening paragraph observes, "Life appears in the union of substance and form. These are the elementals. To be without form is the void of matter, and it is the void of thought."[16] If one wishes to avoid the void, he suggests, one must turn to the natural world. A sermon, he writes, "should be like a tree. . . . It should have deep roots . . . show nothing but its own unfolding parts . . . bear flowers and fruit at the same time like the orange . . . [and] must grow in a warm climate."[17] Therefore, preachers must think, not about "constructing or planning" a sermon, rather they want to design a sermon: "Design is seeing and shaping . . . like making a plant to grow in the form inherent in it."[18]

In the early 1980s, Eugene Lowry urged preachers to be attentive to this need to design, but he replaced the botanical image with one that is attentive to time—the novel or the play—regarding the sermon as "a narrative art form, a sacred story." In *The Homiletical Plot*, Lowry introduced the form that lovingly came to be known as "the Lowry loop." The "loop" is a sequence, not a structure, in which the preacher engages the listeners by first "upsetting the equilibrium, [and] analyzing the discrepancy."[19] Drawing on Scripture, the preacher then discloses "the clue to the resolution, [leading them to] experience the gospel, [and] anticipate the consequences."[20] Fortunately, Lowry's students provided him with a shorthand definition: "oops—ugh—aha—whee—yeah."

Genre

Finally, before we turn to how to teach these various forms, it is important to look at one other possible approach. At the same time that preachers have been imitating trees and plays, it is important to attend to one other approach to form. Genre is a way of speaking of the different types of discourses or literary pieces. Echoing Kenneth Burke's definition of form, Thomas Long uses the term "expectation" "to refer to a person's readiness to read or listen in a particular way, according to one set of rules and procedures and not another."[21] Different genres have different rules and procedures, and they set up different expectations. Long identified five different literary forms, or genres, in the Bible: Psalms, Proverbs, Narratives, Parables, and Epistles. He does so because it is his contention that the form of the sermon preached should relate to the form of the text read: "The sermon's task is to extend a portion of the text's impact into a new communicational situation."[22] It is Long's argument that the preacher must "allow the movement of the sermon to follow the movement of the text."[23] Consequently, if the preacher follows the movement of the text, the sermon preached on Psalm 23 should follow a different form than a sermon preached on the parable of the Prodigal Son.

QUESTION THREE: TEACH ONE FORM OR MANY?

While preachers may accept the fact that sermons should follow a form, and may also be aware of the wide variety of options that are available to them, the next question is one that must be answered by the preaching instructor. Should students, while being invited to answer questions 1 and 2, be allowed to employ a number of preaching forms in the sermons they write for their class, or should they be required to learn only one form? While each instructor must answer this question for himself or herself, I will comment from my own experience.

Although I teach at a denominational seminary, my preaching classes are extremely diverse. In a given class I may have six or seven different denominations represented—and that does not include the students who identify themselves as "nondenominational." With so many different theological approaches, cultural and racial backgrounds, it is almost impossible to identify one preaching form that everyone can agree on. Therefore, I do not even try. I do allow them to experiment with different forms.

However, I have found that it is helpful to force them to try to follow a form. Currently there are two excellent resources available: *Patterns of Preaching: A Sermon Sampler,* edited by Ronald J. Allen,[24] and *Creative Styles of Preaching,* by Mark Barger Elliott.[25] Each book not only describes the different patterns, but each also offers a sample sermon. For the first two sermons they write for our introductory course, the students are required to try two different sermon patterns that are different from a pattern with which they are familiar. In the first assignment they are asked to write a sermon on an Old Testament text. In the second sermon they are to choose a New Testament text. Not only must they identify their principal text and the sermon pattern they have chosen, they must also mark up the sermon to identify the way that they are following the directions for that particular sermon. Therefore, if a student is following the homiletical plot, in the margins I will see, "oops," "ugh," and so on.

As Eugene Lowry notes in the opening of his work, "Reading a textbook on how to prepare sermons often is like looking up a word in a dictionary in order to find out how to spell it—you have to have the answer before you can probe the question!"[26] I have found that the best way to introduce students to the concepts that form matters and that different forms do different things is by forcing them to do it rather than read about it. They also realize how important it is to think about what the different parts of a sermon are doing, learning how the structure moves the work along and engages and guides the listeners, and how complicated the employment of form can be.

Another possible exercise, mentioned earlier, is to read and view a sermon by an accomplished preacher. By having the written text in front of them as they view the sermon, the students are able to both see and hear the moves and transitions as they are made by the preacher. Unfortunately, altogether too many students have arrived at seminary without a firm grasp of writing skills. Therefore, in addition to exploring the important theological dimensions of preaching and the content of what they are going to say, preaching classes must also engage in the remedial work of understanding how a work is constructed.

Finally, as was noted earlier, during the practical phase of their studies, when they preach a sermon to the class and that sermon is discussed, it is important to help, not only the preacher, but the class as well, to analyze and understand the structure developed by the preacher. I frequently find that while a preacher will have the right "parts," she or he has put them in a less than desirable order. Taking the time to identify and lift out the various parts or moves of the sermon and then examine what happens when those parts are put back together in a more strategic and engaging order can be most enlightening.

QUESTION FOUR: HOW DO WE REACH
TODAY'S LISTENERS?

As I noted earlier, my preaching classes are far from homogeneous. Looking out over my classroom, I see that I have students from a wide variety of denominations that represent a broad spectrum of theological and liturgical perspectives. But the diversity does not end there. I have women and men, different races and cultural backgrounds, urban students from inner-city Washington and students serving small congregations on the rural eastern shore of Maryland. I have students from Korea, Japan, and a number of African countries. The class might include students from countries in the former Soviet bloc, students who grew up in an atheist country as well as students who, although they grew up in the United States, also experienced an atheistic upbringing, not attending church until they were adults. I have students who have just finished college sitting next to students in their fifties and sixties who have retired from a wide variety of positions in the government. There might be students who already hold a number of advanced degrees and students who returned to finish college only after raising a family, so that they could attend seminary. In the second chapter of Acts we are told that there were dwelling in Jerusalem "devout [men] from every nation under heaven," and while I may not have any Parthians or Medes in my classroom, they are speaking, metaphorically, a multitude of languages. How do we speak to each in her or his language?

The final question concerning arrangement and form, therefore, is, how does one take into account the effects of diversity? The same diversity that I encounter in my preaching class is quite possibly the same variety that today's preachers will encounter on a Sunday morning.

Telling in Their Own Tongues

In his preaching opus, *Homiletic: Moves and Structures*, David Buttrick set out to examine the "moves," the components of a sermon, and the "structures," its form and arrangement. He did so from a phenomenological point of view, that is, by being attentive to "*how sermons happen in consciousness.*"[27] It is, he argued, important to link our sermons to the way people think, learn, and create the world that they know.

We are presented with a question. Do we all think, learn, create the same way? Are we, as the children of God, made or "hardwired" the same way? There have been a number of challenges. Some would suggest, for example, that women and men may not "think" the same way. Recent works have sought to examine those differences, works such as *Women's Ways of Knowing: The Development of Self, Voice, and Mind*, by Belenky, Clinchy, Goldberger, and Tarule,[28] and Carol Gilligan's *In a Different Voice: Psychological Theory and Women's Development.*[29]

Joseph Jeter and Ronald Allen explore the challenges faced by today's preachers in their book *One Gospel, Many Ears: Preaching for Different Listeners in the Congregation*. Although we preach one God, one gospel, "a given congregation has many different listeners who process the sermon with their own particular sets of receptors," and the preacher "has her or his tendencies of speaking and listening, cultural proclivities, and modes of apprehending the world."[30] In the book they explore differences in the generations, learning styles, gender, culture, class, and political differences. Their work will be helpful as a new preacher seeks to examine ways to "build" a sermon that take these many "different ears" into account.

The Wired World

Another significant challenge to today's perception of form and arrangement comes from the wired world in which we live. When Aristotle and Cicero were describing the fitting structure for a particular context, they described a linear layout because that was the world they inhabited. But it is not the world in which we or our listeners live. What are you doing as you read this book? Is there a television, radio, or iPod playing? You may even be reading this on a computer screen rather than a printed page. In that case, you may also be instant-messaging in the midst of your reading, or switching over to the Internet to order some of the books that are recommended. Today, we rarely do one thing or hear one thing at a time.

We now experience messages all at once, or as what Marshall McLuhan called a "mosaic" of numerous messages. According to Jeanne Fahnestock, we "form opinions from a chaos of fragmented impressions and bits of information."[31] Many of the sermons that will be prepared in the future will not just be made up of the spoken word. That spoken word will be accompanied by visual images of other words, pictures, or film clips.

FORM—MORE, NOT LESS, IMPORTANT

The electronic capabilities that are now available to preachers—computers, PowerPoint, sound and film clips—will have great potential for radically altering the sermon event. Listeners will expect more than the simple spoken word, a format that has changed little since the earliest centuries of the church's history. It is imperative that all preachers become familiar and comfortable with these new possibilities.

As we look at the future of preaching and the increasing use of audiovisual components in the preaching event, it would seem that, in order for congregations to experience a challenging and coherent message instead of "a chaos of fragmented impressions and bits of information," arrangement and form will have to take an even more prominent role in the preparation of sermons. Preachers will not be able to focus on content and let form "take care of itself."

NOTES

1. Aristotle, *On Rhetoric: A Theory of Civic Discourse*, trans. George A. Kennedy (New York: Oxford University Press, 1991), 258.

2. Cicero II *De inventione, De optimo genere, oratorum topica*, trans. H. M. Hubbell, Loeb Classical Library (Cambridge, MA: Harvard University Press, 1976), 41.

3. George A. Kennedy, *Classical Rhetoric and Its Christian and Secular Tradition from Ancient to Modern Times* (Chapel Hill: University of North Carolina Press, 1980), 137.

4. Augustine, *On Christian Doctrine*, trans. D. W. Robertson Jr. (Englewood Cliffs, NJ: Prentice-Hall, 1958), 118.

5. Thomas Long, "And How Shall They Hear? The Listener in Contemporary Preaching," in *Listening to the Word: Studies in Honor of Fred B. Craddock,* ed. Gail R. O'Day and Thomas G. Long (Nashville: Abingdon Press, 1993), 177.

6. Fred B. Craddock, *As One without Authority* (Nashville: Abingdon Press, 1986), 5.

7. Ibid., 53.

8. Ibid., 57.

9. Ibid., 55.

10. Ibid.

11. Kenneth Burke, "Psychology and Form," in *Counter-Statement* (Berkeley: University of California Press, 1968), 31.

12. Ibid., 32.

13. Ibid., 33.

14. Ibid.

15. Edward Corbett, *Classical Rhetoric for the Modern Student* (New York: Oxford University Press, 1990), 317.

16. H. Grady Davis, *Design for Preaching* (Philadelphia: Fortress Press, 1958), 1.

17. Ibid., 15–16.

18. Ibid., 21.

19. Eugene L. Lowry, *The Homiletical Plot* (Atlanta: John Knox Press, 1980), 25.

20. Ibid.

21. Thomas Long, *Preaching and the Literary Forms of the Bible* (Philadelphia: Fortress Press, 1989), 16.

22. Ibid., 33.

23. Ibid., 128.

24. Ronald J. Allen, ed., *Patterns of Preaching: A Sermon Sampler* (St. Louis: Chalice Press, 1998).

25. Mark Barger Elliot, *Creative Styles of Preaching* (Louisville, KY: Westminster John Knox Press, 2000).

26. Lowry, *Homiletical Plot,* 8.

27. David Buttrick, *Homiletic: Moves and Structures* (Philadelphia: Fortress Press, 1987), xii.

28. Mary Field Belenky, Blythe McVicker Clinchy, Nancy Rule Goldberger, and Jill Mattuck Tarule, *Women's Ways of Knowing: The Development of Self, Voice, and Mind* (New York: Basic Books, 1986).

29. Carol Gilligan, *In a Different Voice: Psychological Theory and Women's Development* (Cambridge, MA: Harvard University Press, 1993).

30. Joseph R. Jeter Jr. and Ronald Allen, *One Gospel, Many Ears: Preaching for Different Listeners in the Congregation* (St. Louis: Chalice Press, 2002), 9.

31. Jeanne Fahnestock, "Modern Arrangement," in *Encyclopedia of Rhetoric*, ed. Thomas Sloane (Oxford: Oxford University Press, 2001), 47.

10

Cultivating Historical Vision

JOSEPH R. JETER JR.

Again there are chariot races and satanic spectacles in the hippodrome, and our congregation is shrinking. . . . See how some who heard my previous instruction have today rushed away. They gave up the chance to hear this spiritual discourse and have run off to the hippodrome.

—Chrysostom, ca. 390[1]

Change "hippodrome" to "Churchill Downs" or "Yankee Stadium" or the neighborhood soccer field, soften—perhaps—the word "satanic," and you might have the words of a very annoyed twenty-first-century preacher. Many things change in this world. Some things never change.[2] Some forty of Chrysostom's sermons began, as this one did, with *palin,* "again." We too preach on some texts, some doctrines, some social concerns, again and again and again. Am I the first person who has ever preached from 1 Peter 3:13–22? No. Will I be the last? No. Might it be helpful to me to know something about how this text has been interpreted and preached down through the centuries? Yes.

Taking this text as an example, we find that the first two sections contain an exhortation about suffering for righteousness' sake and hold up Christ as our model. There is little argument about that. The trouble arises in verse 19, which asserts that Christ, having been put to death, "went and made a proclamation to the spirits in prison." This assertion, coupled with 1 Peter 4:6, which claims that "the gospel was proclaimed even to the dead," has given rise to all manner of interpretations down through the centuries, each laden with the baggage of its own time and place. Here are a few of them:

—Some believe that Christ's soul went to the nether world and preached to the spirits there to convert them and bring them to salvation. This belief was the strongest interpretation of the text at work in the early church, and has a venerable history.

149

—Others believe that Christ did go during the *triduum mortis* (the three days he was in the grave) to preach to the spirits, but only to those that had already been converted before death.

—Others say that he spoke only to Noah's contemporaries, a special lot of departed folk.

—Others say that it was the preexistent Christ who spoke through Noah to his contemporaries.

—Others say that the spirits to whom Christ preached were fallen angels that he needed to straighten out.

—Others say that while Christ did preach to those angels, he did not do so during his *descensus* (time in the tomb), but during his *ascensus* (on the way to heaven).

—Finally, lots of people have said that the text refers to a preaching event prior to Jesus' earthly death, in which he preached to those who were spiritually dead, not physically dead.[3]

In this text's interpretive history, the difficulty has generally arisen when people have used one or more of these interpretations to make a case for universal salvation. While most everyone has agreed that Christ is our model in the face of persecution, not everyone has agreed that the dead will get a "second chance." When this text falls to me on the Sixth Sunday of Easter in Lectionary Year A, some understanding of how preachers have used and perhaps abused the text can be of real service. I am convinced that the writer's purpose was to demonstrate the persistent evangelical nature of Christ rather than to provide séance material, but I cannot ignore the theological tension that it has provoked down through the years, even to the present.[4]

This is one reason for us to give attention to the history of preaching in our preaching classes. There are many others. But do preachers have time to consider them in their sermon preparation, and do teachers have the time to deal with them in their classes? Time is at a premium in an introductory preaching course. We must not only teach the processes involved in the preparation and delivery of sermons, we must also deal pastorally with the universal fear of presuming to stand and speak a word from God to people. And then we must save time for student preaching, critique, and one-on-one feedback. So why teach the history of preaching in such a packed agenda? Why not leave it to the history department? The short answer to that is that one learns to preach not only by mastering certain skills and techniques, but also by finding or creating his or her place to stand within the preaching tradition. I am not the first person to preach the gospel. Nor will I be the last. It is important to consider where I, my people, and the good news I have been given to proclaim fit within the larger context of the understanding and transmission of the gospel. Without that, we have neither roots nor wings. The following five sections give some additional suggestions about ways historical material can facilitate the teaching and learning of the practice of preaching.

1. WHAT IS PREACHING?

What exactly is it that preachers do when they stand before people and speak?[5] There is no single definition that encompasses all that preaching is and does. "Preaching" is a tensive and not a steno symbol for a many-faceted human activity. Definitions cover the spectrum from the low and colorless words of English dictionaries: *a speech on a religious subject*, to the high and august Latin of the Reformers: *the Word of God* ("Praedicatio verbi dei est verbum dei"). Other modern metaphors range from "the only public event at which sleep is socially acceptable"[6] to the more lofty paean of Ian Maclaren, "speaking a good word for Jesus Christ."[7] Each preacher and listener eventually arrives at her or his own understanding of what preaching is and does. But these understandings frequently clash.

The form or style of preaching to which most twentieth-century North Americans were accustomed derived from the Puritan sermon of the sixteenth century. This sermon (originally up to two hours in length) consisted of three parts (precursor to the much-maligned three-point sermon): exegesis, theology, and application, in which the text for the day was examined, explained, and applied to daily living. Modern sermons, with shrunken exegesis and often missing theology, still paid lip service to the old model. Newer modes of preaching, from the therapeutic to the technological, often find resistance among people raised on the traditional model.

Homiletician Ronald Allen tells of one layman, a bomber pilot in World War II and dedicated church member, who heard a sermon by a guest preacher in which the preacher said a few words about the biblical text, and then offered a series of images (highly impressionistic in character) that were designed to make the hermeneutical connection between the text and the listeners. The preacher never stated the meaning of the sermon in a proposition. Afterward, another member of the congregation was effusive about the poetic qualities of the sermon: "I have never heard such a wonderful sermon." Our layman agreed that the sermon was beautiful. He added, however, "I got the point, but why didn't [the preacher] just say it."[8]

When "Jesus came proclaiming the good news" (Mark 1:14), he had a broad understanding of what constituted preaching. Among other things he used biblical interpretation, prophetic pronouncements, wise sayings, and parables to communicate his message. Jesus thus became both the model and the content of the Christian preaching that followed. From the pure proclamation (*kerygma*) that "Christ is risen" to the pastoral concern for the community of faith (*paraklesis*) to the work of teaching (*didache*) as it became apparent that the eschaton was not yet, preaching adapted to the needs of the church.

As the Christian message spread, the tools of rhetoric and philosophy were appropriated. Aristotelian audience analysis led to different rhetorical systems that emphasized, respectively, the preacher, the sermon, and the congregation. And the Christian preachers, like their model, were not uncomfortable using different preaching forms to fulfill their task. The synagogue sermon, the Greek homily, the apology, the polemic, liturgical preaching, epideictic, and other forms were all used to advantage. The preachers, as the need arose, were called to herald, to spread good news, to proclaim, to bear witness, to speak, to challenge, to tell, to persuade, to teach, to console, to exhort, to argue, to command, to prophesy, to speak in a tongue, to interpret, to discourse, to deliver a tradition, to train, to bless, and so forth. As Clement of Alexandria put it, "We must use a variety of baits owing to the variety of fish."[9]

The first formal definition of preaching was likely that of Alan of Lille (ca. 1128–1202):

> Preaching is an open and public instruction in faith and behavior, whose purpose is the forming of men; it derives from the path of reason and from the fountainhead of the "authorities."[10]

Most narrow understandings of preaching are at odds with this understanding of the practice. Alan, for example, saw preaching more as formative (standard for a medievalist) than transformative (standard for an early American revivalist), helping to shape the theological and ethical understandings of people. It is interesting that Christian formation is even now rising to the top of many preachers' concern.

Consider now a historical and functional twentieth-century definition by historian Ronald Osborn:

Preaching is human activity characterized by specific marks:

1. it is a sustained mode of public address,
2. dealing with a religious or ethical theme,
3. bearing witness to the faith of the community,
4. rooted in a holy tradition (as defined in a sacred literature),
5. occurring within an assumptive world of rationalized belief,
6. communicated through the person of the speaker,
7. employing the forms of verbal art,
8. possessing the character of immediacy,
9. intending to convert the listener,
10. conveying powers of renewal to those who hear.[11]

While the definitions have some differences (Osborn emphasizes the personal nature of preaching, the character of immediacy, and the goal of conversion—more twentieth- than twelfth-century concerns), they have some striking similarities. Although they were written some eight hundred years apart, both of these definitions lift up the theological *and* ethical concerns of preaching, the public nature and the rational foundation of the sermon. Moreover, the choice of the words "authorities" and "sacred literature" opens the door to noncanonical resources for preaching. I find all this quite provocative and good material for class discussion about the nature and source of preaching.

2. WHO SHALL PREACH?

Students encounter a variety of tensions in learning to preach—some skill-based, some personal, perhaps none greater than "Who am I to do this?" Ronald Allen begins his book *Interpreting the Gospel* with some of the anxieties of beginning preachers:

> Many beginning preachers feel inadequate when they contemplate speaking in behalf of Christian tradition. Students can be perceptively aware of what they do not know about the Bible, Christian tradition, theology, and life. Students can be painfully aware of their own moral shortcomings. Some students cannot name the source of their distress, but feel it deeply. *Who am I to preach?*[12]

Students who feel this way may find it helpful to hear *palin* that they are not alone in this fear of inadequacy. A short excursus from homiletical history can be both useful and fun. Begin with Exodus 4:10–12:

But Moses said to the LORD, "O my Lord, I have never been elo-
quent, neither in the past nor even now that you have spoken to your
servant; but I am slow of speech and slow of tongue." Then the LORD
said to him, "Who gives speech to mortals? . . . Is it not I, the LORD?
Now go, and I will be with your mouth and teach you what you are
to speak."

I have a three-phrase sort of mantra that is part of my daily prayer
life as a preacher and the last words I pray before entering the pulpit. All
three phrases are grounded in the history of preaching. My paraphrase
of verse 12 is the first phrase of that mantra: "'I will give you the words,'
says the LORD." I could not dare preach without that assurance; with it
I will preach till the boiler bursts.

Are we not good enough to preach? Isaiah was a man of unclean lips,
but God touched him and forgave him and sent him out to preach (Isa.
6:5–7). Are we too young to preach? Jeremiah was and pleaded with
God, "I do not know how to speak, for I am only a boy." But God said
to him, "You shall speak whatever I command you. Do not be afraid"
(Jer. 1: 6–7). Too old to preach? Tradition suggests that the elder John
was carried into church to preach that memorable sermon, perhaps his
last: "Little children, . . . love one another" (1 John 4:4–21). Unworthy
to preach? Paul himself was a persecutor, with a thorn in his flesh, who
lacked the eloquence so highly prized in the Hellenistic world (1 Cor.
1:17). And yet, in the words of Ronald Osborn, "No other preacher of
Jesus Christ has done more or exercised so large an influence."[13] How
did Martin Luther put his feelings and fear?

> Although I am old [he was then forty-eight] and experienced, I am
> afraid every time I preach.[14]

> There is no message I would rather receive than that which would
> relieve me of preaching. But . . . there is a man, who is called Jesus
> Christ, who says no.[15]

Do we feel ourselves a failure? Phillips Brooks and Frederick W.
Robertson remain perhaps the most respected nineteenth-century
preachers from the United States and England. And yet they both failed
at almost everything they tried before they became preachers and glori-
fied the office. On the other hand, Chrysostom, considered by many to
be the greatest preacher in Christian history, preached his heart out in
Antioch, the "Queen of the Orient," but within a century his beloved

city would be no more, reduced to rubble. A failure, then? Not if one considers all the lives he touched through his ministry and the way his story and his words are still remembered.[16]

Many have been told they cannot preach because of their gender. From historical investigation we learn that in one way or another women have always preached. The feminization of the ministry in the twenty-first century now necessitates our quest for our elder sisters' stories and words, where available, that their granddaughters in ministry might claim their own hard-won tradition of preaching. A tenth-century German nun named Hrosvitha, who wrote homiletical dramas, said early on that her work was "difficult and arduous for one of my feeble sex,"[17] but came later to call herself "the strong voice of Gandersheim" (*Ego, clamor validus Gandeishermensis*).[18] Margery Kempe, a fifteenth-century Englishwoman, was more straightforward in her reply to a man who sought to silence her: "Sir, methinketh that the Gospel giveth me leave to speak of God."[19] Verily. The concern has not been limited to Europe and North America. Consider this assessment by a Cook Island woman named Akaiti Ama:

> Women do not preach from the pulpit—only men do that. I often wonder why this is so, especially since women clean and sweep the pulpit. If only men are allowed to preach from the pulpit, then why can't they sweep and clean it?[20]

Verily. Our students, in their concern about their own fitness or opportunity to preach, need to know that others have been there before them, and in spite of everything found sound footing whereupon to preach. They also need to know that they are the ones future generations will look to for courage and hope.

3. INTERPRETATION

We preachers need to know the stories and the metastory of the faith tradition, the ways in which these stories have been interpreted, the relationship between these interpretations and the world in which they functioned, and how these influence our interpretations in our world. Seeing how preachers have interpreted texts in the past can give us clues as to how they might, or might not, be interpreted in our time. It has been said that texts are "infinitely translatable."[21] But it has also been said that "this does *not* mean that a text can say anything that a reader wants it to say. Texts have rights, too. Texts have constraints."[22]

Knowing our stories and their interpretive history becomes even more important in the face of the spreading biblical illiteracy of our time. I was doing a Bible study recently for a large group, when I called them to Nehemiah 8, where the Law is read and interpreted to people who have not heard their sacred texts for a long time or ever. I was greeted by the blind stares of people who had no clue about where to find Nehemiah. I helped them, and we went on with our work. A pastor told me afterward that many church people, especially younger ones, do not need to know where Nehemiah is located in the Bible because they just call up N-e-h-e-m-i-a-h on their Internet connection and go right to the text. I stammered, "But then they have no clue about the context, the powerful dislocations wrought by exile and return, by losing and regaining their sacred story." "Yes," he said. "Context is a victim of technology." If this is true, then history can be a kind of liberator.

The content of sermons generally moves back and forth between text and situation, passing through theological filters (when they are present) along the way. Today's preachers often worry—at least I do—about whether we have missed the latest article or commentary on the text for Sunday's sermon, because we know that interpretation is in a great state of flux. Uriel Simon puts it this way:

> Each generation produces its own Bible commentaries, in accordance with what it finds perplexing, its exegetical methods, and its emotional and spiritual needs. A generation that shirks its duty of reinterpretation is shutting its ears to the message that the Bible has to offer. The gates of exegesis are not shut and never will be.[23]

And yet, we are not the first to find our texts and our world perplexing. It is quite true that the gates of exegesis are never shut, but energy flows in both directions. And how different, really, are our emotional and spiritual needs from those of our ancestors?

In the early church a text by and large meant what the apostolic church said it meant. In the medieval period, Scripture was often interpreted according to four senses: literal, allegorical, moral, and anagogic. For example, in Galatians 4:24–25, "Jerusalem" could be interpreted to mean the historical city in Judea (literally), the Christian church (allegorically), the human soul (morally), and the heavenly city (anagogically). Here may be found the second of my three-phrase mantra: "If I forget you, O Jerusalem, . . . let my tongue cleave to the roof of my mouth" (Psalm 137:5–6). I keep the old "cleave" with its double meaning and let the various meanings of "Jerusalem" work their way with me. By the time of the Reformation, biblical texts had essentially one meaning—the literal.[24] Paul Scott Wilson reminds us, however, that the three "spiritual" senses are "authentic theological meanings that make specific connections with congregational needs and practical life. Our forebears have much to teach us about theological interpretation."[25] But only if we will listen.

The tradition does one other thing. Over time, it sifts out those aberrant exegetical and theological understandings of the Word. Ideas often considered heretical when they are new may find their way into general acceptance. But the tradition gives us a standard by which to measure them. We can then, for example, say confidently that Exodus 19:16 is not about a nuclear explosion; Psalm 109:8 is not about the impeachment of Bill Clinton; and Revelation 9:9–10 is not about attack helicopters. We can reassure our children who have been terrified by one of those awful "hell nights" some churches have on Halloween that God does not hate them but loves them unconditionally. The third phrase of my pre-pulpit prayer is a simple variation on the ancient Jesus prayer, "Jesus Christ, Son of God, Savior." I join millions in affirming my faith and affirming Maclaren's compelling call from a hundred years ago that we preachers must "speak a good word for Jesus Christ." A good word.

4. SHAPING THE SERMON

We can learn not only from what prior preachers have preached, but also from how they preached. Rhetoric may not make a sermon, but it can certainly unmake one. Sacred rhetoric is sensitive to theology, text, tradition, and temporality. Rhetorical systems tend not to arise and then disappear, but are rather woven through proclamation history, coming to the fore time and again when the time and the need is right. For example, preaching began in poetry.

> The shaman of the archaic world recognized a power in poetic discourse that was particularly appropriate for the invocation and propitiation of powers within and without the known world. The use of rhythm, cursus, repetition, rhetorical formulae, assonance, reduplication, and even rhyme all point to factors of the poetic. . . . The primitive who chanted their religious stories around campfires, the

classical tale-singers who extolled the gods in epics, the Jews who sang psalms before Yahweh, the medieval preachers of *sermons rimatos*, the African-American folk preacher—these and other examples point to poetry as an enduring element of religious discourse.[26]

After Aristotle's penchant for classification, prose became the dominant sermon form in Christendom, but poetry never disappeared. In these confusing times, with attention spans measured in milliseconds, preachers are giving attention once again to poetic language for one reason if for no other: it commends itself to memory in a way that prose never can.[27]

Sermon forms are legion. Students may be at sea in trying to shape their sermons. While there is no surefire way to arrive at just the perfect form for next Sunday's sermon, there are some hints, many of which are grounded in the homiletical tradition. Here are a few:

—Does the form of the text suggest a form for the sermon? If the text is a parable, we hamstring it by preaching it as if it were a proverb. There are times, though, when we have to preach against the supposed style of the text. If our text presents us with a list of people, events, or ideas, our preaching it as a list will almost assure its non-reception. David Buttrick reminds us to use lists for grocery shopping, not for preaching. In his classic sermon on Paul's list of friends and cohorts to be greeted in Romans 16, Fred Craddock says over and over again, "Don't call it a list."

—Is there a theological point to be made or questioned? Suppose our text from Romans 6 contains the phrase "the free gift of God is eternal life in Christ Jesus our Lord." So what is eternal life? We might find it helpful to survey the various understandings of this doctrine. Does it involve resurrection (a Hebrew concept: God raises the dead) or immortality (a Greek concept: something in me does not die)? Is it physical (like John 20:27) or spiritual (like 1 Cor. 15:44)? Is it subjective like the Pharisees' claim (I will be conscious of my celestial surroundings) or objective like the Sadducees'—and Process theologians'—claim (God can use whatever good I have done to further God's work)? Is it universal (like Rev. 5:13) or limited (like Acts 4:12)? Preachers have affirmed all of these. So what is it going to be like? The only certain answer is Ezekiel's in 37:3: "O Lord GOD, you know." But Revelation also assures us that the door to heaven is open (Rev. 4:1), that someone is on the throne (4:2), that one who lived and died and now lives forever is at the right hand of God (5:7). The end, then, is not an event, it is a person. The end is Christ, and everything is going to be all right.

—Does the goal of the sermon suggest the way we will shape our material and choose our language? Do we wish to teach, delight, and/or move? Augustine's corresponding plain, moderate, and grand styles are still with us. Often we can glean the purpose of the sermon by the style in which it is delivered. We may leave church on Sunday better understanding a difficult text, we may leave with a smile about the joy and humor that swept over us, or we may leave determined to change the way we have been living—all because of the shape of the sermon. An American seminary dean once led a group to Israel. One day they made their way to the top of Masada. They walked around quietly for a while and then they gathered around the dean. He pulled out a copy of Josephus's *Jewish War* and began to read Eleazar's speech to those who would soon fall to the Romans. But the dean's tears soon clouded his vision and he could not finish reading. Words can move us.

—Is the language appropriate to the time, place, and audience? Preachers who lock themselves into one style run the risk of not reaching people for whom that style does not work.[28] Luther was determined to use whatever method was necessary to get the message across to his people. Consequently, his "style" has been called one of "heroic disorder."[29] Interestingly, one can take some sermons from Luther, clean them up a bit, and carry them into the pulpit (which preachers have been doing for four hundred years). They are vivid, clear, and earthy, aspects of preaching that people seem to prefer these days. On the other hand, it would be much more difficult to do that with Calvin. Why? Not because he was a bad preacher, but because his austere manner meets with considerable resistance when found in preachers today.

The point is simple. The crafting of sermons is a practice, not an exact art. A sermon is composed of any number of homiletical strands that, when woven together, can create a tapestry or a dishrag, either of which may be appropriate to the message. We do not control a number of these strands (Spirit, occasion, people), but we can try to weave these strands together in a way that will help our people to hear good news. And, lest we forget, we did not invent either the strands or the weave.

To consider the history of preaching not only illuminates the past and broadens our experience, it also provides some stability in a shaky world and furnishes us with a sense of identity. It helps us to remember those who have labored in this vineyard before us and can move us to awe and to the determination that we will do our best not to let our link in this historic chain be the one that breaks.

5. MODELS FOR PREACHING

Offering an annotated list of major figures and exemplars in the history of preaching is all but impossible. Space limitations would truncate the list sufficiently to cause universal disagreement. There are also denominational and regional implications. It seems better to list some good books in the reading list that follows this chapter and encourage professors and students to create their own list, with these two caveats: First, there should be biblical, early church, medieval, Reformation, and modern preachers. Second, special attention should be given to those sermons we have from preachers whose work was by and large not preserved in large numbers: women and those preachers outside Europe and North America.

Contemporary preachers from outside the students' own tradition can be very enlightening as well. In a recent class, I had several students who were clearly uninterested in the demanding work of exegesis and the crafting of sermons. They just wanted to stand up in front of the thousands who would flock to hear them and talk like a certain megachurch preacher that they admire. So I suggested we watch some of his sermons, and we did.

There was much to admire in the preacher. He came across as both honest and humble. I found myself liking him. His sermons were simple, clear, and visual. Everything he said was backed with video on a massive screen.

I did, however, have several concerns. The exegesis was very flimsy. He would pick a text, take a theme out of it, and ignore the context and meaning of the text. He also ignored any trouble in the text, anything that did not serve his message. While he is clearly an intelligent man, he sometimes made less-than-helpful assertions. When would wars end in the Middle East? Only when Jews and Muslims accept Jesus as their Lord and Savior. The movement was very strange. Sermons often just stopped. No transitions were evident apart from video. Finally, even though he did not use notes, the sermons were carefully scripted, with very little room for the Holy Spirit to come in and walk around.

We had a good discussion in class. Preaching like this may well be the wave of the near future. But it may also be a wave that will crash on the shore and then slide back to sea. I suggest the homiletical "cutting edge" we so covet may cut us off from the preaching tradition, to our peril. As historian of rhetoric George A. Kennedy puts it, "A speaker who has never read Demosthenes or Cicero remains content with the eloquence of his own age."[30] And I fear that the eloquence of our age has become insubstantial and cheap—except, of course, for the technology, which is very expensive.

One reads Demosthenes and Cicero, Aristotle and Augustine, and finds their rhetorical guidance as helpful today as ever. One reads and listens to sermons from past generations and contemporary colleagues for edification, but also for the sparks that can fly when one hears interpretation or sees imagery that evokes our own stories and remembrances.

One of the problems preachers face is that, unlike almost all other professions, we rarely see or hear our colleagues at work. Why? Because we all practice our profession at the same time: eleven o'clock or thereabouts on Sunday morning. It is important for preachers to make time to listen to sermons—recorded or, even better, in person— not just for "continuing education," but also for our souls. Leading worship is work. We also need to worship and hear others preach to and for us. Here follow some excerpts from remarks I made to a group of preachers about learning from our preaching brothers and sisters, quick or gone to glory:

> I want to say a few words about preaching before we go. A sermon has been defined by one of my colleagues as the only public event at which it is socially acceptable to sleep. That's not the loftiest definition I've ever heard, but it's one of the most persistent. So what do we who have been called to preach have to say in response?
>
> I was at a meeting in Atlanta some time back and had a couple of free days before coming home. Students in my classes watch and listen to sermons, and my collection was getting a little ragged. So I rented a car and drove up to Durham, N.C., to spend some time in the Duke audiovisual center, which I knew to be a good one. I picked up some fine sermons there. It had gone so well I decided to press my luck and drive on to Richmond, where I knew the Reigner Library at Union Seminary had the finest collection of sermons on audio- and videotape of anyplace in the world.

Well, what a day! I was like a child in a candy store as I made copies of sermons from many of the great preachers of days gone by and today. They gently pushed me out the door at closing time with my box of sermons and, as I stood there, reality set in. It was getting dark. I was in Richmond. I had a flight out of Atlanta at 6:04 in the morning. I was 535 miles from Atlanta, and suddenly very tired.

Not seeing that I had much choice, I got on I-85 and headed south into the gathering Virginia darkness. Within twenty miles I was struggling to stay awake. The radio offered no help. Pretty soon my head was bouncing off the steering wheel. Desperately, I looked around the car for something to help me stay awake and I saw the box sitting next to me on the seat, the box full of sermons. It may well be socially acceptable to sleep during a sermon, but not while driving. Could a sermon help me to stay awake? I couldn't see the labels, but just pulled one out and plugged it in. . . .

—It was Peter Marshall describing his call to ministry, and I thought of mine and straightened up in the seat.
—I plugged in Jeremiah Wright, who told us that when things are wrong, "Somebody oughtta say something!" a call that echoed through the Virginia night.
—Joanna Adams was next, who said that somebody was at the door. Who is it? We don't know, she said, but he "knocks like Jesus."
—And James Stewart's magnificent account of the rending of the veil from top to bottom, God's doing, not ours, that would have brought me to my knees if I had not been driving.
—Barbara Brown Taylor is one of the best preachers in the country right now, and I listened to her preach five sermons, one after the other, on into North Carolina and all the way to Durham, loving every minute.
—From there it was Gardner Taylor and Samuel Proctor and the exquisite language of Frederick Buechner across the Piedmont and into South Carolina.
—Two brilliant preachers, David H. C. Read and Edmund Steimle, preached beautifully about our suffering and how it is all going to end, and carried me awake and hopeful across the Cherokee Foothills until, listening to Herbert Meza, I saw that big peach on the sign that let me know I'd made it to Georgia.
—The pace quickened as I heard Cynthia Hale and Fred Craddock and Leontyne Kelly and that great sermon by Clarence Macartney that I'd read many times but never heard, "Come before Winter":

Come before the haze of Indian summer has faded from the fields.
Come before the November wind strips the leaves from the trees and
    sends them whirling over the fields.
Come before the snow lies on the uplands and the meadow brook is
    turned to ice.
Come before the heart is cold!
Come to thy God at last![31]

—And finally, just as the faint rose fingers of dawn illuminated the sky-
scrapers of his hometown, I plugged in the last sermon and heard the
preacher say:

I have a dream today.
I have a dream that one day every valley shall be exalted,
    every hill and mountain shall be made low,
    the rough places will be made plain
    and the crooked places will be made straight,
    and the glory of the Lord shall be revealed
    and all flesh shall see it together![32]

I pulled into the Alamo Rent-a-Car lot, and the young man
opened the door and looked at me and said, "Sir, are you all right?"
And I said, "Am I all right? I made it! I'm going home! And I'm filled
with the Holy Ghost!"

Friends, I haven't been preached to glory yet. But I've been
preached to Atlanta. And the question for today is this: If those had
been your sermons or mine in that box on the seat, would I have
made it to Atlanta?

What did those preachers have that not only kept me awake, but
engaged? Well, it wasn't whether or not they were loud or fast or
clever or whatever. Cynthia Hale whooped the good news, while
James Stewart preached with a quiet and winsome Scottish lilt. Barbara Brown Taylor made the Scripture come alive, while Jeremiah
Wright put the message in your face. Gardner Taylor has a great
trombone of a voice, a voice like God's, one person said, only deeper,
while Fred Craddock describes his voice as like unto the wind
whistling through a splinter on the post. They were all different in
many ways. But what they all had in common was a passion for the
gospel. They all had the conviction that what they were doing was
important because the good news of Jesus Christ was important, and
when the preacher believes that, it shows and hears.[33]

From the history of preaching, then, we receive models of rhetoric
and exegesis and sermon crafting to measure against our own; we receive

inspiration for the task before us; we receive a torch to carry forward; and we receive a passion for the gospel if we will only take it. The spirit of those people we walked with when they were alive and those we have met only in books shapes us and stays with us. When I spoke at the funeral of a beloved teacher, I said: "Much of what I have done has been done in the hope that he would not be ashamed of me."

As we scratch our heads over a difficult text, there is comfort in knowing that wiser heads than ours have puzzled over it. Biblical scholar Alfred Plummer wrote over one hundred years ago about the apparently inexplicable parable of the dishonest steward in Luke 16:

> The difficulty of this parable is well known, and the variety of interpretations is very great. A catalogue of even the chief suggestions would serve no useful purpose: it is sufficient to state that the steward has been supposed to mean the Jewish hierarchy, the tax-collector, Pilate, Judas, Satan, penitents, St. Paul and Christ.[34]

That made me feel better. Current interpretation leans toward the fascination with "trickster" language. One might wonder how long this tack will last. The dishonest steward is still there, grinning.

Homiletician Thomas Troeger encourages the practice of imaginative theology in his book *Imagining a Sermon*. He asks preachers to be attentive to what "is" and what our minds "see," and then describes another aspect of the work he does in his attic study:

> I look at the large table in the center of my study where I have piled dozens of books that I have read during the last few years, as well as those I have recently taken out of the seminary library to prepare sermons and classes. The stacks of books look like a model city of skyscrapers, a metropolis of homiletical wisdom built by biblical scholars, theologians, poets, literary critics, media analysts, novelists, and visual artists, some of them going back centuries and some of them very new inhabitants.[35]

In his description of an imaginative process of creating a sermon, he says that it is not all daydreaming. Rather, he still finds the time and the need to return to the "city of books," the "city of homiletical wisdom,"[36] and all those saints and scholars who live there.

In sum, we can join our students in finding historical colleagues who, through their words and stories, enter into dialogue with us as we walk together down the city street toward the pulpit.

We are reminded that we have been baptized with the same water as were the apostles, struggled with Christology like the church fathers and mothers, preached from the same texts as Luther and Calvin, been angry at some times with the church, like almost everyone who ever loved the church.

Preacher and teacher Eugene Lowry told a story about visiting a pastor whose parsonage was but a short walk through a graveyard from the church. The pastor told him that they had discovered that the parsonage had been built over an unmarked slave burial ground. Lowry asked, "How can you prepare your sermons sitting just a few feet above all those bones?" The pastor looked at him and said: "We all do."[37]

We also receive warnings about pitfalls along the way: abuse of texts, underestimating lay folk, proffering cheap grace, and yielding to plagiarism. One danger is that of stagnation, of not moving forward. Theologian Renita Weems recently spoke at a State of the Black Church banquet. Her vivid example from the exodus placed the children of Israel on the edge of the promised land. Their future was in front of them, and the responsibility for entering the land was theirs, because Moses was dead. The world they were entering was different from that of Moses, as our students' world will be different from the one in which we grew up and went to seminary.

Finally, as we labor to speak a good word for Jesus Christ, we need to remember that it will not be very long before preachers, seeking to learn from the past on their own way to the future, will be looking in our direction. We are the future's past. And to complete the circle, I hope those we entrust with that future will not be ashamed of us.

I will give you the words, says the Lord.
If I forget you, O Jerusalem, let my tongue cleave to the roof of my mouth.
Jesus Christ, Son of God, Savior.

SOME OTHER USEFUL EXERCISES

Trying to give even a synopsis of the history of preaching in a single hour-and-a-half class session will be ineffective, if not impossible. Since one cannot "cover" the history of preaching, perhaps the best option is to involve students in a few experiences of living homiletical history. Here are four examples.

1. Show two substantial film clips of an African American folk preacher and a New England–style European-American preacher. Involve the class in analyzing the rhetorical methods used. Then do a

quick time line, tracing each method historically, showing (perhaps to the students' surprise) that the folk preacher's poetic approach far antedates that of the prosy preacher.[38]

2. Explain the three elements of speech making in Aristotle's rhetoric (speech, speaker, audience) and the type of rhetoric each engendered (technical, sophistic, and philosophical). Then ask what happens in a sermon event when one or two of these elements are ignored. Use examples from sermons that are not grounded in the life/world of the people, that puff up the preacher and ignore the gospel, and so forth.

3. Augustine suggested the three duties of the Christian orator are to teach, delight, and move. I heard scholar-preacher Tom Long suggest a few years ago that we were in a homiletical mode of delight, to the frequent exclusion of teaching and moving. With the unfortunate decline of religious education programs, the sermon is often the only instruction in the faith that many people receive. Show students how teaching can be done in an interesting and compelling manner. Invite a discussion of sermons that have moved people in their lives—and hope there have been some! If not, the need is doubly demonstrated. One might also show a delightful, entertaining sermon that, upon analysis, had little or nothing to say, and discuss how it might gain substance without losing its appeal.

4. Give students a choice of classic sermons to read or hear. Invite comparisons between, say, Luther and Calvin, or Royden and Ramabai, and dig to find the reason for the differences: theology, hermeneutic, culture, all of these? Then discuss which of these elements have disappeared from our preaching and which have remained and why.

Exercises like these give students a chance to understand how our work builds on homiletical history. Examples from history can also enrich other subjects or topics throughout the course.

HELPFUL READINGS

A brief bibliography for the history of preaching might include the following:

Required:
Edwards, O. C., Jr. *A History of Preaching.* Nashville: Abingdon Press, 2004.
Kennedy, George A. *Classical Rhetoric and Its Christian and Secular Tradition from Ancient to Modern Times.* Chapel Hill: University of North Carolina Press, 1980.
Kienzle, Beverly, and Pamela Walker, eds. *Women Preachers and Prophets*

through Two Millennia of Christianity. Berkeley: University of California Press, 1998.

Osborn, Ronald. *Folly of God.* St. Louis: Chalice Press, 1999.

Thirty assigned sermons from across the centuries.

Wilson, Paul Scott. *A Concise History of Preaching.* Nashville: Abingdon Press, 1992.

Recommended:

Aristotle. *Rhetoric.* Translated by W. R. Roberts. New York: Modern Library, 1954.

Augustine. *On Christian Doctrine,* Book 4. Translated by D. W. Robertson Jr. Indianapolis: Library of Liberal Arts, 1958.

Other Suggested Books:

Cunningham, Mary, Pauline Allen, Carolyn Muessig, and Larissa Taylor. *A New History of the Sermon.* 3 vols. Boston: Brill, 1998– .

Lischer, Richard, ed. *The Company of Preachers.* Grand Rapids: Wm. B. Eerdmans Publishing Co., 2002.

Oden, Amy. *In Her Words.* Nashville: Abingdon Press, 1994.

Old, Hughes Oliphant. *The Reading and Preaching of the Scriptures in the Worship of the Christian Church.* 4 vols. Grand Rapids: Wm. B. Eerdmans Publishing Co., 1998– .

NOTES

1. Chrysostom, "The Sixth Instruction," *St. John Chrysostom: Baptismal Instructions,* trans. Paul W. Harkins, in *Ancient Christian Writers,* vol. 31 (Westminster, MD: Newman Press, 1963), 63.

2. Chrysostom's concern did not, of course, end with him. In 1618 King James I of England published the *Book of Sport,* which the clergy were asked to read to their people. "It recommended the continuation of such Sunday amusements as dancing, attending harlequinades, and participating in sports." See Harold J. Grimm, *The Reformation Era* (New York: Macmillan Co., 1966), 546–47. English Puritans struggled against this, trying to keep the Sabbath holy. Today's megachurches seek to end-run the problem by erecting huge sports complexes where people can get in shape and get saved at the same time.

3. For a detailed study of the text and its interpretive history, see William Joseph Dalton, *Christ's Proclamation to the Spirits: A Study of 1 Peter 3:18–4:6* (Rome: Pontifical Institute, 1965).

4. See a treatment of the text and its claims in Joseph R. Jeter Jr., "Calling Them as We See Them: Interpreting the Bible in Faith," *Biblical Preaching Journal* 3:2 (Spring 1990): 24–27.

5. Or sit, as in days of yore.

6. Suggested to me by a colleague.

7. See Ian Maclaren [John Watson], *Beside the Bonnie Brier Bush* (New York: Dodd, Mead & Co., 1895), 87–102.

8. See Joseph R. Jeter Jr. and Ronald J. Allen, *One Gospel, Many Ears* (St. Louis: Chalice Press, 2002), 49.

9. Clement of Alexandria, "On Spiritual Perfection," from *Stramata 7:18*, trans. J. E. L. Oulton and Henry Chadwick, in *Alexandrian Christianity*, ed. Henry Chadwick, in the Library of Christian Classics (Philadelphia: Westminster Press, 1954), 165. The previous two paragraphs are based on an excerpt from a paper I wrote for the 2001 meeting of the Academy of Homiletics.

10. Alan of Lille, "The Art of Preaching," cited in *The Company of Preachers,* ed. Richard Lischer (Grand Rapids: Wm. B. Eerdmans Publishing Co., 2002), 4. The claim for Lille's being the first "formal definition of preaching" is made by James J. Murphy and found on p. 3 of Lischer.

11. Ronald E. Osborn, "A Functional Definition of Preaching," *Encounter* 37:1 (Winter 1976): 53–54.

12. Ronald J. Allen, *Interpreting the Gospel: An Introduction to Preaching* (St. Louis: Chalice Press, 1998), 3.

13. Ronald E. Osborn, *Folly of God* (St. Louis: Chalice Press, 1999), 264.

14. Martin Luther, cited in Roland Bainton, *Here I Stand: A Life of Martin Luther* (New York: Mentor Books, 1955), 273.

15. Luther, cited in Gerhard Ebeling, *Luther,* trans. R. A. Wilson (Philadelphia: Fortress Press, 1972), 45.

16. Another value of history is the prodding to remember that the sermons of this "great Christian preacher" contain some of "the most horrible and violent denunciations of Judaism to be found in the writings of a Christian theologian" (James Parkes, cited in Robert L. Wilken, *John Chrysostom and the Jews* [Berkeley: University of California Press, 1983], xv). The damage wrought by Chrysostom's good intentions may perhaps be measured against that of a contemporary filmmaker.

17. *The Plays of Roswitha,* trans. Christopher St. John (New York: Benjamin Blom, 1966), 14.

18. Ibid., xiv.

19. *The Book of Margery Kempe,* trans. B. A. Windeatt (New York: Penguin Books, 1985), 164.

20. Akaiti Ama, in an unpublished paper discovered by this writer at the Pacific Theological College in Suva, Fiji, March 1991.

21. Thomas H. Troeger, *Ten Strategies for Preaching in a Multi-media Culture* (Nashville: Abingdon Press, 1996), 16–17.

22. Danna Nolan Fewell, "Deconstructive Criticism: Achsah and the (E)razed City of Writing," in *Judges and Method: New Methods in Biblical Studies,* ed. Gale A. Yee (Minneapolis: Fortress Press, 1995), 141.

23. Uriel Simon, *The JPS Bible Commentary: Jonah* (Philadelphia: Jewish Publication Society, 1999), vi.

24. See William Baird, *History of New Testament Research* (Minneapolis: Fortress Press, 1992), xiv–xvii.

25. Paul Scott Wilson, *God Sense: Reading the Bible for Preaching* (Nashville: Abingdon Press, 2001), 85.

26. Joseph R. Jeter Jr., "The Development of Poetic Preaching," *Homiletic* 15:2 (Winter 1990): 5.

27. See *Committed to Memory,* ed. John Hollander (New York: Turtle Point Press, 1996).

28. Jeter and Allen, *One Gospel,* 11–13.

29. Elmer Carl Kiessling, *The Early Sermons of Luther and Their Relation to the Pre-Reformation Sermon* (Grand Rapids: Zondervan Publishing House, 1935), 60.

30. George A. Kennedy, *Classical Rhetoric* (Chapel Hill: University of North Carolina Press, 1980), 243.

31. Clarence Macartney, "Come before Winter," in *20 Centuries of Great Preaching,* vol. 9, ed. Clyde Fant and William Pinson (Waco, TX: Word, 1971), 140.

32. Martin Luther King Jr., "I Have a Dream," *20 Centuries of Great Preaching,* 12:357.

33. Joseph R. Jeter Jr., "Is the Devil to Have All the Passions as Well as All the Good Tunes?" a talk delivered at Ministers Week, Texas Christian University, February 8, 1996.

34. Alfred Plummer, *A Critical and Exegetical Commentary on the Gospel according to St. Luke* (New York: Charles Scribner's Sons, 1896), 380.

35. Thomas Troeger, *Imagining a Sermon* (Nashville: Abingdon Press, 1990), 21.

36. Ibid., 23, 25.

37. Remembered from the sermon "Stones and Bones," preached by Eugene Lowry at a meeting of the Academy of Homiletics at Fuller Theological Seminary, Pasadena, CA, December 6, 1991.

38. See Jeter, "The Development of Poetic Preaching," 5–12.

11

Voice and Diction

TERESA FRY BROWN

In my years as a speech-language pathologist, I studied a variety of speech-related topics: phonation and sound production; human transmission systems; sound perception (or hearing); the acoustic, physiological, psychological, and linguistic phenomena of human speech; measurement and assessment of intelligibility and quality of speech; technological processing of speech analysis; and therapeutic principles for remediation of communicative disorders in children and adults. I directed a university speech and hearing clinic for three years and taught anatomy, physiology, endocrinology, and neurology. My experience was acquired as director of private and public school, state hospital, and group-care homes speech and language programs.

The specialized use of the vocal mechanism must also be afforded particular attention in sermon delivery. The preacher's ability to communicate a message clearly and effectively is directly impacted by the type of voice and diction the preacher possesses.

In my preaching classes, I require each student to preach a one- to three-minute sermon on the first day of class. This exercise allows the students to begin listening to each other, helps break the ice for those who view preaching with abject terror, and allows me to hear their voices and theologies. Classes thereafter are punctuated with extemporaneous and scheduled minisermon experiences. One week each semester I teach about voice, sound production, breathing, hearing, and fluency. One section of the peer evaluation for major student sermons also includes a section on the preacher's communicability.

Students who have exhibited voice and diction difficulties such as sound misarticulating (substituting, omitting, distorting, or adding sounds), breathing problems, raspy or harsh voices, inaudible voices, loudness problems, pitch breaks, or ineffective pausing are asked to meet for a one-on-one discussion where they receive a cursory voice and diction evaluation. Referrals to speech and language professionals, hearing specialists, or voice teachers are made for students with major organic or structural complications. Students with functional or manageable problems are given voice and structural diction exercises specific to their issue.

All preaching students receive voice and diction exercises for maintenance of vocal health. Follow-up sessions are scheduled twice a semester, after each major sermon is preached. Each student is encouraged to analyze his or her own audio- and videotaped sermon presentations for voice and diction clarity. Often students have little awareness of communication difficulties until they are in my class.

The following are examples of students I have encountered over the years. Their profiles seem to show up each semester in one manifestation or another.

—Student A holds an earned research doctorate and a law degree. She carefully pronounces each syllable. Her language level and perfectionism, however, lead to occasional overenunciation and affectation. Her plodding rate diminishes her persuasive ability. Each sermon sounds as if she is arguing a case or defending her dissertation.

—Student B is a Black male who grew up in a Pentecostal church in southern Alabama. His primary preaching models are older Black males who evidence a slow, hoarse, staccato, yet rhythmic cadence in preaching. He is caught between his "proper" academic speech and his acculturated speech pattern. The result is an odd blend of "standard" English pronunciation of some words and a regional-cultural dialect, which includes the omission of word endings and substitution of "f" for "th."

—Student C is a senior pastor of a charismatic, evangelical church with twelve years' experience. This student creates words as he preaches, mispronounces biblical names, uses only language from the King James translation, and prolongs or distorts words such as God (*Gahd* or *Goooodud*), Jesus *(Jeezuz)*, Lord *(Lourd or Laard)*, and Bible *(Bahble or Biiible)*. His style is fast-paced with varied inflections, is punctuated with jargon and clichés, and at times is earsplitting in volume. He also has a regular televised sermon on a local public-access channel.

—Student D is diminutive, soft-spoken, and barely audible, with minimal eye contact. The exegesis and content of the sermon are excellent.

—Student E is dyslexic. His presence is disengaged, looking only at the manuscript, and switching syllables in every other line. His peers perceive his misarticulations as ethnic pronunciations.

—Student F is an international student. His overall presentation is marked by spiritual depth, high regard for the preaching moment, excellent exegesis, and recurring narrative content. Substitution errors (such as "l" for "r") and translation errors in word choices are also present.

—Student G presents pitch breaks from tenor to falsetto voice during the preaching moment. Additionally, this student exhibits tremors of the face and upper body while preaching. His complexion takes on a bright-red blush, and occasionally he repeats syllables or sounds at the beginning of words. In peer conversation, these problems are not evident.

—Student H is a pastor of a congregation of approximately 1,500. He preaches three times each Sunday. He is tired physically, and his voice is fatigued. He sounds lethargic, although tapes of his Sunday worship service present a vibrant, energetic, and captivating preacher. His voice is hoarse and wheezy on Tuesday morning. He complains of "losing my voice" and says, "I keep on clearing my throat" during the third service each Sunday.

In this chapter I will provide a brief overview of the areas of voice and diction that I assess with students such as these when I encounter them in preaching classes, seminars, and pastors' schools. By so doing I hope to provide the reader with tools for addressing similar concerns in the pulpit or the classroom. This chapter will also include exercises that have proved helpful for enhancing the communicability of preachers.

SPEECH PRODUCTION

There are three major components of voice or speech production: the breathing mechanism, the larynx, and the vocal cavities or articulators.[1] Respiration, or breathing, is accomplished through the interaction of the lungs, trachea (windpipe), rib cage, and diaphragm (the muscular floor that separates the chest from the abdomen). We exchange oxygen and carbon dioxide approximately eighteen times per minute when sitting and twenty-two times per minutes when standing.

Breathing

The most common breathing problems observed in preaching or public speaking are: speaking too long without a breath, pausing frequently for short gasps of air, too much neck and shoulder movement while breathing, and audible breathing (as if affected by a cold, stuffiness, or exhaustion). Students need instructions in how to breathe deeply—that is, with the diaphragm flat and the abdomen protruding, rather than the militaristic taking in of breath with shoulder elevation. Discussions on the avoidance of smoking, use of certain medications, and eating habits may also prove helpful.

Respiration exercises

1. After taking a deep breath, count slowly, one second per number, in a good loud voice. Repeat until you can count aloud to fifteen slowly. Then repeat until you are able to count to twenty or thirty.

2. Sound the vowel "ah" in a full voice, and prolong it in a monotone until you feel as if all the breath is exhausted. Time each trial. When taking a breath, place your hand lightly on your abdomen. *Diaphragmatic breathing* means that your stomach distends when air is taken in. If your shoulders move up (*clavicular breathing*) and your stomach goes in, you are breathing incorrectly and will have minimal airflow.

Posture exercise

Shoulders should incline slightly forward. Carriage of the chest and collarbones is relatively high. The chin should be inclined forward, slightly. Feet should be approximately 10 to 12 inches apart. Exaggerated, stiff, military posture decreases vocal efficiency.[2]

The Physiology of Sound Production

The larynx (or voice box) is situated in the neck at the upper end of the trachea, and is composed of cartilage and muscles. The larynx modulates airflow with valve action of the vocal folds (soft muscle tissues approximately the size of a dime) that open and close to allow air to pass from the lungs to the mouth.[3] The exhaled air causes the muscle tissue to vibrate, producing sound.

The articulators are the head, teeth, jaw, tongue, palate, and lips. Sound vibrates and bounces across the soft moist tissue of the articulators to produce various sounds.[4]

Sound production problems can be organic or functional. Organic problems include edema or swollen folds resultant from vocal abuse, hoarseness, or laryngitis. Functional loss is attributed to vocal abuse (imitation of another), yelling, and psychological stress (aphonia).[5] I refer all organic voice problems and persistent functional problems lasting more than ten days to medical or voice or speech language professionals.

MAINTAINING HEALTHY VOICES

Volume, Intensity, and Projection

Vocal audibility should be natural and effortless. Adequate breathing is essential to effective voice. Breath control is accomplished by using the correct energy when setting the vocal fold into motion. Proper monitoring of tension, stress, anxiety, and fear in the body can contribute to correct vocal energy.

Homiletician Frank Thomas writes that there are predictable occasions when the preacher's voice sounds unnatural. Among them are: major preaching assignments (when anxiety sets in), occasions when the preacher has not adequately prepared the sermon or herself through prayer, and occasions when the preacher is not well rested or when the mind is preoccupied.[6] In an age of performance-oriented preachers, overwhelming schedules, and style imitators, the content of the sermon is at times lost in the sound of the preacher. The preacher has a duty to care for his or her voice with the same passion used in composing the sermon and speaking with the congregation.

Volume, Intensity, and Projection Exercise

Prolong the "ah" sound softly at a normal pitch level. Gradually increase the loudness of the sound in a monotone as long as the breath lasts. Make sure you increase the sound gradually, imagining that a person is walking away from you. Try to reach twenty feet with your voice. If you feel a tickling, cough, or hoarseness, you are straining your voice. Stop if this occurs. Next, decrease the volume as if the person is walking toward you. Always direct your voice toward the person. Having mastered this distance without strain, try thirty, forty, and fifty feet. Try with the inflection patterns going up, down, and monotone.[7]

Emotion

Emotion in preaching has a direct correlation to message intent. Preachers are human, emotive creatures. My contention is that even though one is called to lead or minister with the people, one is also called as a passionate, compassionate human with emotions that need to be expressed. The challenge is for the preacher not to "bleed all over the congregation," beat up the congregation, expose too much of the self, or ignore the emotional temperature of the listener.

Emotion and Preaching Exercise[8]

The weight of emotion directly affects the tone, duration, energy, volume, and quality of a person's voice. Consequently, I ask preachers to consider their own management of the emotions generated by their individual lives, preaching contexts, and congregational relationships. Some of the individual factors discussed include theology and personal beliefs, effects of culture (isms), family dynamics and support, health, lifestyle, age, gender, authority issues, and relationality. Elements of ministerial responsibility also bleed over into the preaching moment and may affect speech and language production. Congregational demographics and relationships, competing ministerial responsibilities, worship or ritual leadership, and congregational illnesses or deaths all carry different emotional weights and may affect the vocal production of the preacher.

THE PREACHER'S VOICE

In my first year of teaching in Atlanta there was an abundance of preachers who believed themselves to be clones of Martin Luther King, Joyce Meyer, Rod Parsley, and T. D. Jakes. My mantra became, "Be yourself!" The greater struggle was helping students identify who they were and what they really sounded like. David Schlafer provides a helpful manual on "preaching signature" (blueprint, fingerprint, what you are "known for" in preaching). He states that a person's preaching voice modifies over time. Contributing elements include: the context/situation for preaching, types of texts preached, congregational dynamics, subject matter, culture, liturgy, and personal circumstances.[9]

Identification of Preaching Voice Exercise[10]

Think of the last two or three sermons you preached.
What is the color of your preaching?
How does it look?
How does your preaching smell?
How does it sound?
How would it feel if you could touch it?
If the sermon were a meal, how would it taste?

Tonality

Jon Eisenson writes that vocal variation, or intonation, gives melody to speech. It is similar to discreet musical note shifts. The upward and downward shift of the voice colors speech and either energizes the message or yields a monotone presentation.[11] The melody of speech is determined in the mood, emotion, intonation, and flavor of the voice of the speaker. Better speakers produce speech in a range of one and one-half octaves of rising and falling stressed syllables. Monotone speakers produce only one-half octave in expression of feelings and belief.[12]

A problem occurs in preaching class when women students with higher vocal registers believe they must sound like men in order to gain credibility in the pulpit. The "masculine" style or sound with bass baritone, loud, energetic flourishes, hard consonant contact, and broad pounding gestures apparently has a "homiletical stamp of approval" as "real" preaching. I have a friend who says that when people opine, "You don't sound like a preacher," she replies, "The real ones never do!" I caution women, in particular, to consider their unique vocal structure and breathing capacity, and the damage they can do to their voices by imitating others. We practice exercises of sound content, using varied inflection patterns such as running scales, and talk about being authentic preachers. We work at finding their true *pitch*—the level of voice determined by age, gender, and vocal structure. I also advise each student to have an annual hearing evaluation in order to enunciate clearly, project the voice, and monitor both his or her own voice and the responsiveness of the listeners.

Articulation

A critical component of voice and diction assessment is articulation—movement of the lips, tongue, teeth, jaw, palate, and bronchial tube which modify the air stream and produce specific sounds such as "p," "b," and "s." *Phonation* is the production of sound that occurs when your vocal folds vibrate as air passes between them. General misarticulations include the substitution of sounds (e.g., "ax" for "ask"), omission of sounds, distortions, and addition of sounds.

The most common articulation errors in preaching are mispronunciation of biblical names and locations. In order to address this problem, I ask students to obtain a self-pronouncing or phonetic Bible thesaurus or to use one of the electronic programs for correct pronunciation of Greek, Hebrew, Latin, or English words. I caution them to practice the entire sermon prior to preaching. For students with structural difficulties (such as joint misalignment, missing teeth, or dental appliances, lip injuries, or nasal/sinus congestions), location of an alternative word works wonders for improved clarity.

Tight Jaw or Tense Jaw Exercise

If you speak with little mouth opening or you clench your teeth, try chewing exercises. Pretend you have caramel or your favorite gooey food in your mouth. Open your mouth as wide as possible and chew twenty times. With the mouth wide open cough drily and lightly five times. Alternate a few times, resting in between. You might try slow neck rolls also—first clockwise, then counterclockwise, five times each. Phonate "m" softly as you roll the head slowly, thinking of some pleasant event or place.

Dialect

Dialect, or manner of speaking, is defined by one's ethnicity, nationality, culture, region, district, class, or gender. The enunciation of words is decidedly different from "standard" English. A preacher's dialect may or may not interfere with the reception of the preached word, depending on the social location of the listeners.

In my classes, I teach students a form of "code switching"[13] or bilingualism, in order to train them to preach within a variety of cultural contexts. Code switching is a learned behavior that allows members of certain cultural groups (e.g., African Americans) to move in and out of standard English in order to represent their own cultural emotional codes. This facility is important for the emotive content of preaching, and is evident in the multilingual preaching of seminary-trained African American preachers.

Pacing and Pauses

Jon Eisenson, voice and diction professor, says timing is everything. The rate and duration of speech—slow may indicate sadness, fast indicate joy—depict emotion. The use of action verbs, length of sentences, types of sentences used in speaking (i.e., declarative, exclamatory, or interrogatory), and punctuation set the intonation of vocal production. The use of a pause in speech is an indication of control and transition.[14]

The speaker may use the pause as a means of allowing the listener to catch up, integrate what has been said, or arouse expectations of the homiletical event. At times preachers are reticent to pause or fear waiting even briefly for the communication to be transmitted. The pause, however, signals the completion of a thought, and timing for vocal variety. It also helps maintain interest on the part of the listener, allowing him or her to reconnect or attend to the content of the message.[15]

Rate

Rate, or fluency, is the speed of vocal production—too fast, too slow, or variable. Fluency disorders disrupt the flow of speech. The preacher may be speaking at such a rapid rate that clarity of speech is sacrificed. We read faster than we speak, and manuscript-bound preachers may not sense the listener's frustration in keeping up with them. Anxiety, time constraints, fatigue, resistance to preaching, control, manipulation, and disengagement with the listener may prove causative factors of an inappropriate rate.

Prolongation of sounds and repetition of phrases are hallmarks of African American and charismatic preaching. These elements are viewed as "disfluencies" when the listener becomes fixated on a syllable or sound the preacher has difficulty enunciating, and become problematic when the preacher clutters or stutters.

Fluency and Rate Exercises

Speak as rapidly as you wish, as long as you articulate all speech sounds. When you seem to produce numerous pauses and repetitions of words or sounds, or you can't seem to produce the next word without struggle, your disfluencies are termed stuttering. If you speak so rapidly that your speech is generally incoherent or words seem to be connected into one long sentence, your disfluencies are termed cluttering.

1. Practice reading prose or poetry using a tape recorder. Read at your normal rate, read faster, then slower, comparing your clarity. Have someone else listen to the tape and rate your clarity.

2. Read the passage allowing two beats between each word. Use a rate of 60 to 100 syllables (not words) per minute. Prolong the vowel sound in each syllable. Practice with the twenty-foot volume projection mentioned earlier. Attend to the articulation of each sound.

An average reading rate is 135–175 words per minute—often a preacher will use this as his or her speaking rate. The mood, style, and situation of the speaker determine the speed of presentation. As you vary your rate, maintain easy breathing, clear voice production, incisive articulation, proper phrasing, pausing, and inflection.[16]

Presence and Appearance

The final area used for evaluation is the preacher's presence. Depending on the preacher and the context, it may be assessed as fearful, energetic, commanding, domineering, self-righteous, or manipulative. The image projection of the preacher is based on reputation, attitude, knowledge, clothing, status, voice, eye contact, body language, content, and handling of the biblical text. The exercises that follow are used in various preaching classes to assist students in identifying themselves as preachers and engaging the listeners in a more deliberate manner.

Exercise: Presence and Delivery[17]

1. What emotions do you feel before, during, or after the preaching moment?
2. Consider your posture. What does the congregation see?

3. Is your voice generally calm, undulating, muted, loud, "normal," raspy, etc.?

4. Consider your facial expressions. How do you transmit emotion?

5. What can be observed through your body language?

6. through your eye contact?

7. through your use of space while preaching?

Exercise: Attire, Presence, and Delivery[18]

1. What is your attire while proclaiming God's Word? (Robes, suits, dresses, pants?)

2. Is your attire based on tradition, personal preference, senior pastor dictates, other?

3. Is there attire that you think is inappropriate for the preaching moment? If so, why?

4. Is there one or more particular color that you think is inappropriate? Why?

5. Do you alter your hairstyle in any manner when proclaiming? Why, or why not?

6. Is jewelry appropriate in the pulpit? If so, what style, amount, and placement?

7. What about head coverings and shoes?

CONCLUSION

The voice and diction of the preacher are essential to the effective communication of the preached word with the congregation. Clarity of speech may never be perfect. However, the preacher and teacher of preaching can begin by taking small steps to modify glaring hindrances to communicability. This chapter has provided an overview of some of the elements of oral competence—speech production, audibility, breath control, volume, emotion, voice, tonality, articulation, pacing, rate, and presence. This is by no means an exhaustive listing. It is, however, a starting point for the teacher of preachers who strives to assist the student in becoming a person who speaks the truth with a modicum of clarity, and who maintains a healthy voice for the preaching life.

NOTES

1. Jon Eisenson, *Voice and Diction: A Program for Improvement*, 7th ed. (Needham Heights, MA: Allyn & Bacon, 1997), 17–21.

2. Teresa Fry Brown, Voice and Diction Exercises, "Introduction to Preaching" Class, Candler School of Theology, Atlanta, 2004.

3. Eisenson, *Voice and Diction*, 17–21.

4. Ibid. See also G. Robert Jacks, *Getting the Word Across: Speech Communication for Pastors and Lay Leaders* (Grand Rapids: Wm. B. Eerdmans Publishing Co., 1995), for a more "user-friendly" explanation of sound production.

5. American Speech-Language and Hearing Association (ASHA), http://www.asha.org, 2004.

6. Frank Thomas, "Flunk Likes," *The African American Pulpit*, Winter 2002–2003, 22–26.

7. Teresa Fry Brown, Voice and Diction Exercises, "Introduction to Preaching" Class, 2004.

8. Teresa Fry Brown, "Oral Presentation of Scripture and Sermon Class," exercise, 1996.

9. David J. Schlafer, *Your Way with God's Word: Discovering Your Distinctive Preaching Voice* (Cambridge, MA: Cowley Publications, 1995), 9–15.

10. Teresa Fry Brown, "Women and Preaching" Class exercise, 1997.

11. Eisenson, *Voice and Diction*, 110–22.

12. Ibid.

13. Charles E. Debose, "Codeswitching: Black English and Standard English in the African American Linguistic Repertoire," *Journal of Multilingual and Multicultural Development* 13 (1992): 157–67.

14. Eisenson, *Voice and Diction*, 161.

15. Ibid.

16. Exercises listed are recommended by Teresa Fry Brown. See also Jon Eisenson, *Voice and Diction*, 143–80, for exercises on control of loudness, increased clarity, articulation, and rate, and G. Robert Jacks, *Getting the Word Across: Speech Communication for Pastors and Lay Leaders*, 125–48, for general pronunciation exercises and a listing of words preachers mispronounce most often.

17. Teresa Fry Brown, "Introduction to Preaching" Class exercise, 1997.

18. Teresa Fry Brown, "Women and Preaching" Class exercise, 1997.

SECTION THREE

Assessment and Formation

12

Marks of Faithful Preaching Practice

PAUL SCOTT WILSON

In the previous sections we have been considering preaching as a practice that already exists, and which therefore has something to tell us about ways in which it might be taught and significant components of it. In this section we will tease from the practice certain features that have particular significance, both for the practice itself and for the evaluation of faithful practice. If preaching is in fact a learning-centered practice, it participates in what God is doing in the world, and some of its features must be key in effecting that participation. Our purpose here is not to identify a set of rules that apply to all sermons, nor is it to name the components of good preaching, aware that they may be in some ways determined by the occasion or the culture. It is, rather, to hold up some elements that may be employed in various ways and combinations and are key to contributing to faithful proclamation of the gospel.

KEYS TO FAITHFUL PREACHING

Preaching is situated in the practice of worship. This means that preaching participates in a larger act of praise and thanksgiving honoring God. It is part of a ritual practice that has form and structure and that as a whole retells something of the metanarrative of the community of faith through its prayers, hymns, songs, offering, sacraments, and other parts. Services take place often within seasons of worship that have

185

their own portion of the Christian story to tell. Moreover, the symbols of worship and artwork such as banners and special windows all contribute to the larger story. In coming before God in gladness (Ps. 100:2) and with a prayerful attitude, people expect to hear God's word and be emboldened to rededicate their lives to Christ's mission.[1] The word is delivered to that specific gathering of people in that specific time and place, whether it is the regular Sunday service, a wedding, funeral, or some other occasion. One important implication of the setting of worship is that preaching is not the sole vehicle of the Christian story, and the sermon may appropriately rely on other elements of the service to help frame what is said.

Preaching brings people into relationship with the preacher, the congregation, and God. Primary among these, of course, is God, who gathers the community, addresses and blesses it, and sends it forth into the world to do Christ's work. The preacher's relationship with the congregation is established both through the office as well as through the sermon, according to the various issues that are discussed. Who the preacher is as a person is made clear in and through the sermon by the kinds of things that are said, how they are said, and what is not said. A preacher establishes both the pastoral and prophetic dimensions of ministry each week, not least through the sermon. Preaching is not an individual action, however; it is taken on behalf of the community. While God calls and empowers individuals, the church tests, trains, and otherwise equips them and sets them apart for the ministry of Word, sacrament, and pastoral care. The community supports the preacher spiritually, and in other ways that allow for adequate sermon preparation time through the week; physically and audibly in the preaching moment, through gestured acknowledgments or oral response; and critically, by offering feedback that helps to ensure the preaching is doing what it needs to do. Both the preacher and the community have responsibility to ensure that the word is proclaimed and appropriated. Thus to a large degree the community is made known by the practice of its beliefs in the worship and the preaching, for here its actions throughout the week find their explanation and motivation clearly stated.

Preaching brings people into the presence of God. The practice of preaching demonstrates something of the purpose of exegetical study, that is, it leads to a theological understanding of the biblical text. One way for the sermon to accomplish this is by focusing on God's action that connects the Bible and the present-day situation. This reflection on God may be normally engaged through lifelike conversational style that introduces God not in abstract propositional ways, but in narratives, images, ideas, and metaphors that resemble how life is typically lived and experienced. The sermon is thus not simply information about God, or communication of certain doctrines, though it certainly and importantly includes these. God speaks in and through the sermon, and people appropriately listen to sermons with the expectation of hearing Christ speak. Preaching is an announcement of what God is doing, an encounter with the living God, who wills to be known in this way, for, as Christ said, "Where two or three are gathered in my name, I am there among them" (Matt. 18:20). When preaching is understood in faith to be one manner of Christ meeting and equipping his followers, preaching may also be understood to participate in the action of God: our preaching does not make God present, but rather God chooses to come to Christ's followers in and through the proclamation of the Word.

Preaching significantly engages a biblical text. Teaching preaching from the perspective of practice does not presuppose that one approach will be followed by the preacher in arriving at the sermon or that the sermon will present the text within the sermon in a predetermined way. The text will be viewed differently in different settings, and the practices of exegesis vary widely according the gravitational center and focus of each text. The sermon variously engages the worlds in front of, behind, within, and around the biblical text. Normally this will include historical-critical treatment of the text and scholarship in order to ensure that the text is accurately heard within its own settings, as well as literary engagement of the text that enables it to be heard with various emphases and focuses within the contemporary world. Since exegesis is an art, not a science, it is not appropriate to think of the text as a cadaver and the process of interpretation as an autopsy, as seemed once the case; some more dynamic activity offers a better analogy—perhaps a dance or a musical performance. The manifestation of textual analysis in the sermon is an effective communication of one unified understanding of the biblical text in a clear and reliable manner.

Preaching is a practice that enrolls listeners into its worldviews and values. It takes seriously the world of the listeners as both the hearing place of the text and the place where it will be lived out. This practice is communal and has the effect of transforming hearers into an authentic community that does justice, loves kindness, and walks humbly with God (Mic. 6:8). It has to do with proclaiming the gospel of Jesus Christ, and with our lives being conformed to his purposes. He ordained preaching when he instructed the church to "proclaim the good news to the whole creation" (Mark 16:15). He was pointing to the content of preaching, which is not narrowly the biblical text at hand, but more largely that portion of the larger story or metanarrative of faith to which an opening is given by a particular text. While different individuals or denominations might define what is meant by the gospel in different ways, it has to do with what Scripture says was accomplished in the life, death, resurrection, and ascension of Jesus Christ.

Preaching is formed by and forms the particular nature of the community at hand. As a practice, preaching takes seriously the setting in which it occurs, the nature and sociological composition of the congregation as well as the particular history of that community, their faith warrants, theology, and mission. An exegesis of the congregation is necessary in order to become aware of its elements and dynamics. All these considerations are reflected in the sermon in the way the preacher earns trust, meets needs, evokes emotion, and develops a message as an effective communication of the gospel. Comments and stories that have been told by members of the community inform sermon composition in everything from biblical interpretation to referring to events in the news. In other words, the sermon seeks to be heard by that particular individual community of faith, not by communities of faith in general, and its evaluation is not by one fixed set of standards, but arises out of considerations of how the practice contributes to that community's theological and ecclesial commitments. At the same time, preaching is a process of forming a community of faith, and it accomplishes this by participating in God's informing, transforming, and empowering activity. The identity the community complacently assumes for itself is often undermined by the Word, who calls and equips disciples into new ways of being in the world that are sensitive to issues of freedom, justice, race, gender, and culture. There is then a necessary tension between preaching that is formed by and preaching that shapes the community of hearers, a tension that serves to build up the body of Christ into a community of mutual care, support, and outreach.

Sermons both demonstrate form and generate it. There is no set form for preaching, although many classical and contemporary forms are identified in homiletical literature. Preachers may benefit from trying models that are different from their familiar ones. In some ways the only limitation on the number of identifiable forms is one's patience for categories and the practicality of naming minor variations. Said another way, sermons evolve out of a dialogical set of relationships between the preacher and the biblical text, God, the people, the news, culture(s), former preachers and teachers, and the scholarly community. Each occasion of preaching gives rise to a new set of dynamics that themselves help to dictate the form of the sermon, both as a whole and in the various forms that make up the whole. Ideally the macroform will be determined by the purpose or function of the individual sermon, determined in large part by the biblical text and its interpreted theological significance for today. The microforms of the sermon include various linguistic devices like images, doctrinal pieces, metaphors, sentence structures, stories, set pieces, and rhetorical units; sound devices like use of voice, inflection, intonation, timing; and physical gestures that include everything from stances to hand movements to facial expressions. When preaching is viewed as a practice, form becomes a larger and more fluid issue than genre or the arrangement of ideas on a page, and each sermon's form is unique. Preachers are thus wise to be attentive to preaching through all the ages for ways in which, both at a micro and macro level of form, they may learn from their forebears. Arguably the most significant issue of form is the organic manner in which the central idea or theme sentence of the sermon is developed to give unity and coherence to the sermon.

Preaching as a practice both reflects experience and creates it. The language of preaching reflects experience both in the Bible and in the contemporary world, and to a considerable extent the two overlap. Even biblical experience that employs good exegetical processes and scholarly research is still rendered in the sermon with our own language, culture, and worldviews shaping the discussion. The biblical witness is always an interpreted witness, and the same is true for the manner in which our world is sermonically represented. With regard to both, the preacher seeks to identify with the listener by reflecting in a pastoral manner what has been seen and heard in the community and the world at large. This identity is established through use of common words, expressions, ways of oral expression, various appeals to logos, pathos, and ethos, as well as by the bringing to memory of past experience and creation of new experience in and through the sermon itself. The sermon itself is an experience, not just in its words, sounds, and visual dimensions within the church, but also in its pictured worlds that receive life in the minds and hearts of the listeners. These worlds are not transferred in a sterile fashion into the sermon; they are created through the language and imagination of the preacher. They involve choices at every level by both the preacher, who has to decide what and what not to include, and the listener, who has to decipher and imagine the world that the preacher speaks; in other words, these worlds involve active participation of speaker and hearer. Thus when the preacher pictures the world as God intends it to be, the congregation experiences it in that moment, though it may only be a foretaste of the reality God intends. Language shapes consciousness.

Preaching is a living and dynamic art, and the principles that mark its faithfulness emerge from it in differing ways according to the congregation. The marks that we have identified, while not exhaustive, are at least representative of some of the features that emerge from preaching as a practice, yet they do not stand as rules that now function to dictate how the process of that practice develops. If one adds them all up, they do not explain how to arrive at a good sermon. In fact, as we have discussed them, they are more descriptive than prescriptive, more indicative of values than of how they are to be lived out or accomplished. Even to call them marks of faithful preaching is to make them into static elements, when in a sense each one describes a dynamic that needs to be released and set in motion. In short, they are activities that come into play in the process of faithful proclamation, and how they are put into play may vary from occasion to occasion as the preacher enters into the wonderful and terrible prayerful creativity that we call sermon composition and delivery.

NOTE

1. To the extent that street preaching emerges out of the sacred community, it too may be considered as being within the worship context.

13

Methods of Assessment

DANIEL E. HARRIS

ASSESSMENT AS A PASTORAL PRACTICE

Preaching assessment usually bears the stamp of the individual homiletics professor and the particular classroom situation. This chapter does not propose a *best* method of assessment, since no single method can address the variety of homiletics curricula, faith traditions, and unique styles of each classroom. This chapter offers suggestions for sound sermon assessment that individuals will need to adapt to local circumstances.

Despite the variety of methods and styles used to assess sermons, many homiletics professors report their common experience of approaching this aspect of their teaching as a pastor as well as professor. On the one hand, homiletics teachers attempt to apply objective criteria in an evenhanded style, aimed at helping students arrive at a balanced appreciation of the strengths and areas for growth in the sermon being assessed. On the other hand, teachers sometimes find themselves needing to nuance feedback in ways that can most effectively help a student grow at his or her particular pace. Professors who see themselves as pastors will at times reserve especially sensitive sermon critique to a private meeting with the student. In all cases, their role is to critique the practice of preaching, not to criticize the preacher as a person.

Who Assesses Preaching?

Since this text is for homiletics teachers, this chapter primarily addresses methods of assessment in classroom and laboratory settings. However,

191

it is important to remember that everybody connected with the sermon assesses preaching—the preacher himself or herself, peers in the classroom and ministry, and, of course, the congregation. As important as all of these voices are, the preacher's self-assessment becomes pivotal, in the sense that he or she is ultimately the one who will continue to build on perceived strengths and work to improve perceived areas for growth. The following suggestions for preaching assessment therefore aim to help a preaching student become a healthy self-critic.

Do We Assess the Whole Sermon?

When I began learning digital video editing, the training tape that came with the software advised the novice to start with a very simple project. Begin with a few video clips. After learning how to arrange these clips in the storyboard mode, then move on to video transitions, later to special effects, and on and on. It was excellent advice. I was glad that I did not try to produce *Gone with the Wind* in my first effort. Preaching, as both art and craft, is best learned in small steps. Alvin Rueter suggests this gradual approach in *Making Good Preaching Better*.[1] Rueter cautions the homiletics instructor that students can be set up for failure if they are asked to present a full, well-crafted sermon early in their education and formation. He cites his experience of presenting preaching workshops where time limits allowed only three-minute sermons on videotape. He brought this same technique into the classroom so that students can gradually grow in confidence.

In addition to starting with briefer sermons, the instructor might also consider a gradual approach when assessing the qualities of a student's sermon, regardless of its length. In chapter 12, Paul Scott Wilson discusses how good preaching is marked by effective biblical interpretation, theological discernment, ethical and faith goals, and rhetorical construction. Is it realistic for a beginning student to master the integration of all four critical elements in his or her early preaching? Perhaps early assessment might focus on each of these aspects of preaching one at a time. For example, in the first round of preaching in a foundational homiletics course, the feedback could center on rhetorical construction. Although preachers need to realize that all four homiletic pillars need to be in place in each sermon, the assessment process, especially in the case of students who are new to preaching, might best focus on just one aspect as a strategy to help the student appreciate the specific skills needed to strengthen that one pillar of preaching.

The Preaching Laboratory and Assessment

Preaching, as an act of ministry, needs an appropriate physical space where both student preachers and the congregation can enter the spirit of celebrating the Word of God, not just engage in developing a set of skills. Most seminaries and schools of theology have facilities for video recording either in a chapel or in a preaching laboratory that resembles a worship space more than a classroom. A control room separate from the preaching space can allow the instructor to view the sermon and take notes without distracting the preacher. Even if student preaching is done before parish congregations and viewed in class on video, it is important to maintain an atmosphere of worship while viewing the recording. Since preaching is intended to elicit a faith response from believers, it is unfair to critique a sermon without including this integral aspect along with comments geared to improving skills.

Just as the preacher is encouraged to enter the spirit of ministry in presenting the sermon, it is important that the congregation made up of peers listen as believers more than as critics. It is nearly impossible to enter the spirit of worship if the congregation is taking notes on the "performance." As noted, if the instructor finds it helpful to take notes during the preaching, he or she may consider viewing the sermon from the video control room. Some instructors use this option so that they can enter comments and evaluations directly into a computer during the class.

In-Class Verbal Feedback from Peers

After the sermon is preached and heard in an atmosphere of worship, preacher, peers, and the instructor now shift mental gears to assess the sermon. Unless the group is experienced in offering feedback, it will be essential to agree on norms for the peer feedback process. All group members bring expectations to any process. Unless those expectations are voiced and negotiated, some will find the process frustrating, since the group is not offering them what they expect. Unfortunately, they may never have bothered to tell the group what they need or expect. The ultimate goal is for the preacher to become a good self-critic. But as a participant in the homiletics class, the preacher is asked to look at himself or herself through the eyes of others.

Norms for Feedback

1. Each member of the class is expected to contribute feedback even if another student has made the same observation. All preachers know the frustration of having to guess how the congregation has heard the message. Did they "get" my main idea? Did the examples speak to their faith lives? Does the word make a difference? Homiletics classes allow preachers to hear what each listener heard.

2. The instructor and peers criticize the sermon, not the preacher as a person. There is a difference between saying that some sections of a sermon are boring and saying that the preacher as a person is boring. The assessment process focuses on the art and craft of preaching, not on assessing the personality of the preacher.

3. Observations are supported with a specific example from the sermon when possible. Vague comments such as "I liked the sermon" or "At times my attention drifted" may be honest reactions, but they are not especially helpful in guiding the preacher's growth. Whenever possible, observations should be supported with a specific reference to the sermon.

4. Feedback should be balanced. To the extent possible, peers should offer feedback that mentions both the strengths of the sermon as well as areas for further growth.

Establishing a Healthy Critical Atmosphere

Organization strategists often employ brainstorming as a strategy for generating new ideas. A crucial element of brainstorming is that all members of a group know that it is safe to voice their ideas because others in the group are not allowed to comment on the merits of the statements. Group members can criticize an idea only after the brainstorming is finished. The strategy is obvious. If people begin verbally reacting to ideas, especially if the reaction is negative, others may be reluctant to speak up, and some good ideas may be buried. When peers are offering feedback to preachers, it is important for the preacher to listen quietly so that all in the class will feel that they will be heard.

There is an additional reason why preachers ought to listen to feedback without interrupting or commenting. In preaching, as in all communication, it is the listener who creates the meaning, not the preacher.[2] On Sunday morning a few parishioners might stop to ask the preacher questions for clarification, but most people walk away with what they have heard. It can be very instructive for student preachers to hear the meaning that their listeners have created—especially when that meaning is not the one intended by the preacher. After everyone in the class has commented, the preacher can be given the opportunity to comment on the feedback or ask questions of the listeners.

Directing the Feedback Process

In advanced courses where the participants have had experience with healthy group feedback, the instructor may simply open the floor for comments when the sermon concludes. When a group is new to the process, it is important that the instructor direct the process so that useful feedback emerges. As mentioned above, the feedback might focus on just one aspect of preaching: biblical interpretation, theological discernment, ethical and faith goals, or rhetorical construction.

The instructor may also begin the feedback process with an openended question intended to generate feedback on some aspect of preaching with which the student has been dealing. For example, the group might be asked to comment on whether the sermon used examples that would speak to the faith experience of the intended congregation. The preacher himself or herself might pose this opening question to hear the kind of comments that would most help with specific areas where he or she needs to grow. Note that these sample open-ended questions designed to generate feedback address the sermon itself, and not the preacher as a person:

—What was the central idea of this message as you heard it?
—Did any particular part of the sermon stand out for you? Why?
—Is there any part of the sermon you would eliminate or change? Why?
—How did the sermon allow the Scripture reading(s) to speak to the listeners?
—What is the one main suggestion you would offer for improving this sermon?

Written Assessment

Written feedback from peers has several advantages. If each student submits a written assessment, the preacher has a permanent record of the comments that can be consulted at a later time. Some students who are reluctant to speak openly in groups may be able to offer more honest and complete feedback on paper. On a very practical level, there may not be enough time in class for extensive verbal feedback.

Internet-based courseware such as *Blackboard* facilitates written feedback by allowing students to engage in threaded discussions as a way of offering sermon assessment. Students can offer comments directly to the preacher, and other students can comment on each other's observations. Some students who have English as a second language find these threaded discussions to be far less intimidating than speaking in class.

Private Review with the Instructor

Some homiletics professors conduct personal review sessions of video-recorded sermons with individual students. In many cases, it is the student who is able to name his or her strengths and areas for growth as the student observes the preaching through the objective eye of the camera. However, circumstances in the contemporary seminary or school of theology may make it unfeasible for professors to meet privately with each student to review each lab preaching. There may be too many students enrolled in classes to allow for individual work with the instructor. The full-time resident seminary student is becoming a rare phenomenon, making it difficult to schedule these one-on-one sessions even if the professor has the time. Some schools employ teaching assistants or visiting pastors to meet with preachers on an individual basis. This practice can introduce a completely new set of challenges if these outside resource persons are not qualified to provide professional assessment. Homiletics teachers may need to exercise great creativity in finding ways for students to have some type of experience where at least one other individual, if not the professor, helps them develop sound habits of assessing their preaching practice.

During the Sermon

For the first twenty years of teaching, I have listened to in-class preaching as a member of the "live" congregation. In the last few years I have found that I can listen more actively from the video control room because I am able to consult computer documentation on individual students without distracting them. Students submit a full preaching manuscript by e-mail one week before the sermon is to be preached in class. I make comments in a red-colored font and return the manuscript by e-mail. Students then submit a revised text by e-mail no later than the morning they are scheduled to preach. The original and revised manuscripts are therefore available on my computer so I can see how the student responded to my suggestions.

In addition to these preaching manuscripts, I have all previous assessments for each student available on the computer. A copy of that assessment form is attached later in this chapter. In particular, while the sermon is being preached I can monitor the specific areas for growth on which the student is working. At the conclusion of each preaching interview session, the student and instructor agree on a specific goal for the following sermon. As instructor, I have those goals available during the preaching class. I enter a few initial reactions on the assessment form as the student is preaching. After listening to the in-class feedback I may enter a few additional comments or questions for the interview.

After the Sermon

Before viewing the video with each student, I usually remind him or her of a particular insight or question raised during the in-class feedback session. Since the preachers are given an opportunity to react after hearing from all their peers, their reaction often becomes the focus of that pre-viewing issue. These initial comments are one way to focus viewing. We "pause" the video if either the instructor or the student wishes to make a comment—we never speak over the sermon. Pausing the video immediately after a vague or misleading statement, for example, can be a helpful way for the preacher to realize how a listener might create a meaning quite apart from the one intended.

While viewing the video with the student, I typically add more entries on the homily assessment form. However, I limit this typing in order to attend to the sermon. Students are comfortable with my computer entries because I assure them on our first meeting that they will receive a complete copy of everything that I write about their sermon. I keep no assessment notes that the student does not see.

One of the most common skills that students need to develop is the ability to find examples or concrete experiences that connect the world of the Scriptures with the lives of the believers. In their excellent document on the liturgical homily, the American Roman Catholic bishops call preaching a moment where the lives of the listeners are interpreted in the light of the Scriptures.[3] Student preachers typically have a deep faith experience behind or under their carefully crafted sermon texts, couched in safe theological and biblical abstractions. I have been repeatedly moved and inspired when these students talk about those experiences in our interview. Most agree that it would be a good idea to bring that material more explicitly into the actual preaching moment.

At the end of the review, I refine and complete my written comments on the assessment form and e-mail the document to the student. As mentioned, this written assessment always includes a particular goal that both the preacher and instructor will monitor during the following sermon. I check that written goal when I receive the first draft of the student's sermon manuscript.

The following two pages contain a sample sermon assessment form and a brief description of the criteria for assessment. It can be tempting to use a printed form as the primary means of assessment. We encourage instructors to also use face-to-face feedback within and outside of class, as well as written feedback from peers. Students receive a rating of 1 to 10 for each category. The large space is for written comments that describe the numerical rating.[4]

Feedback from the Congregation

This chapter has dealt with preaching feedback in the classroom setting. Any complete homiletics program needs to include the congregation. Student preachers have used the following form most frequently during their internship year serving in a parish. It differs significantly from the Preaching Assessment form, which is designed for use by an instructor or peers who can focus on particular preaching skills. The following form on pages 201 and 202, intended for the congregation, avoids terms more familiar to those who know the grammar of homiletics. The form also tends to center more on the response of the listener than on the skills of the preacher. The intent of the form is to help the preacher hear the meaning constructed in the faith lives of the listeners.

PREACHING ASSESSMENT

Rating   Preacher _____

	Rating	
Introduction		
So What?		
Organization and Central Idea		
Concrete		
Witness		
Scriptures		
Vocal Qualities		
Main Area for Improvement		
Miscellaneous Comments		

Overall Rating:

USING THE PREACHING ASSESSMENT

Each category on the Preaching Assessment form receives a rating from 1 (lowest) to 10. The larger space after the categories is for written comments.

Introduction		Does the introduction gain the interest of the congregation? Will listeners say, "This message has something to offer me"?
So What?		Does the sermon meet the realistic spiritual needs of the congregation? Does it make a difference? Has it left the people changed in some helpful way?
Organization and Central Idea		Is there one simple, clear, central idea? Are the various movements or areas of development arranged in a way that makes the sermon easy to follow?
Concrete		Are there enough examples and illustrations to help the congregation relate the message to life experience? Is the language too abstract? Is the sermon down to earth?
Witness		Is the preacher talking from personal faith experience? This witness can be explicit or implicit.
Scriptures		Is the message rooted in one or more of the readings from the particular liturgy being celebrated? Is the preacher merely explaining the reading, or proclaiming the message?
Vocal Qualities		Is the voice animated and lively? Does the preacher sound enthusiastic about the message? Comments here might refer to rate, pitch, variety, volume, projection, etc.
Main Area for Improvement		What is one main area where the preacher can improve this sermon? This comment can refer to a specific skill, element of content, organization, approach to Scripture, or any other issue that needs significant attention.
Miscellaneous Comments		The evaluator can add anything here that was not covered in earlier comments.

Feedback from the Pews

Preacher's Name _____   Your Name _____

The preacher has asked you to provide honest comments on the sermon. There are no correct or incorrect answers. Please respond to the questions according to the most recent sermon you heard from this preacher—not to his or her preaching in general.

I. Circle the word that best expresses your reaction to each item:

1. The message was very clear

    Strongly Agree   Agree   Uncertain   Disagree   Strongly Disagree

2. The sermon had one main idea

    Strongly Agree   Agree   Uncertain   Disagree   Strongly Disagree

3. The sermon was too long

    Strongly Agree   Agree   Uncertain   Disagree   Strongly Disagree

4. The sermon was too short

    Strongly Agree   Agree   Uncertain   Disagree   Strongly Disagree

5. The message helped me appreciate the Scripture reading(s)

    Strongly Agree   Agree   Uncertain   Disagree   Strongly Disagree

6. The preacher sounded interested in the message

    Strongly Agree   Agree   Uncertain   Disagree   Strongly Disagree

7. The message kept my interest from start to finish

    Strongly Agree   Agree   Uncertain   Disagree   Strongly Disagree

8. I will probably think more about this message

    Strongly Agree   Agree   Uncertain   Disagree   Strongly Disagree

9. The preacher seemed to understand my life

    Strongly Agree   Agree   Uncertain   Disagree   Strongly Disagree

10. The message had interesting examples

    Strongly Agree   Agree   Uncertain   Disagree   Strongly Disagree

II. Please complete the following sentences:

The main point of the sermon was . . .

The part of the sermon I most appreciated was . . .

I wish the preacher had said more about . . .

The sermon would have been better if . . .

Add any further comments you wish:

Using the Form

Preachers should not distribute this form before the worship service. If they do, people in the congregation will be filling it out during the sermon. Even if people do not fill out the form during the service, their assessment will likely enter the mind-set of evaluators. It has been more successful to introduce the form at the conclusion of the service.

Student preachers who distribute this form randomly after the service, asking people to mail it back, will typically see about a 20 percent return. Therefore, if preachers want to actually examine twenty-five responses they will need to distribute over a hundred blank forms. Students who have received the most successful return have asked members of the congregation to remain after the service to fill out the form. If the congregation understands that this extra effort on their part will help a student preacher's formation, most tend to be eager to engage in the process.

Parish Assessment Group

Aquinas Institute in St. Louis, Missouri, practices the *Partners in Preaching*[5] process, in which DMin students invite a group of parishioners to meet after the preaching to offer feedback on the sermon. The parishioners are given a printed form with a few brief, open-ended questions. Reuel Howe, author of the process, suggests these questions among others:

What did the preacher say to you?

What difference do you think the message will make in your life, and where did it touch you and how?

What advice do any of you have for preachers and their communication?[6]

The preacher turned on an audiotape recorder and left the room, so that the people would feel freer to speak to one another rather than to the preacher. This and many variations on the process can be used to help preachers hear what ultimately matters—does the Word feed God's people?

Preaching Evaluation Forms

Twenty-five years ago, Don M. Wardlaw and other homiletics teachers produced *Learning Preaching: Understanding and Participating in the*

Process.[7] That undertaking had the same purpose as this present book: to serve as a resource for homiletics teachers. An appendix to Wardlaw's work lists over twenty sermon critique forms used by various homiletics teachers who responded to his survey. A recent search (April 2008) of the Internet, using the search engine Google, produced 500,000 results when the term "sermon evaluation form" was entered. There are many sermon evaluation forms in use, both in the homiletics classroom and in our churches. The authors of this work chose not to provide a sampling of those forms. We encourage those who use this book to determine what they would like to measure and then choose or devise an instrument that will help them assess a student's strengths and areas for further growth.

NOTES

1. Alvin C. Rueter, *Making Good Preaching Better: A Step-by-Step Guide to Scripture-Based, People-Centered Preaching* (Collegeville, MN: Liturgical Press, 1997).

2. See J. Randall Nichols, "Communication," in *Concise Encyclopedia of Preaching*, ed. William H. Willimon and Richard Lischer (Louisville, KY: Westminster John Knox Press, 1995), 85.

3. The Bishops' Committee on Priestly Life and Ministry, National Conference of Catholic Bishops, *Fulfilled in Your Hearing: The Homily in the Sunday Assembly* (Washington, DC: United States Catholic Conference, 1982), n. 20.

4. All assessment forms are from Daniel E. Harris, *We Speak the Word of the Lord: A Practical Plan for More Effective Preaching* (Chicago: Acta Publications, 2001).

5. Reuel L. Howe, *Partners in Preaching; Clergy and Laity in Dialogue* (New York: Seabury Press, 1967).

6. Ibid., 113–24, passim.

7. Don M. Wardlaw, ed., *Learning Preaching: Understanding and Participating in the Process* (Lincoln, IL: The Lincoln Christian College and Seminary Press, 1989).

Preaching in the Curriculum

14

Designing the Introductory Course in Preaching

BARBARA K. LUNDBLAD

DECISIONS THAT WILL SHAPE
THE INTRODUCTORY PREACHING COURSE

"Good preaching can be taught and learned." That conviction, set out in the introductory chapter, has shaped all that follows. The capacities needed for good preaching have been laid before us like a banquet table, rich with possibilities. Those who teach and those who learn may look at this abundant table and not know where to begin. The capacities outlined in the previous chapter could fill three years of seminary work. We also know that won't be possible. Time is limited—for both faculty and students. Other courses in the curriculum demand attention. Some students will be coming to class while working full- or part-time. Several won't follow the catalog description of three sequential years of study, but will extend their studies over a longer period of time. Before we enter the classroom, decisions need to be made about how "good preaching can be taught and learned" in our particular location.

What Preaching Courses Are Required, If Any?

While almost every survey of congregations puts "good preaching" at the top of the list of desired ministerial qualities, preaching is seldom given adequate time in the seminary curriculum. Preaching requirements vary greatly from one seminary to another. In some cases there is no requirement at all. Some schools require one semester, while others require one course every year. One yearlong required course is recommended as a minimum for master of divinity students. An alternative is a one-semester introductory course for all students, plus a required elective chosen to meet particular needs or interests (e.g., Preaching and Pastoral Care, Preaching the Epistles, Preaching in the Black Church Tradition). Some seminaries offer a yearlong introductory course in worship and preaching to emphasize the organic connection between the two disciplines. In almost every seminary, learning to preach requires more time, rather than less. Simply put, the practice of preaching requires practice. Such practice includes preaching several sermons in class as well as in the seminary chapel, at fieldwork sites, and, for some students, during a parish internship.

When Should the Introductory Preaching Course Be Offered?

There are assets and drawbacks for each of the following options:

—First Year: Preaching classes are often community-building experiences, encouraging students to respect each other across differences, to pray together, to engage texts with body, mind, and soul. Thus, a preaching class is an important part of pastoral formation and fits well in the first year. In many seminaries, students do fieldwork in their second year, and it's helpful to have some preaching experience before beginning work in a congregation. If one semester of preaching is required, it can be scheduled for the second semester of the first year, after at least some foundational work in biblical studies and theology.

—Second Year: Placing the required course in the second year allows for more grounding in biblical studies and theology. While students may be less prepared for fieldwork, their parish assignment will give them the opportunity to preach in a congregation as well as in class.

If the second option is chosen, the first year of seminary can still provide important groundwork for preaching. Colleagues who teach Old or New Testament can be encouraged to assign a sermon as part of the exegesis process. Courses in speech and movement are very helpful for preaching and don't depend on biblical background. A one-credit course in dance or movement can help students become more embodied in their preaching. Encouraging students to get out in the community to listen to a variety of preachers can help them discern what "good preaching" sounds like. The first year of seminary may be the student's last chance to worship in different congregations before fieldwork and full-time pastoral ministry.

What Practices for Good Preaching Are Learned in Other Courses?

To maximize learning needed for good preaching, collaboration across the curriculum is essential. The initiative for such collaboration may indeed come from those who teach preaching. How can the exegetical methods learned in biblical courses relate more closely to preaching? How can introductory theology courses help students speak about theological concepts in down-to-earth terms? There are several different models for working together more closely across fields:

—team teaching the introductory preaching course, or at least parts of it, with a member of the biblical or theological faculty;

—offering the introductory preaching course in tandem with a biblical exegesis practicum; biblical and homiletics faculty members work with the same texts and respond to student sermons;

—encouraging theological and biblical faculty members to meet with a small preaching practicum group.

Preaching courses will be greatly enhanced by working with colleagues in other disciplines. This isn't a matter of "applying" what is learned in systematic theology or biblical studies to preaching. Preaching *is* doing theology; preaching *is* interpreting biblical texts. Other courses in the curriculum will also be greatly enhanced by working more closely with colleagues who teach preaching.

One semester or more required? First year or second? Teaching worship and preaching together? Decisions about these questions cannot be made by the homiletics faculty alone, but with other faculty colleagues and the administration. How these questions are answered will shape the design of the basic preaching course.

THE SHAPE OF THE INTRODUCTORY CLASS

It can be overwhelming to read back over the capacities outlined in Section 2 of this volume and realize you have only approximately twelve weeks to learn them all! While a yearlong course is desirable, the following broad outline assumes a one-semester introductory course common in many seminaries. Hopefully, students preparing for parish ministry will elect to take additional courses focused on such areas as preaching particular books of the Bible, topical preaching, preaching and social transformation, and so on. Everything cannot be accomplished in one introductory preaching course; however, there are basic skills that can be learned and practiced even in twelve short weeks.

Providing a Safe Environment to Foster Excellence in Preaching

Students bring many different gifts, fears, and experiences to their first preaching class. Some have never preached and are terrified, while others may have preached many times and feel confident, perhaps even set in their ways. Some come with rich backgrounds in other careers, including years of public speaking as teachers, actors, or lawyers. The class may include students who are Pentecostal, Episcopalian, Baptist, African Methodist Episcopal, Lutheran, Metropolitan Community Churches, Unitarian Universalist, and "uncertain." Even in a class where everyone is the same denomination there are wildly different theological perspectives in the room. While such differences affect discussion in other classes, these differences often feel more personalized and threatening in a preaching class. No longer are students speaking *about* the sources in Genesis or Paul's eschatology, they are speaking words that claim to be "the gospel" or "the Word of God," and distance is no longer possible. Part of the teacher's role is to help create a space for honoring differences, for giving and receiving criticism, for taking risks. This respectful environment needs to be fostered in every part of the class from the beginning, not only when giving feedback to sermons.

Mapping the Course

As noted earlier, the capacities described in Section 2 need not be learned in a certain order. Students will learn by reading classic and contemporary sermons, listening to lectures, watching tapes of living preachers, telling stories, working on texts in small groups, keeping a journal, reading Scripture aloud, walking the neighborhood, moving their bodies, preaching sermons, and responding to sermons. Because preaching is a specific practice, there are many resources available to guide students in learning this complex task. Will one text or several be required? Will you provide a course reader with selected chapters from many different books (with proper copyright permission, of course)? What Internet resources can be helpful? Before finalizing the course syllabus, it's important to ask questions such as the following:

—Are there readings by women as well as men?
—Will the voices of different cultures and traditions be heard? (This is important even if everyone in class is the same denomination and race.)
—Are theological perspectives from the worldwide, ecumenical church present?
—Are there readings that are grounded in our particular location, as well as those that help us see communities that are very different from our own?
—Do readings introduce us to the practice of preaching through the centuries?
—Are there readings that spark the imagination and encourage creativity? Any poets or storytellers, artists, or musicians on the list?

The course syllabus is not only a schedule of readings and assignments, but an introduction to resources and conversation partners for the life-long practice of preaching.

Practicing Preaching in Plenary Sessions and Practicum Groups

The introductory preaching class is time- and labor-intensive. The size of the class will vary greatly from one school to another. A required course might number over a hundred or less than twenty. Even with a smaller enrollment, it's impossible to allow ample time for presentations and preaching with only one weekly meeting. In most seminaries, the practice of preaching will be taught and learned in plenary sessions for the whole class and in smaller practicum groups. Both large and small group sessions include practicing.

What Practices Are Learned in the Plenary Session?

The plenary session is often a two-hour weekly meeting, though other options can be considered. Even though the group may be large, practicing is an important component. Breathing exercises and body work can start a class. A student leads opening prayer, practicing what it means to be grounded in her body, to speak clearly, or to expand his imagery for God. Short speaking experiences (e.g., telling a short story, describing a walk around the city block, reading a biblical text aloud) give opportunities to practice speaking in front of a group. Lectures can model a variety of ways to fully engage listeners. Students can pair up and talk to each other about their personal response to a biblical text. The plenary session itself can provide guidance about speaking to each other across differences with respect.

Understanding Where We Stand within the Larger Practice of Preaching

Before students begin to engage biblical texts or prepare sermons, it's important to acknowledge the perspectives on preaching that each one brings to the class. Each student's approach to preaching is shaped by theology, denomination, race and ethnicity, family background, class, and many other factors. Such perspectives will shape how students engage biblical texts, as well as their convictions about the purpose of a sermon. There are many ways to begin these discussions, guiding students in how to respond to differences with respect.

—View three or four videotaped sermons from different preachers. What does each sermon say about God, about Jesus Christ, about God's actions in the world, about the nature of human beings, about the work of the Holy Spirit?

—Read three or four different theological perspectives on preaching, including both historical and contemporary texts. Write a paper responding to the readings and ending with a description of your own theology of preaching.

—Exchange your "theology of preaching" paper with another student, then either online or in class respond to each other's papers with prompts such as:
  (1) What I appreciate most about your theology of preaching is . . .
  (2) I wondered what you meant by . . .
  (3) Here's where my theology differs from yours . . .

—Write one paragraph responding to each of the following:
  (1) In my denomination, preaching is defined as . . .
  (2) In my home congregation, people think preaching is . . .
  (3) At this time in my life, I think preaching is . . .

It's important to help students understand how such perspectives shape the way they think about preaching. Does preaching usually move toward an altar call or toward the Table? Does every sermon call for personal or social transformation? How is the "gospel" different from the Bible? Such questions will be asked again and again as students begin to preach, but it's important to ask them early in the semester, to encourage people to respect the differences within the class and to hone their own understanding of what preaching is.

Engaging the Biblical Text for Preaching

Hopefully, students have some background in biblical studies and exegesis as they enter the class; however, it's possible that students have very little understanding of the Bible or have learned an exegetical method that doesn't work well for preaching. The plenary session can be a time for everyone to experience one model together, working on the same text from first reading to crafting a sermon. In interpreting texts for preaching, the whole person is engaged—body, mind, and spirit. All the senses participate in responding to the text. One model might begin with some of the following experiences:

—Listen as one person reads the text aloud, then respond to it by writing without stopping for ten minutes—no censoring!
—Read the text together, moving around the room, responding to the text with your body. (It helps to have a classroom that doesn't have stationary chairs.)
—Read the text in pairs, then tell each other what the text means to you personally.

As a group, lift up questions about the text that need further clarification. Note odd details in the text that spark your curiosity. Share insights about this text from biblical courses, by recalling the larger context of the chapter or book, and so on. Help students discern what further work is needed to move toward deeper understanding of this text.

Before the next class, students should read the text in three different locations (e.g., a hospital waiting room, a Laundromat, a video arcade, a beauty shop), then jot down how they hear the text in that place. While this work is going on in plenary, students can begin to "exegete" their practicum group: How will the people in my small congregation hear the text? (Someone just had a baby, someone's mother is very ill, someone was hurt by last week's discussion, one person's theology seems very different from most in the class.)

After these initial engagements with the text, dig into the passage more deeply, recalling the questions and insights shared in class, as well as responses from reading on location. Small groups can be assigned specific parts of the interpretive task: work with the original language or interlinear text, setting of the text within the chapter and/or book, word studies of key words, analysis of the texture of the passage, historical background of the text, and so on. It's important to expose students to biblical interpretation from a variety of cultures and interpretive positions. As the process of moving from text to sermon moves on in the plenary session, students may also collaborate with others in their practicum group to engage the text for their first sermons.

Discerning the Sermon Theme or Focus

The choice of a clear focus is one of the most important and most difficult steps in the practice of preaching. The sermon theme considers not only exegesis of the biblical text but exegesis of a particular congregation. The theme, or focus, is the word that seems most urgent or needed or compelling at this particular time and place. Give students permission to omit several important insights about the biblical text. Help them see that many of their creative ideas need to be left behind or put in the ragbag, the compost pile, or computer file to be used another day. There are different ways of framing the sermon theme and several readings to help guide the process of discernment:

—Focus and function statements (Thomas G. Long, *The Witness of Preaching*, Westminster John Knox Press, 2005)
—Behavior purpose statement (see "Sermon Worksheet," in Frank Thomas, *They Like to Never Quit Praisin' God*, Pilgrim Press, 1997)
—One simple declarative sentence (Fred Craddock, *Preaching*, Abingdon Press, 1990)

Students can work in small groups within the plenary session to determine possible sermon themes for the text the class has been engaging together.

Deciding on the Sermon Form

Read two sermons, each with a different form, and analyze each sermon using questions such as the following:

1. How does the sermon begin, and how does the introduction lead into the sermon?
2. How is each paragraph connected to the next?
3. How does the sermon move?
4. How does the sermon end, and what does the ending say about the purpose of the sermon?

Help students understand the organic connection between form and content. Some basic background in rhetoric provides insights into the relationship between sermon purpose and sermon form. Reading a selection of historical and contemporary sermons can help students see how rhetorical strategies are used for different purposes. What do you hope for listeners at the end of the sermon? Will you build to a celebration or end with a question? What connectors, such as repeated refrains or the reappearance of a central image, will help people move with the preacher?

Working with the same text that has been the focus of the plenary thus far, several insights are now available to the class:

—multiple hearings of the text (in class, in the streets, with your body);
—imagined congregational responses to the text;
—deep communal study of the text;
—decision about sermon theme or focus.

Using these materials, offer one or two models for how a sermon on the chosen theme might take shape. While there are many possible sermon models, it is best not to overwhelm students with too many in the introductory course.

Practicing the Oral Art of Preaching

Moving from written words to spoken words is an enormous transition for many students, since most of their academic work has focused on writing papers. Hopefully the class has been structured to give students several chances to practice speaking before they preach their first sermon. Some teachers ask students to preach their first sermon without any notes, or using only one note card. This option clearly emphasizes the oral nature of preaching, but students may find it more difficult to be intentional about movement and organization. Others assign a written sermon before students preach in class. While this option seems to emphasize writing rather than speaking, it offers the chance to give feedback on the sermon, including attention to oral language, before the student stands up to preach. Whatever method is chosen, it's essential for students to practice preparing to *speak* rather than write. If a written text is used, offer guidelines for crafting a sermon "script" rather than a manuscript:

— Talk aloud while you write; avoid big words and theological jargon; create language that is compelling and colorful, inviting rather than scolding (see Robert Jacks, *Just Say the Word,* for example).
— Type in large print, double-spaced, with margins wide enough for written cues.
— Write only on the top half of the page, to avoid looking too far down the page.
— Leave spaces to indicate pauses or transitions; circle key words; don't break a sentence at the page turn.

Encourage students to create a script that leaps off the page into speech, knowing listeners have only one chance to hear the words as they fly by.

Becoming Part of the "Company of Preachers"

The introductory course is often front-loaded with skills needed to prepare and preach sermons in the practicum groups. Part of this preparation has already involved attention to theology and biblical studies. Hopefully, the readings have also introduced students to historical sermons as well as those of living preachers. As the semester moves on, it will be important to devote some time to the history of preaching. Chapter 10 has laid out many possibilities for helping students see themselves as part of a great cloud of witnesses. Engaging lectures and assigned readings can give students an overview of preaching since New Testament times. Students might choose a preacher from the past, perhaps from their own tradition, and write a reflection paper on that preacher. If the plenary isn't too large, students could speak in the voice of their chosen preacher in class: an early church father, a Reformation pastor, a slave preacher.

The larger "company" also includes preaching beyond the seminary community. If students are working in a parish, at least one sermon in the course can be prepared for that congregation. While it's important for students to preach to the actual living people in their practicum groups, it's equally important to think about preaching within communities beyond the seminary. Several resources are available to help students begin to exegete congregations as well as biblical texts (see chapter 5). Introduce students to some of the resources from the areas of congregational studies and the sociology of religion, as well as excellent books written by those who teach preaching. Such texts can help students pay attention to cultural and racial diversity within congregations, differences in theo-logical perspectives, particular needs of various age groups, resistance to change, and the like.

For students to see themselves as part of the company of preachers means knowing that this class is not the end. The practice of preaching will continue to be learned in a lifetime of preaching, in congregations large and small. Throughout the semester, and especially toward the end, present ways for students to be intentional about lifelong learning. Give them clues for organizing resources, stories, and creative ideas in computer files or manila folders. Help them evaluate Internet preaching sites without wading through the thousands that pop up when you hit "preaching." Encourage students to develop concrete plans to give adequate time for sermon preparation in the parish. Though this will make little sense until they are in the congregation, the seed can be planted now: good preaching takes time. Ordering your days to make room for adequate preparation does not deny the work of the Holy Spirit.

Modeling a Sense of Excitement and Urgency about the Practice of Preaching

"Every event of preaching involves multiple actions and skills for which preachers can be educated and trained." That conviction, set out in the introductory chapters, has shaped this book. "Good preaching can be taught and learned," but it is also a mystery that cannot be fully explained. The preaching class respects this mystery even as skills are taught and learned. Each week of the course pays attention to this indecipherable aspect of preaching: time for silence and for prayer, time to speak to one another about what a text means to you personally, time to keep a daily journal. There must be room in the preaching class for inspiration and excitement, for the intangible offerings of creativity and recognition of a deep urgency to proclaim the Word of God. Perhaps we can borrow words from the poet Mary Oliver to speak of this. Hopefully, we can hear the word "sermon" where she speaks of poems: "For [sermons] are not words after all, but fire for the cold, ropes let down to the lost, something as necessary as bread in the pockets of the hungry."[1]

What Is Best Learned in Small Practicum Groups?

The practicum group is the locus for the most intensive practicing. In most cases these small groups meet weekly alongside the plenary sessions. Practicum groups must be small enough to allow students to preach at least twice, preferably more. In some cases the instructor meets with each small group, but with large classes this is almost impossible. Small-group leaders must be carefully chosen and trained to work with student preachers. Though it is unlikely that group leaders can participate in every plenary session, it's essential for leaders to be well acquainted with course goals and the ongoing work of the larger class.

Practicum Group as Learning Community and Congregation

Work in the practicum groups can begin before the first sermons are preached. The small group may be the best place for students to discuss their theologies of preaching and learn to honor differences among them. Students can practice communal interpretation of texts, receive feedback on sermon theme or focus, or practice a possible sermon introduction. Community building is an important part of the practicum because this group also functions as the listening congregation. In order to exegete this small congregation, it's helpful for students to talk with each other about "who I am besides being a seminarian."

Planning for Preaching in the Practicum Group

Because of time limitations, students will probably preach before even the basics have been covered in the plenary sessions. This will be very frustrating to some, but also a very helpful way to learn. Students might draw a text at random in the first meeting and preach a two-minute sermon on that text. While this is a very scary experience, it emphasizes preaching-as-practice, something done on the ground. Others will want to spend more time in getting to know the members of this small congregation before preaching. Even in a course that is only twelve weeks long, there are several options for laying out a schedule for preaching over the semester:

—Begin by preaching a sermon without notes or with only one note card, the second sermon using a manuscript, and the third using either one.

—Begin with a written sermon to receive evaluation and suggestions from the professor before preaching in the practicum group.

—Preach your first sermon twice, with specific goals for improvement based on feedback from the group and from watching a videotape.

—Follow appointed lectionary readings: one sermon on an Old Testament text, another on the appointed Gospel, and a third to be preached in a congregational setting.

—Preach three sermons: Gospel, Epistle, and Old Testament texts; or move from five-minute to ten-minute to twenty-minute sermon over the course of the semester.

Many find it helpful to limit the first sermon to five minutes so that students can maintain a clear focus and work on beginnings, endings, and transitions. Students gain a great deal from receiving feedback on a sermon draft before they preach. Even if the first sermon is to be preached without notes, students can speak their sermon to one or two others before preaching to the practicum group. Such feedback allows the student to make changes to improve a sermon before getting up to preach. It can be frustrating to preach a sermon, receive feedback, then move on to a different text and sermon without a chance to improve the original.

The Preaching Moment

If possible, schedule preaching in a worshipful setting. The school chapel or a smaller devotional chapel may be available, but even a classroom can be set up to enhance the sense of preaching as part of worship. When the introductory class includes preaching and worship together, students are encouraged to choose a hymn, litany, or other liturgical element that relates to their sermon. Though traditions vary within the class, encourage students to volunteer to lead the congregation in prayer for the preachers and the listeners. If sermons are

videotaped, make the taping as nonintrusive as possible. (If possible, a
work-study student might be paid to do the taping so this task doesn't
fall to the teacher or a member of the practicum group.) During the
sermon people in the congregation listen rather than take notes. If
written comments are part of the evaluation, leave these until later.
When two or more students are preaching in the same session, leave
a space for silence after each sermon. Then leave the discussion until
after all have preached.

Responding to Sermons

Responses to student preaching may be oral, written, or both. Oral feedback allows everyone in the group to learn from each other. Over the
semester listeners can build their skills in discerning theological perspectives, different approaches to biblical texts, sermon organization and
movement, effective introductions, distracting or effective body language, and so on. What are the most helpful ways to respond orally to
the student preacher? Whatever method is chosen, it is essential to establish a safe environment for the preacher and for listeners. Even for students with substantial experience, preaching to seminary classmates and
teachers is often very threatening. Ground rules need to be established
from the beginning to diminish threats and encourage respect. Suggestions such as the following may be helpful:

—Begin with affirmation rather than condemnation.
—Encourage respondents to claim their own comments: "What I
    remembered most was . . . ," or "I got lost when you talked
    about. . . ."
—Focus on what would make this sermon stronger, rather than on
    why this sermon was bad.
—Be as specific as possible, rather than making sweeping general-
    izations.
—Draw on collective understandings gained from plenary sessions
    in assessing work with Scripture, theological perspectives, unity,
    and organization.

If the group is responding to more than one preacher, it's helpful to
appoint a timekeeper so no one is shortchanged.

Written responses give students something tangible to refer to in
preparing goals for their next sermon. Such responses might be a set

form that remains the same throughout the semester, so students learn to recognize elements of a good sermon. Forms can also be designed to focus on specific aspects of preaching that may differ over the course of the semester: effective beginnings and endings, working with epistle texts, preaching without notes, for example (see chapter 15, especially pp. 199–200). There are other options as well: responding to three questions on a note card, writing online to the preacher within two days of hearing the sermon, making oral comments in class and filling in a written form to be returned the following week.

Videotaping is also a form of assessment and can be used in several different ways. Taping is especially effective in helping students hear their own voices and see what their bodies are doing. Though watching a tape can be discouraging, it's the best way to detect distracting gestures, observe rigid posture, hear vocal problems, and, in general, to see ourselves as others see us. Students may watch the tape on their own and write specific comments including goals for their next sermon. Teacher and student can watch the tape together, stopping to comment on body language, voice, or organizational problems. Though time-consuming, such conversations can be especially fruitful to encourage the preacher toward new practices.

If students preach from a written text, responses can be made on the manuscript itself. Computer programs allow instructors to make specific comments within the body of a sermon text submitted online. Responses to written sermons can focus on oral language, theological jargon, movement and transitions, ideas that aren't related to the central theme or focus, and the like.

Coordination between Plenary and Practicum

It will probably be impossible to keep plenary and practicum sessions running on complementary tracks. A plenary devoted to the history of preaching won't coincide with historical sermons preached in the small group. Yet the two types of learning situations are complementary. Students can be encouraged to review their first sermons when the plenary focuses on sermon movement or beginnings and endings. Encourage students to listen to an ongoing conversation between the two groups. *What great ideas did I have to set aside to keep my focus clear for this sermon? How did the preaching of Julia Foote inspire me to be more courageous? After people in our practicum group preached, I saw how hard endings are—how can we do better next time?*

Even as preaching courses are not simply places to *apply* other disciplines in the curriculum, the practicum is not the place to apply what is learned in the plenary. The relationship between the two sessions is much more dynamic, a lively conversation in which learning in each one enhances the other.

NOTE

1. Mary Oliver, *A Poetry Handbook* (San Diego: Harcourt Brace Jovanovich, 1994), 122.

15

Finding Support from School, Denomination, and Academy

GREGORY HEILLE

The authors in this book have distinguished a number of integral components to both the practice of Christian preaching and the practice or ministry of teaching preaching. A discussion of homiletics education would be incomplete without consideration also of communities of practice. Just as Christian preaching is constitutively associated with interrelated communities in local congregation, larger denomination, and society, so too preaching is taught in constitutive contexts of school, denomination, and academy. We encourage teachers of preaching to pioneer in animating these communities of practice for teaching preaching.

CROSS-CURRICULAR PRACTICES IN OUR SCHOOLS

Preaching today is taught in freestanding and university-related seminaries and graduate schools of theology and ministry, as well as in non-degree ministerial formation programs. Preaching offerings in Master of Divinity programs range from one three-credit course to eight or nine credits distributed over a number of courses throughout the curriculum. While loyalties in some schools are more often to individual departments or to the university than to formation for ministry, faculties in other schools are exploring ways to support one another in their desire for more integrated approaches to pastoral preparation—with either preaching or theological reflection being named as an integrative discipline for the entire ministerial curriculum. When asked about desired interdisciplinary avenues for collaboration, teachers of preaching name virtually every discipline of the curriculum, starting with Scripture and worship, stressing a need for closer alliances with systematic theology, and mentioning also church history, moral theology, pastoral theology, and field education. The point is that all departments can work together to support educational formation for the practice of preaching. This interdisciplinary collaboration will be approached variously in different schools, and can include some team teaching of cross-disciplinary courses and will include many examples of syllabi strategically designed to coordinate content and assignments between disciplines, to take advantage of opportunities in the curriculum for preparing students for the preaching ministry.

For example, one community of practice, Aquinas Institute of Theology in St. Louis, has made preaching education a priority in its mission—offering a Doctor of Ministry in Preaching, a Master of Arts in Pastoral Ministry in Preaching, and a summer Preaching Institute. Faculty and students have committed themselves to five cross-curricular practices in every discipline and in every course: (1) close reading of texts, (2) excellence in written and oral communication, (3) analysis of social context, (4) theological reflection, and (5) collaboration. Additionally, in the fuller experience of ministerial formation, students and faculty commit themselves to such cocurricular practices as common liturgical prayer and preaching, shared meals, friendship among colleagues, and intentional spiritual formation. All these cross-curricular and cocurricular practices support the common project of preparation for the ministry of the Word.

A theological grounding for such a common project can be found in the tradition of first-order and second-order theology (*theologia prima* and *theologia secunda*). In the Hale Memorial Lectures of Seabury-Western Theological Seminary in 1981, Benedictine liturgist Aidan Kavanagh made a claim "that a liturgical act is the act of primary theology par excellence, the act from which other acts of secondary theology take their rise within that life of right worship we call the worshipping assembly, the community of faith, the Church."[1] How can preachers be freed to see systematic and biblical and liturgical second-order theology in its diaconal relationship of service to the first-order pastoral exigencies of pulpit, worship, and world—and how might this be reflected in cross-disciplinary collaboration in the ministerial curriculum?

This question challenges the traditional division of seminary biblical studies, systematic theology, liturgics, homiletics, pastoral studies, and field education into separate "academic" and "pastoral" disciplines, even as it opens new possibilities for interdisciplinary pedagogical practices—the goal being a preaching that is theologically, biblically, pastorally, and culturally relevant to our times.

The *First Naiveté–Critical Enquiry–Second Naiveté* hermeneutical process of Paul Ricoeur suggests one interdisciplinary pedagogical approach. In Ricoeur's First Naiveté, the student takes the posture of looking at the world as a child does. Personal experience is the first horizon as the reader assumes the worldview of the author and notes first impressions of the text. Then, in Critical Enquiry, the reader proceeds to the second horizon of interpretation, digging below the surface and studying scholarly interpretations of the text. Ultimately, in Ricoeur's third horizon, Second Naiveté, the reader appropriates or reappropriates the text, proclaiming it anew on behalf of his or her Wisdom Community.[2]

Mary Margaret Pazdan, O.P., Professor of Biblical Studies at Aquinas Institute of Theology, distills this approach in an interdisciplinary *Contemplo–Studeo–Praedico* hermeneutical process for interpreting Scripture for preaching. This dynamic hermeneutic is in tandem with the ecclesial core practices of prayer, study, community, and ministry of the Word, as well as with the *Poetics* of Aristotle and Ricoeur's hermeneutic.

Contemplo (I contemplate) extends the First Naiveté of Ricoeur, while drawing on the deep mystical tradition of the church. In its approach to scriptural texts for preaching, it includes many ways of praying that recognize reflection on relationships with God, self, others, and cosmos and with body, mind, and spirit. One way of praying with the scriptural text for preaching is the Benedictine practice of *lectio divina,* or Holy Reading.[3] In its particularly Christian context, *Contemplo* fuses the horizon of knower and known, because it does not ascribe to the Aristotelian definition of *theoreo,* i.e., to observe from a detached point that can separate the knower from what is known.

Studeo (I study) shapes Ricoeur's Critical Enquiry process. It is a serious inquiry about the worlds of the text, using diverse interpretive procedures and employing commentaries, journal articles, and Web resources. It corresponds to the Aristotelian *poieo,* to bring to birth or create understanding (of a text).

Praedico (I preach/proclaim) is one expression of Ricoeur's Second Naiveté. What is essential here is to proclaim anew what is experienced and learned from the First Naiveté and Critical Enquiry. The individual and community declare a claim, a wager, a commitment to the new discovery. It is a way of witnessing to the truth. *Praedico* corresponds to Aristotelian *prasso*, i.e., I practice (act repeatedly) the understanding to achieve the goal.

The following outline exemplifies a distillation of the *Contemplo–Studeo–Praedico* hermeneutical constellation of practices for use in Bible and preaching classrooms.[4]

I. *Contemplo*. I contemplate. [cf. *theoreo*. I observe.]

Reflect on relationships with God, others, and cosmos and self with body, mind, and spirit:

—Recognizing blessings to articulate gratitude and praise
—Recognizing concerns to articulate anxiety and stress
—Recognizing blessings and concerns in ecclesial and political arenas
—Recognizing blessings and concerns of liturgical and yearly cycles
—Creating a few images with particular colors and phrases to express discoveries

Let lectionary texts wash over body, mind, and spirit:

—Reading them aloud (chanting, singing, moving with images, phrases, symbols)
—Reading them silently

Be still and know that I am God! (Ps. 46):

—Beg for the Spirit's breath, energy, and insight.
—Listen for a connection: word, image, and symbol.

II. *Studeo*. I study. [cf. *poieo*. I create.]

—Gather materials to create new understanding: read widely.
—Establish context within a biblical book.
—Attend to structure of the book and its literary genre(s).
—Choose a biblical commentary (or two). Select a preacher's commentary, including Web reflections.

—What new insights broaden and deepen personal contemplation?
—What new insights relate to personal interpretation of the community, liturgical season, situations in the church and world?

III. *Praedico.* I preach. [cf. *prasso.* I practice.]

—Appropriating contemplation and study anew
—Moving from personal/community appropriation to specific preaching contexts

Student preachers in this process are freed from turning willy-nilly to biblical commentaries. Rather, they turn first to the text itself, engaging it contemplatively through a practice such as *lectio divina.* Contemplative engagement between text and student, each on their own authority, in turn suggests questions or intuitive insights to be taken to Critical Enquiry through biblical study. Scholarly commentaries then can be selected according to worlds of the text as suggested through contemplation. Having thus appropriated the text first through prayer and then through study, the preacher at last is ready to consider a message, strategy, and form for preaching.

Whether in the biblical studies or the homiletics classroom, students can learn both Bible and preaching through pedagogical applications of this process. In Bible classes, students can be asked to write a homily; in preaching classes, students can be asked to identify and employ online and print resources for studying the worlds of the text. The following journal assignment asks students to document their engagement in the *Contemplo–Studeo–Praedico* hermeneutical process:

> Prepare to preach for five to seven minutes, focusing your preparation on one of the lectionary texts for one of the upcoming two Sundays. Prior to preaching in class, submit a written journal of your preparation process, with entries describing each step of your *Contemplo–Studeo–Praedico* hermeneutical process of moving from scriptural text to preaching. Demonstrate engagement of the text through *lectio divina,* your study of at least two different hermeneutical approaches to the text, with sources, and your preaching strategy, expressed in terms of your intended homiletic focus, function, and form.

This *Contemplo–Studeo–Praedico* hermeneutical process is one example of the kind of interdisciplinary collaboration for teaching the practices of preaching that was called for by the authors of a 1998 denominational study demonstrating that only 27 percent of the Roman Catholic Sunday preachers sampled appeared to engage in sound exegetical preparation.[5] This study made some basic recommendations for collaboration in curriculum:

The curriculum in biblical studies. Preachers need to learn how to bring their exegesis of the biblical texts into dialogue with the reality of the congregation. Courses should help students develop skills for moving between the biblical situation and the contemporary world. Students appreciate what they learn in biblical courses, but not all are convinced that they themselves can interpret a text well enough on their own. Our study suggests that neither courses in biblical studies nor courses in preaching help the students develop an effective method for moving from text to homily. While they develop an exegetical method, they do not always develop a technique necessary to communicate in preaching what they have learned about the text.[6]

The curriculum in preaching. Included in the evaluation of the homily should be a critique on how well the homily flowed from the Scriptures and whether it reflected use of sound exegesis in the preparation. Homileticians should require students to describe their exegetical techniques.[7]

In a pursuit of these recommendations, twenty-seven senior and junior teachers of Catholic biblical studies and homiletics gathered twice in St. Louis during the 2003–2004 academic year for a problem-based inquiry into interdisciplinary approaches for teaching Bible and preaching.[8] In an exercise in syllabus design, the teachers sketched out collaborative syllabi to exemplify the formational, hermeneutical, pedagogical, and transformational priorities of the group. Two of these interdisciplinary syllabi in the making follow here.

Contemplo–Studeo–Praedico

This is a course in biblical interpretation for preaching, following a prerequisite introductory course in biblical method.[9]

Purposes: to develop a habitus of interpreting life through the Scriptures; to be able to use contemporary biblical methods for preaching.

Benefits: development of a biblical spirituality that leads to a passionate proclamation of the gospel; growth in facility for uncovering, appreciating, and engaging the multiplicity of meanings within a text; engagement in ongoing conversation between text and congregation.

Goal: to learn a *Contemplo–Studeo–Praedico* hermeneutical process for preaching.

Objectives: Contemplo: prayerful engagement with the text using methods such as individual or group *lectio divina. Studeo:* critical inquiry by which students learn to appropriately engage a variety of biblical methods, employ skills of theological reflection for preaching, and do analysis of social location. *Praedico:* articulation of a focused gospel message in an appropriate form for achieving the purpose intended.

Theory: adult learning, experiential/active learning, collaborative learning (preaching and evaluation involving peers), using some lecture, preaching practicum, and perhaps problem-based learning.

Content: Contemplo: methods of *lectio divina* with theory in depth. *Studeo:* review of biblical methods learned previously in introductory course; introduction to key user-friendly resources that appropriate biblical methods for preaching; uncovering and examining the theological presuppositions of the student/preacher and of the congregation; a process for negotiating and integrating the theological pluralism of speaker, message, and audience; methods for doing social analysis; the question of interpretive context: liturgical rites, seasons, and events. *Praedico:* help students arrive at a message that is biblically responsible, theologically appropriate, and pastorally relevant; familiarize students with a repertoire of rhetorical forms for preaching; familiarize students with various functions of preaching, e.g., evangelization, catechetical, liturgical, prophetic, pastoral.

Alive and Prophetic

This interdisciplinary course emphasizes social transformation.[10]

Purposes: to recognize that preaching and interpretation always effect social transformation for better or for worse—to identify the values driving social transformation; to acknowledge that the scale of social transformation is very small most days—not sweeping change, but rather a word, a conversation, a simple action or encounter; to realize that we can choose to be subjects rather than objects in preaching and social transformation; in the Catholic context, to make *Fulfilled in Your Hearing* alive and prophetic; to understand that preaching either colludes with or breaks inequality in society.

Benefits: an understanding of preaching as a creative act; ability to conceptualize social transformation in small ways; beginning discovery of one's own sounding (voice and depth) for preaching, involving critical thinking processes.

Goals: to form wisdom community—this will be especially useful in the lab portion of the course: deeper, better preaching critique will come out of relationships that have a high level of trust; be ethical and intentional about choices in preaching; articulate assumptions about social transformation, the Bible, and students' own social locations; concretely discuss inequality.

Objectives: to articulate social location and its relationship to interpreting Scripture and to preaching, including reflection on the student's social location in relationship to others and her/his point of insertion; to explore and encounter an identity group not one's own; to begin to find one's own prophetic voice.

COURSE CONTENT AND TEACHING STRATEGIES

Prior to the Course

Discern and include resources that deal narratively with social transformation, such as Jonathon Kozol's *Ordinary Resurrections* and Heidi Neumark's *Breathing Space;* find and assign texts that value diversity in the area of homiletics, such as work by André Resner and Christine Smith; also use texts that focus on social location and social interpretation when teaching biblical hermeneutics, such as *Return to Babel: Global Perspectives on the Bible*, edited by John R. Levison and Priscilla Pope-Levison, or *Then the Whisper Put on Flesh: New Testament Ethics in an African American Context*, by Brian K. Blount; arrange for local ministers and preachers to come as collaborators in teaching and in living the connection between preaching and social transformation.

Beginning the Course

Begin the class with a hermeneutical self-inventory with regard to issues pertinent to them and their vocations; move to individual and group goal-setting for the course; begin exploration of homiletics by theologically establishing that social transformation is critical to preaching and that to engage in social transformation is to be alive and prophetic.

Throughout the Course

Arrange for people from the field to preach and share experiences; maintain an environment that invites participation and deepens level of communication; listen to the students, inviting them to listen to themselves, to one another, and to voices around them.

Content Areas

History: Acknowledge the church's history of both collusion with injustice and action on behalf of denouncing injustice. *Social Analysis*—In order to avoid the paralysis of analysis, teach and practice the analytical process of see, discern, act, evaluate, celebrate. *Creativity and Imagination*: Unlock students' creativity and imagination through exercises that allow students to listen to their own voices from their places of transformation, such as the following. Word bowl: Fill a bowl with small slips of paper, each with a noun or a verb written on it, and at the beginning of class pull out three words and have the class write for ten minutes. Three letters: Pick three letters at random and ask each student to devise a slogan using the letters. Photographs: Select a photo and ask one person to give the individual a first name, then ask another for a last name, and then have the class write about the person. Poetry: Read a random line of poetry to the class, and ask them to write. *Biblical Interpretive Methods*: Review modes of biblical interpretation according to the worlds behind, in, and in front of the text—working in collaboration with members of the Biblical Studies faculty. *Homiletic Form:* Demonstrate various kinds of homiletic form, as discussed in the homiletic literature, and enable students to integrate various approaches in a way that leaves them resourced but free to develop their own forms and style. *Preaching Lab:* The environment of acceptance and critical reflection will enrich the peer and instructor evaluation of student preaching.

At the End of the Course

Do another hermeneutic self-inventory and invite conversation about areas of growth and areas of challenge for the future.

DENOMINATIONAL PRACTICES IN SUPPORT OF PREACHING

We certainly hope that denominations will support their teachers of preaching by working with them to promote the practice of preaching. The Catholic Association of Teachers of Homiletics (CATH) is one example of a forum for mutual scholarship and support that can lead to the professional development of teachers of preaching within a denomination. CATH works to underscore the significance of preaching as a means of proclaiming the good news, serves as a resource to bishops in their responsibility for the continuing formation of priests respective to their duty to preach, develops programs in homiletics for the preparation of ordained and nonordained ministers, and functions as a unified movement toward the development of advanced degree courses in homiletics within Catholic theological schools.

In 1992, the "CATH Report on Homiletics Curriculum and Preaching Professor Certification" called for integrated approaches to curriculum design, discussion about the integrative role of worship in seminary curricula, and emphasis on preaching supervision in field placement. Additionally, homiletics was put forward as an integrating factor for seminary curricula:

> CATH proposes that seminaries and theological schools use homiletics as an integrating factor in the curriculum. . . . Students ought to be helped to learn scripture, theology, and other elements of the curriculum not as ends in themselves, but as means to bring their faith to others in the Church. In this sense, preaching is not only a necessary aptitude for successful ministry, but is a primary reason for doing theology at all. For this reason some seminaries have found in preaching a useful focus for integrating the study of theology and the practice of ministry.[11]

In 2002, working from a bishops' decree that "homiletics should occupy a prominent place in the core curriculum and be integrated into the entire course of studies,"[12] CATH delineated a list of preaching competencies, as well as pedagogical strategies and professional competencies for teaching preaching.[13] This denominational organization of homiletics professors once again proposed that in "a healthy homiletics program, . . . the overall curriculum recognizes preaching as an important, integrative discipline"[14] and spelled out this proposal in several pedagogical strategies:

Some schools understand the preparation of preachers to be a primary function of the institution. This vision may be prompted by the school's perception of its mission, or it may be a personal commitment of individual administrators. In either case, *commitment at the administrative level* can lead to the initiation and encouragement of many of the other practices described below.

At the level of the graduate faculty, various strategies may be employed to facilitate homiletic integration, including *team teaching* (e.g., "Preaching from the Hebrew Scriptures"), *coordination of courses* (e.g., sacramental theology and sacramental preaching), *and interdisciplinary assignments* (e.g., a homily rather than a research paper in a Christology course).

Integration of theological courses through preaching can also be the result of *curriculum design*. Classes can be sequenced in a way that clarifies the relationships between other theological studies and preaching (e.g., offering introductory courses in scripture and theology before introduction to homiletics). Some schools have *integrating projects* in the final year or throughout the courses in which preaching can play an important role.

Worship itself helps students to see the relationships among their courses. In many schools *models of preaching by the faculty* within the seminary community or outside it demonstrate for students the relationship between the professor's scholarly work and the preaching task of ministry.

Finally, the *students' preaching* before the seminary community and in the context of field education shows their ability to bring together what they have learned through their theological education. Within the seminary the entire faculty can participate in feedback processes to help students use their theological learning in their homilies. Field education supervisors should be trained to help students with their parish homilies in content as well as in delivery.[15]

In addition to supporting teachers of preaching and outlining curricular and pedagogical goals for preaching education, denominations can set strategic goals for promoting the practice of preaching throughout the denomination. For example, since 1989 the Catholic Coalition on Preaching, now comprising twenty-one member organizations, has recognized the primary importance of preaching in its denomination and has sought to promote and energize quality preaching in the United States.[16] The goals of the coalition are collaborative in nature:

—To research the problems and corresponding needs in preaching today and provide resources in this major ministry

—To sponsor workshops and programs for the shaping of effective preaching

—To help to create supportive and motivating networks of preaching throughout the local churches

—To support the United States Conference of Catholic Bishops in their efforts to create a national consciousness about the primary importance of the preaching ministry

—To influence seminaries and theological schools to intensify their focus on preaching in the formation of their candidates for ministry

—To address the needs, problems, and possibilities related to the empowerment of Sunday preaching on the local level

—To suggest ways to involve hearers of the Word in appreciating, evaluating, and developing preaching

In response to a charge from its denomination's bishops, the Coalition proposed a set of strategic goals for continuing implementation of the denominational document *Fulfilled in Your Hearing*.[17] These goals, written in 2000, detail a broad denominational vision for collaborating locally, institutionally, and nationally to promote the kinds of practices that in turn will support the practice of preaching:[18]

Parishes and Local Ministries

—Invite parishioners to participate with preachers in the ministry of the Word of the local congregation—through Scripture study, faith reflection, and involvement with preaching preparation and evaluation.

—Use the three-year lectionary cycle and the liturgical year to engage the community in living a robust faith that does not place undue emphasis on one aspect of the mystery of faith over another.

—Address the necessity of providing competent preachers to meet the diverse needs of the community, and provide training and current exegetical, liturgical, and preaching resources to assist readers and preachers in their ministry.

—Coordinate preaching with other parish ministries, including music, environment, catechesis, pastoral care, action for justice, and the weekly bulletin.

—Give priority to the ministry of the Word in role descriptions and working relationships of priests, deacons, and pastoral ministers, and provide adequate time for preaching preparation.

Dioceses and Religious Institutes

—Take every opportunity to celebrate excellent preaching and recognize preachers at diocesan and regional gatherings, especially in the celebration of Morning and Evening Prayer and the Eucharist.
—Encourage and support diocesan and regional opportunities for preachers to engage communally in Scripture study, theological reflection, and preaching formation.
—Articulate standards and competencies for the initial and continuing formation and evaluation of preaching.
—Offer opportunities and resources for language and cultural study to preachers called to serve in the culturally diverse context of today's church.
—Motivate preachers for continuing education through workshops, sabbatical study, conferences, and advanced degree programs in preaching.

Training Centers for Ministry and Preaching

—Nurture spiritual formation and growth in virtue, and recommend these habits for ministerial life.
—Prepare curricula for the training of preachers, and employ highly qualified teachers of preaching, prepared for this ministry when possible by doctoral study in homiletics.
—Make preaching the integrating discipline of priestly and diaconal formation. (see *Program for Priestly Formation*, 4th ed., chap. 3, #377; *Directory for the Ministry and Life of Permanent Deacons*, chap. 2, #25.)
—Foster theological formation of candidates for presbyterial, diaconal, and ecclesial lay ministry—especially when preparing diaconal and ecclesial lay ministers to lead and preach at Sunday celebrations in the absence of a priest.
—Teach students of homiletics how to move from exegesis to interpretation of Scripture for liturgical proclamation.

National Organizations

—Promote *Fulfilled in Your Hearing.*
—Develop and encourage the use of the best online resources for preaching.
—Continue to study Catholic preaching in the United States and develop specific plans for helping preachers and local faith communities to make better preaching a priority.
—Identify appropriate competencies for preaching.
—Sponsor conferences, colloquia, scholarly research, and publication in the academic discipline of homiletics and liturgical preaching.

The Academy of Homiletics

Finally, in this sketch of institutional possibilities for supporting teachers of preaching, we issue an invitation to all teachers and doctoral students in homiletics to join and actively participate in the Academy of Homiletics.[19] The Academy of Homiletics was founded in 1965 and now claims some four hundred members from across North America and other regions of the world. Its purpose is to promote the practice of homiletic scholarship through participation in scholarly work groups and an annual meeting and through publications of the Academy's journal, *Homiletic.* The Academy of Homiletics aspires to work in close partnership with other organizations, including the Catholic Association of Teachers of Homiletics, the Evangelical Homiletics Society, the Religious Communication Association, and *Societas Homiletica,* an international society of homileticians.

———

Dear preachers, the ecumenical and interdisciplinary privilege of working together to promote the practice and component practices of preaching and to prepare ministers for the preaching ministry is most certainly an inspiring challenge. Opportunities and challenges abound—in our denominations and schools, in the work of each academic discipline and through interdisciplinary collaboration, and of course in each local congregation and pulpit. What has been offered here, not only in this chapter but throughout the book, is by way of invitation to join in a marvelous common project. As St. Paul reminds us:

How are they to call on one in whom they have not believed? And how are they to believe in one of whom they have never heard? And how are they to hear without someone to proclaim him? And how are they to proclaim him unless they are sent? As it is written, "How beautiful are the feet of those who bring good news!"[20]

NOTES

1. Aidan Kavanagh, *On Liturgical Theology* (New York: Pueblo Publishing Co., 1984), 96. See also Gordon Lathrop, *Holy Things: A Liturgical Theology* (Minneapolis: Fortress Press, 1993), which is organized according to this understanding of first- and second-order theology: Part 1, Patterns—Secondary Liturgical Theology; Part 2, Holy Things—Primary Liturgical Theology; Part 3, Applications—Pastoral Liturgical Theology.

2. See Mary Margaret Pazdan, "Developing a Wisdom Community as a Feminist Hermeneutic: Pedagogy for a New Millennium," p. 418 in National Association of Baptist Professors of Religion, *Perspectives in Religious Studies* 27:4 (Winter 2000): 413–25.

3. See Luke Dysinger, O.S.B, "*Lectio Divina*" at www.valyermo.com/ld-art.html for a discussion of this process for private or group *lectio divina*, involving *lectio* (reading/listening), *meditatio* (meditation), *oratio* (prayer), *contemplatio* (contemplation).

4. Attributed to Mary Margaret Pazdan, O.P. While the focus here is on the individual, doing this process communally, whether in a shared *lectio divina* or some other format, discloses the richness of the Word encountered.

5. Barbara E. Reid, O.P., and Leslie J. Hoppe, O.F.M., "Preaching from the Scriptures: New Directions for Preparing Preachers" (Chicago: Catholic Theological Union, 1998), 21.

6. Ibid., 13.

7. Ibid., 14.

8. The Biblical Preaching Project of Aquinas Institute of Theology was funded by the Wabash Center for Teaching and Learning of Theology and Religion and addressed the following Problem Statement: "Catholic teachers of preaching name the critical issue in teaching homiletics to be the formation of M.Div. graduates who are not only familiar with the hermeneutic process and a spectrum of methods for biblical interpretation, but who also can employ those hermeneutical approaches in effective biblical preaching."

9. The following teachers worked on this syllabus: Biblical Studies: Dianne Bergant, C.S.A., and Barbara Reid, O.P., Catholic Theological Union, Chicago; George Boudreau, O.P., and Seán Charles Martin, Aquinas Institute of Theology, St. Louis; Seung Ai Yang, Saint Paul Seminary School of Divinity, St. Paul. Homiletics: Alan Bowslaugh and Gregory Heille, O.P., Aquinas Institute of Theology; James Wallace, C.Ss.R., Washington Theological Union, Washington, D.C.

10. Biblical Studies: Catherine Corey, University St. Thomas, St. Paul; Juan Escarfuller, Vanderbilt University, Nashville; Homiletics: Martha Brunell, Aquinas Institute of Theology, St. Louis; Deborah A. Organ, Saint Paul Seminary School of Divinity, St. Paul; Ray John Marek, O.M.I., Oblate School of Theology, San Antonio.

11. Unpublished manuscript, drafted by James Burke, O.P., Dominican House of Studies, Washington, DC; Daniel Harris, C.M. Kenrick Seminary, St. Louis; James Motl, O.P., Saint Paul Seminary School of Divinity, St. Paul; and Robert Waznak, S.S, Washington Theological Union, Washington, D.C.

12. National Conference of Catholic Bishops, *Program of Priestly Formation,* 4th ed. (Washington, DC: United States Catholic Conference, 2001), #377.

13. "The State of Homiletics in the Seminaries and Graduate Schools of Theology in the United States," online at www.cathomiletic.org, drafted by Rev. Stephen DeLeers, St. Francis Seminary, Milwaukee; James Motl, O.P., Saint Paul Seminary School of Divinity, St. Paul; Rev. Richard Stern, St. Meinrad School of Theology, St. Meinrad, IN; and Honora Werner, O.P., St. Mary's Seminary, Baltimore.

14. Ibid., 6.

15. Ibid., 7–8.

16. The CCOP home page can be found at www.preachingcoalition.org.

17. Bishops' Committee on Priestly Life and Ministry, *Fulfilled in Your Hearing: The Homily in the Sunday Assembly* (Washington, DC: United States Catholic Conference, 1982), online at www.usccb.org/plm/fiyh.htm.

18. These strategies were reviewed by the United States Catholic Conference Bishops' Committee on Priestly Life and Ministry in September 2000 and remain the work of the Catholic Coalition on Preaching and of Gregory Heille, O.P., their author.

19. The home page of the Academy of Homiletics can be found at www.homiletics.org.

20. Romans 10:14–15.

Contributors

Teresa Fry Brown is Associate Professor of Homiletics at the Candler School of Theology, Emory University, Atlanta, Georgia.

Anna Carter Florence is Associate Professor of Preaching and Worship at Columbia Theological Seminary, Decatur, Georgia.

Daniel E. Harris is Professor of Homiletics at Aquinas Institute of Theology, St. Louis, Missouri.

James Henry Harris is Professor of Pastoral Theology and Homiletics at the Samuel DeWitt Proctor School of Theology at Virginia Union University, Richmond, Virginia.

Gregory Heille is Academic Dean and Professor of Homiletics at Aquinas Institute of Theology, St. Louis, Missouri.

Lucy Hogan is Professor of Preaching and Worship at Wesley Theological Seminary, Washington, DC.

Joseph R. Jeter Jr. is the Granville and Erline Walker Professor of Homiletics at the Brite Divinity School of Texas Christian University, Fort Worth, Texas.

Thomas G. Long is the Bandy Professor of Preaching at the Candler School of Theology, Emory University, Atlanta, Georgia.

David J. Lose is Academic Dean and the Marbury E. Anderson Associate Professor of Biblical Preaching at Luther Seminary in St. Paul, Minnesota.

Barbara K. Lundblad is the Joe R. Engle Associate Professor of Preaching at Union Theological Seminary, New York.

James Nieman is Professor of Practical Theology at Hartford Seminary, Hartford, Connecticut.

James W. Thompson is Professor of New Testament at the Graduate School of Theology of Abilene Christian University in Abilene, Texas.

Leonora Tubbs Tisdale is the Clement-Muehl Professor of Homiletics at the Yale Divinity School of Yale University in New Haven, Connecticut.

Paul Scott Wilson is Professor of Homiletics at Emmanuel College of Victoria University in the University of Toronto, Toronto, Ontario.